A Theology of the Jewish-Christian Reality

PART III
CHRIST IN CONTEXT

A Theology of the Jewish-Christian Reality

PART III
CHRIST IN CONTEXT

Paul M. van Buren

1817

HARPER & ROW, PUBLISHERS, SAN FRANCISCO
Cambridge, Hagerstown, New York, Philadelphia, Washington
London, Mexico City, São Paulo, Singapore, Sydney

FIRST EDITION

Library of Congress Cataloging-in-Publication Data
van Buren, Paul Matthews.
   A theology of the Jewish-Christian reality.

   Includes bibliographical references and indexes.
   Contents: pt. 1. Discerning the way — pt. 2. A Christian theology of the people Israel.
   1. Theology, Doctrinal   2. Judaism (Christian theology)   I. Title.
BT78.V28   1987   231.7'6   79-27373
ISBN 0-06-068823-8 (pbk. : v .1)

88 89 90 91 92 RRD 10 9 8 7 6 5 4 3 2 1

To the
Theologische Fakultät
Ruprecht-Karls-Universität Heidelberg
in appreciation.

Contents

Foreword

Having done what I could in *Discerning the Way* (Part 1 of *A Theology of the Jewish-Christian Reality*) to clarify the path into which we Christians believe ourselves to have been called by the One who has condescended to be known as the God of Abraham, Isaac, and Jacob, and then having attempted what must come first, *A Christian Theology of the People Israel* (Part 2), I turn in this third part to the next task for Christian reflection: an understanding of the Christian reality, how it has come to be, what it is, and where we are going. It needs no great insight to see that this means clarifying the central Christian confession concerning Jesus Christ. The task before us, then, is to develop a Christology for the Jewish-Christian reality.

If the reality within which the Church finds itself today includes the Jewish people and their eternal covenant with the God whom the Church serves through Jesus Christ, and the Church since Vatican II has confessed just this again and again (cf. van Buren, *Discerning*, 174–175; *People Israel*, 351–52*), it follows, for theologians as well as for biblical scholars, that responsible work can be done for the Church today only by those who take the trouble to learn and understand Jews and Judaism from Jews and Jewish sources. The present volume could not have been written without having first worked through the subject of *People Israel*, and I

*For a guide to abbreviations used in references, please see Abbreviations, p. 301. For complete bibliographic information, see Bibliography, p. 304.

urge readers to set it aside until they have done the same. Only then will it be clear that the covenant that the Jewish people live with God is not primarily the Abrahamic covenant or the Davidic covenant, but what we may call the Great Covenant, the covenant of Sinai. Jon Levenson's *Sinai and Zion* should be required reading on this subject.

Christology, the Church's understanding of "the things concerning Jesus of Nazareth" (Luke 24:19), is a rich and complex subject, lying as it does at the heart of the Church's identity and bearing on every aspect of its life. It is well, therefore, to make clear from the beginning that I have made two fundamental decisions that determine how I have chosen to address the subject. The first is to follow the rule of Scripture which James A. Sanders has detected, that "God is the subject of all the verbs of the Torah-Christ story" (Sanders, *Canon and Community*, 59). The second is to give priority in the apostolic witness to the theme of solidarity between Jesus and his people rather than the theme of conflict.

The grounds for the first decision are provided by a consistent series of notes sounded in the apostolic witness to Jesus and echoing a central theme of the whole scriptural witness. Jesus is presented as having said to one who addressed him as "Good Teacher," "Why do you call me good? No one is good but God alone" (Mark 10:18, Luke 18:19). The Johannine community felt able to include in its witness a presentation of Jesus as saying, "If I glorify myself, my glory is nothing" (John 8:54), although the words following, "it is my Father who glorifies me," may not be ignored. And in one of his letters reciting—but perhaps modifying and expanding—an early Christian hymn, Paul wrote "that at the name of Jesus every knee should bow . . . and every tongue confess that Jesus Christ is Lord, to the glory of God the Father" (Phil. 2:10,11). On this basis we formulate the following rule: *Every proper Christological statement, however "high," will make clear that it gives the glory to God the Father.*

The reasons for the second decision may not so clearly be given in texts, since it is, even more obviously than in the first, a judgment to give more weight to some texts than to others. We make the choice in favor of the witness to solidarity between Jesus and his people because it stands in greater continuity with the witness to God's covenant and therefore confirms the faithfulness of

God. If God is faithful to his people, and Jesus was faithful to God, then his solidarity with his people would follow. But beyond this general consideration lies one relevant to our own situation: this choice serves to support the church's recent formal rejection of, and efforts to abandon, the anti-Judaic tradition which began in the Apostolic Writings and became dominant in the Church from at least the second century. If the Church means to stand by its recent affirmations of the covenant between God and Israel, then it will have to let the original witness to that covenant become truly Holy Scripture in the Church, and show that it reads it as more than merely an "Old Testament" subservient to the Apostolic Writings (the "New Testament"). For these reasons, we formulate a second rule: *Every proper Christological statement will make clear that it is an affirmation of the covenant between God and Israel.*

I am happy to acknowledge the help of Clark Williamson, a colleague in the cause of responsible theology, for having led me to improve an earlier formulation of the reasons in support of this rule. (See his essay "A New Context for Christology.") This remark can also serve as a place to say that I shall continue in this volume to use small-print paragraphs to handle matters that are digressions from or subservient to the main line of argument.

I am well aware, as will be anyone familiar with the Church's theological tradition, that to follow these two rules is to take sides on matters that have been and are controversial. The whole of this volume will constitute an argument in their support. I give them in this lapidary form and without further argument in this foreword, in order to alert the informed reader as to the direction in which I shall be moving. Suspicions as to a "subordinationist" tendency (with the first rule), and to an abandonment of the Church's universality (with the second), will be addressed, if not allayed, in the book itself.

Finally, I would urge the reader also to keep in mind the difference between what is indisputably necessary to the health of the Church—its affirmation of the Jewish people—and what it debatable—any proposal about how this is to be done. What is offered in this volume is a proposal about how the Church, at a crucial point, might go about doing what it must.

CHAPTER ONE

The Place of Christology

The church of God lives by its understanding of "the things concerning Jesus of Nazareth" (Luke 24:19). How it understands and speaks of these is therefore decisive for its account of God and itself and for its conduct and life. Its Christology is both this understanding and speaking, and also its critical reflection upon them.

1. THE CHURCH AS STARTING POINT

i. The fact of the Church

As there is a Jewish reality in this world, so there is a Christian reality. The name of the former is the Jewish people, or the people Israel. The name of the latter is the Church. The Church is as visible, as much a historical entity, as is the Jewish people. Jews sometimes worry about who is a Jew. Christians sometimes worry about who is a Christian. In both cases, the worry is about the inclusion of actual people in an entity that is itself part of our actual world. The Church with which we shall be dealing, then, is a historical entity, in the same sense in which the Jewish people is a historical entity.

As a historical entity, the Church is visible. One need not be a believer to see that there is and has been the Church as an identifiable historical factor in the history of the world, and especially of the West, since the first century of the Common Era. The be-

liever may see the Church in other ways than the unbeliever, but both are looking at the same historical entity.

The visible historicity of the Church has been made problematic for some because of an old tradition, sharpened in the Reformation of the sixteenth century, of distinguishing between the visible and the invisible Church. (For a critical analysis of this distinction and its history, see Karl Barth, *CD*, IV/1, 652–54.) The laudable intent behind the distinction is to confess that the Church of God is defined by God (so its limits are known only by God), not by our human decisions as to its (visible) boundaries. The distinction was sharpened by the conviction that there is a true Church as distinct from a false Church, or an obedient Church in contrast to a disobedient Church. But if such could ever be determined, assuming that it is conceivable that there ever was a Church that did not need daily to pray, "Forgive us our trespasses," it would still be the case that an obedient Church, being made up of men, women, and children, would be just as visible as a disobedient Church. It is therefore preferable, following Karl Barth's suggestion, to say that the Church is always and only visible, but that which makes this visible community to be the Church is always invisible.

Indeed, the most important claim which believers can make about the Church refers to that which cannot be seen: its divine calling. The Church understands itself to be a gathering of persons called together by God out of every nation to trust and serve God and God's cause. As called, the Church may also be designated "the elect," but since it knows its election (its being singled out and set in a new Way) by means of the calling of Jesus Christ to follow him as his disciples in the service of his Father, "calling" would seem to be the more appropriate term to use. This call is what creates and sustains the Church and makes it to be the Church, and this call of Jesus to discipleship, *heard as the call of God*, is of course invisible.

Nevertheless, those who are called are visible, whatever others may think about their call. Reasons both good and bad may be found for why people call themselves Christian and members of the Church, but both those called and those who think themselves to be called are visible people. During nineteen centuries, countless Gentiles learned in the Church to call upon the God of Israel, established schools and hospitals in God's name, and sought to bring the kingdoms of this world under God's rule.

There is, however, an ambiguity in the existence of the Church, to a degree related to, yet quite different from, the ambiguity that we saw in the existence of the Jewish people as the Israel of God (van Buren, *People Israel*, 184–89). The ambiguities are related because both the Church and the Jewish people are visible, historical entities that are invisibly called by God. The ambiguities differ because the histories of the two entities have been so different. Even if the Church's claim to have been called by the God of Abraham, Isaac, and Jacob be granted, the assertion is surely true that the Church has manifested a history deeply colored by anti-Judaism. Both the claim and the assertion apply to exactly the same historical reality. Therein lies the particular ambiguity of the Church's existence. As we shall see, the Church has manifested other negative characteristics, notably intolerance, pride, and patriarchal sexism. Serious as these are, however, none of them has manifested the ambiguity of the Church's existence more consistently and pervasively than its anti-Judaism.

The negative side of this ambiguity is intimately related to the positive side. Called by the God of Israel, the Church, by the end of the first century, came to see itself as the true Israel of God, a construct grounded in its Gospels and especially in its passion narratives, which portrayed the Jews as the enemies of Christ and responsible for his death, and so no longer the people of God. One aspect of this anti-Judaic theme is the note of intolerance: If your understanding of the things concerning Jesus of Nazareth are not identical with mine, then you are the enemy of the truth and fit only to be cast aside. This theme was sounded in the name of the inclusive love of the Maker of heaven and earth who had graciously included the Gentiles in the history he had begun with Abraham. As the Church increasingly came to exercise some degree of authority in the empire, and continuing until secularism and nationalism took its power away, the Church carried out its desire to draw the nations of the world into the service of God with a spirit of pride that some have named "triumphalism," although its calling has been to follow the humble one who came to serve. Finally, from its early conflict with Marcionism, the Church consistently put women "in their place," although it had been called to be a society in which "there is neither male nor female . . . for you are all one in Christ Jesus" (Gal. 3:28). The negative side of the Church has become visible precisely in that into which it had been called as the Church.

The church's self-critical reflection has to take both the Church's calling and also the negative aspects of its history into account. It may not deal with the one first, and then, in a later volume, so to speak, turn its attention to the other. Its focus needs to be always on the visible Church that has been invisibly called by God, for that is the only Church there is or has ever been. All Christians live as members of just this Church and for just this Church all are called to pray.

ii. The Church of God

The Church exists because it has been called by God into existence to walk in his ways alongside his people Israel. By its very existence and its course through history, therefore, it is called to respond to the One who calls it and to answer to him for the manner in which it makes its Way in the world. Its existence being due solely to this calling, it belongs fully to God as his special possession, even as Israel lives as God's special possession.

The One to whom the Church belongs is the One who has been pleased to be known as the God of Israel. So was God known by Israel before the Church even began to be. The Church knows no other God than the God first known by Israel as the God of Abraham, Isaac, and Jacob. In short, the Church, predominantly Gentile though it be, has been called by, belongs to, and worships Israel's God. No assertion about the Church can be more fundamental than this (cf. van Buren, *Discerning*, 32–37).

What does it mean to say that the Church belongs to Israel's-

God? It means that the Church hears Israel's story of reality, believes it to be true, and then goes on to tell that story as also its own. *Also* its own, not exclusively its own. To say that the Church belongs to Israel's God is to say that it tells Israel's story as Israel's first of all, and therefore still as Israel's continuing, unfinished story. It then begins its own story by telling Israel's, adding its own chapters to it, alongside and not in place of the chapters of Israel's continuing tale. The Church's memory is therefore grounded in Israel's memory and its hope is built on Israel's hope.

At an early stage in its history, the Church failed to recall that the God to whom it belonged was Israel's God, *still* Israel's God, and bound to Israel by an eternal covenant. The result was that it began to tell Israel's story as exclusively its own, and the chapters it added were written in intentional ignorance of the chapters that Israel was writing at the same time. In a word, the Scriptures of Israel became for the Church its "Old Testament," as we shall see, and Israel's further history was ignored. Recognizing this failure and showing how it can be corrected is now an essential task of any responsible theology. Today, no theologian who wishes to serve the Church may ignore its belated recognition of its past failure to acknowledge and affirm the Jewish people as the Israel of God in its continuing covenant with God.

The One who calls the Church into existence and beckons it into God's future is Israel's God, but the way in which God has chosen to call and beckon it is through the Jew Jesus of Nazareth. Jesus is the Church's actual starting point and therefore incomparable for it to anyone or anything else. He is for the Church, we might say, what Sinai is for the Jews. He is the point at which their entry into Israel's story begins, for Jesus himself lived from and in Israel's story. Because Jesus was born into and lived within that story, he is able to be the beginning and entry for the inclusion of the Church in the story that begins with Abraham.

The Church's doctrine of the Trinity is its way of asserting the continuity of its own story with Israel's, of confessing that with the story beginning with Jesus, the story of the God of Israel and the Israel of God continues. (See Ritschl, *Logik*, 178–79.) The trinitarian confession takes into account the Jewish-Christian reality, making it possible and necessary for the Church to tell its story so as to include both that of the people Israel and now also that of the Gentile Church.

It may therefore be said that the Church belongs to Jesus Christ, and that in no way contradicts its belonging to God. The Church is at once the Church of Jesus Christ and the Church of God. It is God's Church by being Christ's Church, or it can be called Christ's because Christ is God's (cf. 1 Cor. 3:23). In making clear the logic of this confession in its christology, the Church makes clear its own identity before God.

iii. The Church and the churches

The Church is the place where the understanding with which we are concerned takes place. In other places the things concerning Jesus of Nazareth may be and in fact are understood in one way or another. Our concern in this volume, however, is with the understanding that arises, develops, and is reflected on critically within the Church that calls itself the Church of God and of Jesus Christ.

The Church of God, however, exists in fact in the form of a number of churches, distinct groupings of local churches having identifiable structural, organizational, and doctrinal bonds. The fact of division and distinction between different churches, e.g. the Roman Catholic church, the Greek Orthodox church, the Lutheran churches, the Reformed churches, the Anglican Communion, and the Baptist churches, to mention a few of many groupings, is a matter of concern in the ecumenical movement of this century, which arose in order to confront and to work toward overcoming these divisions. All of these churches agree in saying that the Church is called to be one and that therefore these divisions are a sign of the Church's disobedience. Nevertheless, the fact of the Church includes the fact that the churches are divided.

However, for the purposes of a theology of the Jewish-Christian reality, and indeed for any theological reflection worthy of the name in our time, the division of the churches is overshadowed by their common participation in a tradition of having rejected the Jewish people as the Israel of God and in a recent common recognition that this rejection was itself an act of disobedience. From the perspective of the ecumenical movement, the churches are not disunited with respect to the Jewish people, in the past and in the present.

This fact confirms Karl Barth's assertion to the Vatican Secretariat for Christian Unity in 1966. Having spoken most positively of the ecumenical movement in general, he went on to say: "There is finally only one really great ecumenical question: our relations with the Jewish people." (Evangelishe Kirche, *Erneuerung*, 102.)

The Church in all its branches faces a common challenge concerning its relationship to the Jewish people. With respect to this issue, the divisions among the churches appear less than decisive. As the Commission on Faith and Order of the World Council of Churches discovered in 1967, a deep division in understanding the relationship between the Church and the Jewish people cuts right across denominational lines. Every Christian community is equally confronted and to some extent divided by the questions of whether it understands itself to be called and beckoned by the God of Israel, and whether it understands that calling to place it necessarily in a positive and cooperative relationship to the Israel of God, the Jewish people. Whether a community understands itself in this sense to be the Church of God and of Jesus Christ may be the new form of the question of membership in the *oekumene*.

A particularly interesting case is that of the Church of the Latter Day Saints, known popularly as Mormons. They clearly see themselves as the Church of God and of Jesus Christ, yet their early tradition is singularly lacking in anti-Judaism or a theology of displacement. If this still holds, then surely the churches are called upon to begin finally taking this church with greater ecumenical seriousness than has been the case thus far, and for this church to consider whether it might not have a responsibility to the rest of the Church that it ought to fulfill.

2. THE THINGS CONCERNING JESUS OF NAZARETH

i. The one name

It does not take a believer to know that the name of Jesus is central to the Church. The Church and its individual members worship, preach, pray, bless, forgive, and act in his name. The name of Jesus is therefore, at the least, formally central for the Church.

The question may be asked whether the centrality of this one name is more than formal, but there is no neutral place from which an answer can be given. Believer and unbeliever can note the formal centrality, but the judgment that it is only a formal centrality distinguishes the judge as standing outside the Church. One standing within the Church will judge that the name is indeed the name of Jesus himself present to his Church. For the Church, the expression "the name of Jesus" functions in a manner similar to that of "the name of the LORD" in Israel's Scriptures: it means Jesus present with and active among and through his Church. The name is formally central because the Church believes Jesus himself to be materially central to its life and activity.

The name "Jesus of Nazareth" indicates, both by the personal name and the place name, a particular setting—a point which Karl Barth emphasized in his first lectures in post-war Germany (Barth, *Outline*, 72–74): it refers us to the Jewish people, to Israel, and therefore to Israel's story. The centrality of this name for the Church brings with it the centrality of the story in the context of which this name was given and borne, and apart from which it would lose its meaning. That Jesus Christ was born a Jew (and here we go well beyond Luther's essay of this title) is therefore crucial to his identity and to the faith of the Church. If it matters for the Church that he was born at all, then it matters that he was actually born a Jew, not a Gentile, growing up (if not born) in the village of Nazareth in the Galilee.

His name is Jesus of Nazareth. He was also known, probably in his lifetime, as "the Anointed," *ho Christos* in our Greek accounts of his story. However "the Anointed" was understood at first, from an early time it became a part of his name, so that he came to be called "Jesus Christ," or simply "Christ." The apostle Paul, our earliest written source, called him Jesus, Christ, Jesus Christ, and Christ Jesus, more or less interchangeably, and the Church has generally followed this pattern until the most recent time.

Recently, there has been a new development: the Greek has been translated back into the original Aramaic or Hebrew, and the name "Christ" has been replaced by a title, "the Messiah." Those who have taken up this practice seem to take it for granted that the title "Messiah" is clear, or was in the first century, and that the early Christian confession was that Jesus is the Messiah, ignoring the evidence of Paul that the early confession was that Jesus is Lord (*kurios*). Paul Tillich helped to popularize the resulting expression: "Jesus as the Christ." The latest novelty in this development has been to call Jesus "Israel's Messiah," as in the Rhineland Church's synodical declaration of January 1980.

It is the duty of a theology of the Jewish-Christian reality to point out that this shift away from the language of the classical tradition is an exceedingly misguided and dangerous one which ought to be abandoned, for the following reasons:

1. As there was no unitary Judaism in the last decades of the Second Temple period, so there are no grounds for assuming the existence of a unified "Jewish idea" of the Messiah. The Jewish concept of the Messiah was neither unitary nor fixed in the first century. As we can see from early Christian usage, the term *ho Christos*, "the Anointed," could refer to "the anointed high priest," as in The Epistle to the Hebrews (so called), or to "the anointed son of David," who would restore Jewish sovereignty, or to "the anointed Son of God," a use not altogether clear in its implications, or to "the anointed prophet of the last days." The Babylonian Talmud has preserved a host of "Messiah" figures and functions. (On this see Neusner, *Messiah in Context*, especially the list on 216–18.) What, then, would one be confessing if one confessed Jesus as the Messiah?

2. Judaism never did develop a unified concept of Messiah, but the Messiah figure, in one form or another, has been of great importance in the life and faith of the Jewish people throughout its long history. In at least one important strand of this complex tradition, the Messiah is a figure whose appearing will be either the cause or the accompanying signal of God's restoration of a Torah-faithful Israel and, along with Israel, of

the whole of creation. According to this tradition, the Messiah (and what else would he be but the Messiah of the Jews?) will appear to a sanctified Jewish people. As their fortunes are restored, the nations will cease to make war, and sickness, destruction, and suffering will come to an end on this earth. In the light of daily events, not to speak of the cumulative history of the past nineteen centuries, it is simply absurd to say that any of this was brought about with the coming of Jesus or has happened to this day. The claim that Jesus is the Messiah of the Jews as Jews have understood the term—and whose term is it?—is refuted decisively by the anti-Judaic behavior of the Church over almost two millennia, not to speak of the events reported daily in the newspapers. To make that claim is either an attempt to rob the Jewish people of one of their own central symbols of hope, or it is to say to them that their hope and this symbol are of no value and need to be replaced by different ones, namely those of the Church.

3. Whichever image of the Messiah we take, be it one of those many available in the first century of the Common Era or that only somewhat less elusive figure developed in the Jewish tradition, it will not be adequate for the Church's confession of Jesus Christ. It is a task of a Christology after Auschwitz and Vatican II to point out that none of the possible uses of the term "messiah" is sufficient to catch even a modest part of what the Church wants to say of the things concerning Jesus of Nazareth. The term "messiah" says far too little. The Church would therefore do well to continue its traditional use of "Christ" as a proper name and to recall that Christology has been its teaching and critical reflection on the importance of this person, not a doctrine concerning the Jewish concept of the Messiah.

ii. Things present

The Church speaks of the things concerning Jesus of Nazareth first of all in the present tense. It speaks of Jesus Christ now, present to the Church, calling it ever anew into existence before God and beckoning it on into God's future. Jesus is central for the Church as the one in whom it discovers ever anew God's call and claim upon it, and discovers itself anew as called and claimed by God. It preaches and enacts the story of Jesus (in word and sacrament) as a story continuing into the present. If the things concerning Jesus of Nazareth did not include the present life of the

Church, there would be little point in telling of the things that happened long ago. Jesus as the founder of the Church can only be of interest if he is right now the one who ever anew refounds the Church and gives it life. If he once confronted people with the gift and claim of God's love but does so no longer, there would be no Church and so no Christology at all. Things present are therefore at the center of the Church's confession of Jesus Christ and so of its Christology.

Friedrich Schleiermacher saw this clearly. His conception of the religious self-consciousness may be too indebted to Romanticism for modern tastes, but at least he was clear that the dependence of Christian faith on Christ in the present was the heart of Christology. (See van Beeck, *Proclaimed*, 554–566, for a subtle discussion of this.)

The concern with the present has two sides. The Church's confession of Christ begins with its confession of *his* presence, and it confesses him as Lord of the present concerns of the Church. These are large and important matters which will call for extended treatment, but at this point they should be defined briefly.

First, Christ present implies Christ alive. The Church's confession that Jesus lives is therefore the logical foundation of its Christology. The point is made classically by reference to the resurrection, but that can obscure the point. The term "resurrection" can mislead one to think of something having happened "back then." It bears reminding ourselves that nowhere in the Apostolic Writings is "the resurrection," as an event that happened at a time in the past, ever described, for no one claimed to have been a witness of such an event. Instead, we are told of Jesus being present to his disciples in one way or another, and for shorter or longer moments. That Jesus lives, and can and does become a reality for his Church from time to time, lies at the heart of all that the Church has to say concerning him.

Second, the confession of Christ alive, and present from time to time with his Church, implies that he is present as Lord of the present Church and of all the present concerns of human beings that it shares. (This is a major theme of F. J. van Beeck's *Christ Proclaimed.*) In the Church's Christology, the name of Jesus will be shown to preside over every serious human concern, be it for peace between nations and groups, for social and economic justice, or for the liberation of the poor and oppressed from all that hinders the development of their human potential. Because human beings, and the visible Church with them, have come to define their concerns in different ways in different periods of history, Christology will also change with time as it takes into account each age's new conception of the fundamental concerns of human beings. In this way too, the Church's expression of the things concerning Jesus of Nazareth will begin with things present.

In taking account of present concerns of human beings, the Church will therefore inevitably have to review and sometimes modify the Christologies of past ages. The growing awareness of the Church's own anti-Judaism, exclusivism, triumphalism, and sexism, against which its past Christologies provided no resistance, will lead it to seek to speak in a new way of the things concerning Jesus of Nazareth, one that assures that the name of Jesus Christ presides over and judges these attitudes and actions as inadmissible for the Church today.

We recognize that, judged by the order we have deemed it necessary to follow, all classical Christologies prove to be deficient. We are departing from the tradition so as to follow an order better adapted to meet the two rules that we find binding on a Church that has been awakened by Auschwitz and the birth of the State of Israel to its relationship to the Jewish people. The present tense comes first if the Church means to give the glory now to God the Father, and if it means to affirm today the covenant between God and Israel.

iii. Things to come

The Church speaks of the things concerning Jesus of Nazareth, second, as an unfinished story, as things for which the Church hopes. If the first tense of Christology is the present, the second is the future. It is clear from the earliest forms of the apostolic witness through the history of the Church's confession of Christ that the Church has always believed that, in Jesus, God was accomplishing things of eternal importance. When one looks in fact at the history of the Church, not to speak of its surrounding environment, and even when one looks at the lives of the most exemplary of the Church's members, the evidence of something accomplished is at best ambiguous, and much of it is frankly negative. Death continues to reign. Suffering and evil abound. Where is the mighty transformation of which the Church speaks? To speak of a transformation in the past tense is to make oneself incredible, and this is indeed what has happened to the Church. The redemption, reconciliation, and new creation of which the Church has spoken so often will always be incredible if the Church pretends that it can speak of these matters in the past tense. A credible Christology will make it clear that the Church lives in hope and that the Jesus of which it speaks is one who will come. A credible Christology will therefore make clear that every claim that it advances is put forward in hope, and not least its answer to the question, "Have you been saved?"

Much of the Church's Christology suffers from ignoring the priority of the future tense over the past. It has consequently claimed as accomplished that for which it can only hope. It has failed to follow the lead of the Apostle to the Gentiles, who placed the adoption of Gentiles as children of God and the liberation of all creation in the future, as that for which he and they were waiting (e.g., Rom. 8:18–25). Salvation was for him something ahead of him, not behind him (Rom. 13:11). And the author of Hebrews could even conceive of Jesus' whole ministry and work as something happening now and in the future, for which of course the past was the necessary preparation (e.g., Heb. 4:11–16). Care should be exercised, therefore, in speaking of the things concerning Jesus of Nazareth, so that the future tense, the need for hope, not be forgotten.

A crucial problem will arise in dealing with the ancient confession that Jesus Christ is Lord. The present tense may not be dissolved into a future, but neither should it be allowed to stand without reference to it. The Church's claim in the present tense is a claim made always in hope of that which has not yet come and does not yet appear. Paul could make the claim of Christ's lordship in the present tense, yet he also said that that lordship was not yet realized, and that when it would be, it would be dissolved into the lordship of God alone (1 Cor. 15:25–28).

Franz Rosenzweig's observation that the Church has never made much use of this verse is quite correct. "Classical" Christology is simply not adequate to this text because of its failure to prevent the past from preempting the future.

iv. Things past

We come only in the third place to the past tense. The things concerning Jesus of Nazareth refer to him in the present and then in the future. In that framework they refer also to the past. There was a man, a Jew, born of Mary, who lived and taught and did things in Galilee and then in Judea and Jerusalem, who was put to death by the Roman occupation forces under Pontius Pilate, and who then appeared to his disciples (cf. 1 Cor. 15:3–8). We know about this past from the Apostolic Writings, especially the Gospels. These writings present that past in the form of a story of this man as one who had confronted his hearers with the gift and claim of the unbounded love of the God of Israel, and their authors told that story in the evident expectation that those who heard it would be confronted as were those who had heard and seen that man.

The various authors and editors of this story told it in different ways and with different emphases, and the resulting stories have been heard and read by the Church in different ways in different times. Today, as a result of critical study of these texts, we are aware that they reflect the circumstances of the communities out of which they arose. These texts, as well as the Church's later reading and interpretation of them, tell of the things concerning Jesus of Nazareth in close association with the deepest concerns of the authors and communities that produced them. Those concerns were themselves grounded in the conflicts and tensions that marked the lives of those communities. The result was that the Church has received its earliest accounts of the things concerning Jesus of Nazareth wrapped in, and to some extent warped by, the things concerning the Christian communities of roughly the last quarter of the first century. It should be noted that any Christology useful for the Church today will be wrapped in, and therefore of course to some extent warped by, the present concerns of the Church.

The reconstruction of the things concerning those communities is a relatively new field of study and it is perhaps too early to speak of a scholarly consensus. Nevertheless, the study of the social circumstances of early Christianity is beginning to take shape. (The subtitle of John Gager's study *Kingdom and Community* (published in 1975) was *The Social World of Early Christianity*.) Examples are Howard Kee's study of the church that produced Mark's Gospel, *Community of the New Age,* and Raymond Brown's work on the church or churches that produced the Johannine Gospel and Epistles, *The Communuity of the Beloved Disciple.* What begins to emerge is a picture of a number of quite different Christian communities coming increasingly into conflict with the developing consolidation of Judaism, even as their membership was in most cases becoming increasingly Gentile. (For evidence of exceptions even as late as the sixth century, see the article by Shlomo Pines, "The Jewish Christians of the Early Centuries According to a New Source.") In addition, toward the end of the first century the dominance of a Johannine tradition was challenged by some, of whom the leading figure was a Christian named Marcion, who thought that Paul had been the only apostle truly to have understood the things concerning Jesus of Nazareth. (On this, most recently, see R. J. Hoffmann's controversial study *Marcion: On the Restitution of Christianity.*)

The result of the conflicts of some of the early communities (and the ones that were later to be classified as orthodox or catholic) with Judaism and Marcionism is that their versions of the things concerning Jesus of Nazareth were deeply influenced by their anti-Judaic and anti-Marcionite concerns. Their own rejec-

tion by the synagogue led them to interpret Jesus' violent end as
the result of his having been rejected by his people: the Jewish
rejection of the followers of Jesus must have seemed to them to
have been the inevitable consequence of a Jewish rejection of Jesus himself (cf. G. Sloyan, "Response," 14–16). That, in any case,
is how they told his story, especially in their passion narratives.
And as for the challenge posed by Marcion, the "orthodox" set
out to reclaim Paul by presenting him as having been fully in accord with a united Jerusalem community (from which all existing
communities were claimed to stem), and whose leadership was
held to be the foundation of all authenticity, "the Twelve" having
been themselves fully authorized by the risen Christ over a goodly
period ("forty days"). Thus we have the Acts of the Apostles, the
Pastoral Epistles ascribed to Paul, and the final edition of the Gospel according to Luke as the refutation of Marcion's position. I
would not claim a scholarly consensus for this hypothetical reconstruction, but I do see it as having the merit of accounting for the
"Paul" of Acts and the Pastoral Epistles, so different from the author of what are widely regarded as the authentic Pauline letters.

If it is indeed the case that the Apostolic Writings, the so-called
"New Testament," present the things concerning Jesus of Nazareth interpreted through the things concerning the Church of
the late first century so as to give them an anti-Judaic (and anti-
Marcionite) cast, then the Church today is faced with certain difficulties. The Church throughout almost its whole history has held
these texts to be canonical (normative) for its understanding of
the things concerning Jesus of Nazareth. In what sense can they
remain so for a Church whose present concerns run in part
counter to those of the Church that produced these writings?
Having seen in the Holocaust the ultimate fruit of the way the
passion narratives were written, the Church is turning its back on
its traditional anti-Judaism. But that means it no longer accepts
the canonical passion narratives as definitive for its understanding of the things concerning Jesus of Nazareth. (Having slowly begun to recognize that its treatment of women has been
oppressive, the Church is learning to give less weight to at least

one anti-Marcionite element in its canon, giving long-delayed attention to texts that indicate that women held positions of leadership in some of the Pauline/Marcionite churches.) In fact, it is difficult if not impossible to find a theologian, past or present, who has not used the Church's canon selectively. The question, so crucial for the Church of today and tomorrow, is not whether to be selective, but how the selection is to be made. Our proposed rules for a helpful Christology are offered as a contribution to an answer.

Two interrelated points call for immediate notice in this matter. First, in letting its present concerns shape its understanding of the things concerning Jesus of Nazareth, the Church today is doing precisely what the Church did from the beginning and which I am endorsing by maintaining that the primary tense of Christology should always be the present. We cannot criticize the early Church, therefore, for its concern over its rejection by the Jewish leadership of the day. It had reason for concern. However, we may and must criticize it for turning this concern into a fundamental counterrejection of Judaism and the Jewish people, and we shall develop this criticism on grounds to which the early Church appealed: its presentation (or at least important parts of it) of the things concerning Jesus of Nazareth. In short, while appreciating the early Church's conviction that it had been called to its own distinctive Way, the Church today need not and should not take that response as in all ways normative.

The second point to be noticed, which follows from the first, is that just these grounds for developing our criticism, and so a Christology for the Jewish-Christian reality, are in fact available to us in the early Church's presentation of the things concerning Jesus of Nazareth. That is, through precisely the Apostolic Writings and through the witness of the Church based on them, by its own confession the Church has been again and again, and continues to be, confronted by the one in whom it encounters the gift and claim of God's gracious love. It happens, in other words, that the Church still lives as the Church of God and of Jesus Christ. This fact of the continuing effect of Jesus Christ is what makes possible a Christology today, a present investigation of the things concerning Jesus of Nazareth, things present, things to come, and things past. In short, Christology today should make clear that the impact of Jesus on the Church today outweighs, without negating, his impact on the Church of the past. Christ present will preside over each moment of the life of a Church that does not in effect relegate his lordship to the past.

3. THE CHURCH'S UNDERSTANDING AND CONDUCT

i. *The power of God*

The Church of God lives by the power of God's having called it into being and beckoning it into the future that God wills for it. So the Church has always believed. But what is this power of God? According to the Apostle to the Gentiles, it is the preaching of Christ crucified, or the word of the cross (1. Cor. 1:18, 23), the public portrayal of the crucified one (Gal. 3:1), Jesus of Nazareth in his weakness, humiliation, and death that Paul seems to have regarded as the central and decisive event of Jesus' life. (That Paul's judgment was widely shared can be seen from the major place given to the passion narrative in each of the Gospels.) In short, the power of God which creates, sends, and supports the Church is the story of the crucified one, the story of Jesus of Nazareth. That story can be the saving power of God because it confronts the hearer with the utterly free gift and total claim of the infinite love of the God of Israel to whom heaven and earth belong. The story confronts the hearer. It comes to us from outside of ourselves. It is not, first of all, our story. It is first of all Jesus' story, and it is that in two senses. It is the story that Jesus is presented as himself telling. Jesus' story in this sense is the story of God, a story about God. Second, it is the story the witnesses tell about Jesus, and so it is also his story in being about him. When so received, as God's gift to and claim upon the hearers, it can become also the hearers' story, as they discover themselves the recipients of that gift, and so the possession of the one who lays claim upon them. From this power the church lives.

The Church lives by the power of God, but it lives in its understanding of that story. As it hears and understands that story, so it understands God and itself. Were the Church to hear that story and understand it only as the story of a pious Jew who lived a long time ago, from which interesting or even important teachings stemmed, it would cease to be the Church of God. As God's Church, it hears that story as the story of God and of itself. It does so because the story was intended to confront, and again and again it has succeeded in confronting, the Church with God and with itself. The Jesus it presents is Jesus authorized by God to do this. To hear the story of Jesus and to find oneself confronted by God is to understand the story and know it as the power of God. Just this, Schubert Ogden has argued (correctly, in my judgment), is the point of Christology (in his book of that title).

That the Church is confronted in the story of Jesus by God, and also discovers itself so confronted, is powerfully underscored by the doctrine of the two "natures" of classical Christology. That doctrine, however, is also misleading in that it appears to be answering a puzzling question about the composition of Jesus of Nazareth, rather than the vital question of the relationship between God and ourselves with which the story of Jesus can confront us. A "divine nature" of Jesus could not be of any benefit to us if it were not a "divine nature" for us, as gift and claim. Melanchthon's epistemological rule is in order here: To know Christ is in fact to know his benefits.

The crucifixion as the decisive event in the story of Jesus is a recurring theme in Paul's letters. We shall have to reflect on the possibilities and the limitations of this interpretation of the things concerning Jesus of Nazareth; indeed, we are invited to do so by the fact that, in contrast to the subject of the person of Christ and his relation to the Father, no single theory about his death became "dogma." Nevertheless, to understand the story of the crucified one as the power of God, so that one comes thereby to know oneself confronted with the gift and claim of God's love, is a humbling form of understanding. It is humbling to learn that that love comes to us a totally unmerited gift, and that its total claim is one which we spend our lives evading. It is humbling because it is shown to us in the humility of Christ and therefore shows us how humble is the power of God, how different it is from what we call human, or more precisely, male power. To understand the story of the crucified one is to begin to understand the humility of God, and that is to begin to understand ourselves as the servants of such a God.

ii. The Church's understanding

The Church's understanding takes place on many levels, but at every level it is an understanding of the story of Jesus whereby one finds oneself confronted by the love and judgment of God, such that these are one: this love is a judgment upon us, and this judgment is an act of love. Such understanding is called faith. Faith in the gospel concerning Jesus is trust that this story and its effect upon the Church is not an illusion, not our own invention. At another level, understanding involves critical reflection on how the Church expresses its understanding. On the first or primary level, the Church trustingly understands the gospel, and on this primary level, its understanding *is* the gospel. The Church has no gospel, no good news, except in its own human words and according to its own human understanding. This is true of the Church today as it was true of the earliest disciples. On the second level of critical reflection, understanding involves raising questions about the fittingness of the way in which the Church expresses its primary understanding. Such critical reflection is called theology. Because all understanding of the story of Jesus is human understanding, and therefore subject to correction both in its articulation and in drawing its consequences, theology is continually necessary and helpful for the Church. Theology is not the gospel, and the theologian is not a deeper or better Christian than others. Theology is the activity of the Church. To one degree or another every member of the Church is engaged in it from time to time, by raising critical questions about, and offering proposals for improving, the way in which the Church speaks of the things of God. As a central part of theology, Christology is the questioning and proposing with respect to the way the Church speaks of the things concerning Jesus of Nazareth.

The immediate purpose of doing theology and Christology is correction of language. But to change the way in which we speak is to change a central part of our behavior. The ultimate purpose of theology is therefore a correction of the Church's behavior. It is concerned with the Church's language because talking is such an important part of our behavior. A Christology for the Jewish-Christian reality will be centrally concerned with how the Church speaks of the things concerning Jesus of Nazareth, and how it is to do this in ways that affirm the people Israel. The ultimate concern in such a task is how the Church can act to affirm the Jewish people in their calling as the people of God.

Theology, then, sometimes called systematic theology (from a concern to think matters through with care and comprehensiveness), is always practical in its concern. A systematic theology that was not at every point also an eminently practical theology would be a theology that had lost sight of its task.

iii. The Church's conduct

The Church's conduct is and has always been a function of its understanding. This can be shown with reference to the major problems that exist in the Church's past conduct. How the Church has understood the things concerning Jesus of Nazareth has shaped its conduct in those matters most needing to be reformed today. We refer primarily to the Church's traditional anti-Judaism, and then to its pride and patriarchalism. All are interrelated.

From a stage early enough to have left its mark on the Gospels, the Church understood the things concerning Jesus of Nazareth as the story of a conflict between Jesus and his own people. As the Prologue to the Gospel of the Johannine community summed it up, "he came to his own [home] and his own [people] did not receive him" (John 1:11). (See van Buren, *Discerning*, 84, for a critical discussion of this verse.) Above all in the passion narratives, Jesus is portrayed as the victim of Jewish animosity: he is betrayed, arrested, tried, accused, condemned, and turned over to the Roman occupation forces for execution—and in each case, by Jews. From this understanding of Jesus, the Church has understood God as having rejected the Jews and it has understood itself as having displaced the Jews in God's favor. This understanding of Jesus in an antagonistic relationship to his own people is the root of the Church's anti-Judaic thinking and behavior.

In this specific sense, we can agree with Rosemary Ruether that anti-Judaism is the "left hand" of Christology, but not as she meant it. It is not because the Church confessed Jesus as Lord and Son of God, nor any particular conception of the incarnation, that leads necessarily to anti-Judaism, as Eugene Borowitz showed in his *Contemporary Christologies.* It is the anti-Judaic Jesus of at least important parts of the Apostolic Writings that is the source of the sickness. An important task of any responsible Christology for the Church after Auschwitz will be to argue that, since this anti-Judaic Jesus was unknown to Paul and is not the Jesus of important strata of the Gospels (however dominant it became in the final versions of the Gospels and then in the Church), the Church today is responsible for deciding how it shall understand the relationship between Jesus and his people.

The Church has thought to exclude not only Jews from the love of God; it has excluded any and all who disagreed with its dominant understanding of Jesus and so of God and itself, whether "heretics" within or "heathen" without. The connection is evident in the predilection of the early Fathers for calling any and all enemies "Judaizers," even when the issue at stake had nothing to do with Jews or Judaism. (On this see David Efroymson, "The Patristic Connection" in Davies, *Anti-Semitism,* 98–117.)

Coupled with this exclusivism is the Church's pride in assuming that it alone has the truth and right on its side, and that, as the body of the triumphant Christ, it is destined to triumph on earth. The Christological foundations of this attitude and its resultant conduct are an understanding of Easter as Christ's unqualified victory over sin and death, such that the Church can be regarded already as the coming of the Kingdom of God that Jesus proclaimed. Understanding Christ as the victorious king, the Church proceeded to act as if it were a victorious kingdom.

With an understanding of the things concerning Jesus of Nazareth that portrayed him as the anti-Judaic, exclusive, and royal master over all, it is hardly surprising that the Church has been a traditional bastion of ancient patterns of patriarchalism. The connection between Christology and sexism is perhaps clearest in an argument raised in objection to the ordination of women: the fact that Jesus was male is taken to be the justification of an exclusively male leadership in the Church.

All these tendencies are interconnected in the Church's Christology. As the Church understands the things concerning Jesus of Nazareth, so it understands God and itself before God, and so it behaves. Because its conduct is a function of its actual Christology, one may hope that an actual reformation of its Christology will lead to a reformation of its conduct. Any Christology helpful for the Church today will have this practical goal in mind.

4. THE PLACE OF CHRISTOLOGY

i. Place as location

Christology, as the understanding of the things concerning Jesus of Nazareth, confronting the hearer with the gift and claim of God's love, takes place in the Church. That is true by definition, for Christology in this sense makes the Church to be the Church. Where there is Christology in this sense, there is the Church, and where there is the Church, Christology in this sense occurs. There could not be a Church without a Christology.

Christology as critical reflection and suggested correction of the Church's understanding of the things concerning Jesus of Nazareth also takes place in the Church, but not with the same necessity. If Christology as critical reflection takes place, that is because it is sensed in the Church that something has gone wrong. It may not be seen at first as a fault in its understanding. The sense that something is wrong may well begin by attending to the Church's conduct, its action. When the Church, or some within it, begin to see that the Church has acted or is acting wrongly, its criterion for making this judgment will refer, sooner or later, to the things concerning Jesus of Nazareth. In proposing that the Church's conduct does not square with the things concerning Jesus of Nazareth, it will in fact be challenging the understanding of him that made possible that conduct. Thus the sense that all is not well with conduct leads eventually to the awareness that all is not well with the Church's Christology.

Others, not members of the Church, may also have their ideas about Jesus and the things concerning him, the Church's Christology not excluded. If they do, it would be well for the Church to keep its ears open and its voice low. It may have important new things to learn, such as the fact that Jews have long known our traditional Jesus as evil because of what he led his followers to do to the Jewish people. On the other hand, the Jewish theologian Eugene Borowitz's *Contemporary Christologies* has made a singular contribution to a better understanding of the relationship between various Christologies and attitudes toward the Jewish people. Generally speaking, however, christological criticism has come from within the Church, as when black Christians have pointed out how white the Jesus of a predominantly white Church has been, or when women Christians have pointed out how patriarchal is the Jesus of a Church run by men.

ii. Place as function

Christology, as an understanding of Jesus that is nothing less than an understanding of oneself before God, gives the Church and every believer their identity as Church and Christian. Christological differences within the Church, therefore, are at once and emphatically differences over self-understanding. The issue is Christian identity. Christological discussion, then, is not a matter of proving who is right about Jesus; it is a matter of finding our uncertain way before God. Of course this takes place with constant reference to Jesus. He is certainly the subject of the discussion, but not in isolation. If the discussion is christological, then God is our ultimate subject of conversation, and we ourselves before God are our immediate subject (the thesis of Ogden's *The Point of Christology*).

Christology at the level of critical reflection arises when a problem becomes evident, when it is seen that all is not well with the Church, when we have difficulty recognizing ourselves as the Church of Jesus Christ. The function of critical Christology, then, is to help the Church, and so each of us, to see how we went wrong, how the problem arose, and how we might correct the situation. This general formulation, however, calls for specification in each time and situation. For the present situation of the Church, we have identified the problem as being at root the anti-Judaism of the Church's classical tradition, and then the pride and patriarchalism that accompanied that anti-Judaism and further marred the tradition. Christology today, therefore, will seek to rid the Church of these problems. That is what it is for.

If the function of Christology has been properly identified, then a proper Christology for the Church today should free the Church to affirm God and itself in Christ without having to negate others (the proper concern of Joseph Monti, *Who Do You Say that I Am?*). It will be an important part of its task to develop a form of that affirmation that does not entail the negation of Jews first, and then women, blacks, "gays," and many others, so painfully characteristic of the Church's past behavior.

iii. Place as authorization

In determining the place of Christology, there is further the question of its authorization. Why should this be done? The answer follows directly from the function of correcting failures in the Church's conduct. The criterion by which a judgment concerning conduct may be made is given by the primary sense of Christology: the Church is confronted in the gospel, in the story of the things concerning Jesus of Nazareth, by the call and claim of God. In hearing this call and claim, the Church knows itself as God's possession and as answerable to God, responsible for the way in which it follows Christ. Called to let itself be conformed to Christ, the Church is therefore always open to the question of the adequacy of this conformation, whether its conduct is appropriate to its gospel.

If it be alleged that the Church can never live fully according to its gospel, that it knows it is always in need of forgiveness, this (however true) may not be used as an excuse for being satisfied with a Christology which does not challenge its failures. The Church's confession of its need of forgiveness is itself an admission that all is not well and is therefore the reason for critical reflection on its understanding of the things concerning Jesus of Nazareth.

The reason for doing Christology can also be expressed in terms that may be more helpful for a Church still deeply influenced by the Enlightenment and by Bultmann's program of "demythologization." We could say that the Church understands itself to be called and claimed by that which it is utterly unable to define or control—indeed just that is what it is to be "religious": it is to want to say to oneself, "it really matters ultimately what we do, but the ultimate is too far beyond us to be nameable." To be a Christian, however, is to let the name of Jesus stand for that which cannot be named. That is what makes it possible for Christology to be a quite practical critical reflection on the relationship between conduct and what matters most for Christians.

iv. Place as context

Reflection on the place of Christology, finally, raises the question of its context. There is no understanding without reference to the context of what is to be understood. The Church's understanding of the things concerning Jesus of Nazareth is no exception: it will depend on the context in which the Church sees them. Assuming the Jewish-Christian reality as defined in *Discerning the Way* and *A Christian Theology of the People Israel*, we shall have to consider the bearing of that context on the Church's understanding of Christ.

The starting point of such reflection will be Israel as the context of Jesus Christ, not only because it was indisputably the historical context of his life, but because the apostolic witness to him presents him and his whole significance within and in the terms provided by Israel's story. There is where he confronts us and where we confront him. But then we shall have to reflect upon the new context that begins with the fact of that witness: standing within the context of Israel, Jesus called into existence a new context of those who acknowledged him as God's invitation to belong to God. A Christology for the Jewish-Christian reality will have to show that, just as Jesus cannot be rightly understood apart from Israel, so he cannot be rightly understood apart from the Church.

Finally, the God of Israel and of the Church is the Creator, and because Israel and the Church have been called by this God out of his concern for his whole creation, we shall need to see the world as an essential part of the context of Christ if we are to understand him properly. That "God so loved the world" (John 3:16) will also have to be considered in a Christology for the Jewish-Christian reality, for that reality is part of the whole visible ecosystem that includes the physical world on which the human world depends. It includes what the tradition has called "nature," as well as the socioeconomic and political world of human activity (see Ritschl, *Logik*, 32–33). All this too is part of the context in which the Church comes to its understanding of Christ.

One last introductory comment is in order about the context essential to the Church's understanding of the things concerning Jesus of Nazareth. Because Israel is the primary element of it, the context needs to be seen in the terms of Israel's story, and that story is not finished. Israel, the Church, and the world, then, stand today in the midst of a story that is still going on. Christology today will need to make it clear that the context up to this point is not the whole story. To understand Christ in context (and we shall argue that only so is he understandable at all) means to understand him as one with a future. And that means that Christology will make clear that there is a future not only for him, but for his whole context before God, and therefore for God too.

CHAPTER TWO

The Function of Christology

Christology, as critical reflection, as well as confession, is the Church's response to the love of the God of Israel with which it is confronted in Jesus Christ, "the same yesterday and today and for ever." It is, consequently, the Church's service to God's goal of reconciliation, which it owes to God and to the world.

1. CHRISTOLOGY AS LANGUAGE

i. *Language: words in context*

"To understand a language is to understand a form of life" (Wittgenstein, *Investigations*, Sect. 19). This is because we acquire our own language by learning to use words as others use them, interwoven with the activities of which they are an integral part. Language consists not only of a vocabulary controlled by a grammar; it always also presupposes a context, apart from which the words that are spoken cannot be understood.

Wittgenstein illustrated the point with an example: " 'After he said this, he left her as he did the day before.'—Do I understand this sentence? Do I understand it just as I should if I heard it in the course of a narrative? If it were set down in isolation I should say, I don't know what it's about. But all the same I should know how this sentence might perhaps be used; I could myself invent a context for it. (A multitude of familiar paths lead off from these words in every direction.)" (Wittgenstein, *Investigations*, Sect. 525.)

The point can, of course, be made on other metaphysical foundations than those provided by Wittgenstein. I happened to learn it from him, but William James made the same point earlier on the basis of his pragmatism. Clark Williamson learned the same point from Whitehead (Williamson, *Rejected*, 11–12). I take it to be an epistemological consensus of our day that context is essential to understanding.

This is as true of Christology as it is of any other use of language. The Christian's confession of Jesus Christ as Lord, and also any statements that arise from critical reflection on that confession, indeed all that the Church has said or says today about the things concerning Jesus of Nazareth, have a context, and if it is not understood, neither will be the use of language that we call Christology. To understand Christology, however, we need to be aware of its triple context: that of Israel's story, that of Christian faith or the Church, and that of the world of human language.

The first context is the story that the people Israel told and tell of their history with God and God's history with them, a story that underlies even such a nonnarrative and ahistorical tradition as that developed by the rabbis. This part of the context of Christology is not one that the Church has supplied. It was there already in the earliest traditions concerning Jesus, where it met and meets the Church as the environment in which Jesus is presented as living and seeing himself. Israel, with its story of the God of Israel in his mercy and judgment, is there in the first word the Church hears or has ever heard of Jesus. This story is the context in which alone the proclamation of the reign of God drawing near and the call to repentance could have made any sense. It is the context in which alone one could understand a question about the greatest commandment, or a word of God through whom "all things were made" and who "became flesh and dwelt among us" (John 1:3, 14). This context was not produced by the Church. It was there already as the framework within which alone it could be of interest to speak of the things concerning Jesus of Nazareth.

Second, Christology, being the church's language about Jesus Christ, has the responding Church as part of its context, for Christology is always and at every level a response of faith. It is a use of language in which the speaker—that is, the Christian or the Church—has an immense investment, for in speaking of the things concerning Jesus of Nazareth, the Church speaks of the grounds of its own identity and calling. The Church in its faith, or the faith of the Church, is therefore also a part of the context of Christology.

Finally, Christology is, after all, one use of our ordinary human language. Every word used can be found in any standard dictionary of the natural language of the speaker. Determining the most reliable sources and sorting out what parts of them represent earlier and later forms of the preaching of the early Church are matters that are settled by the same historical methods that can be and are used of other human texts. The world of human questioning and of searching for answers, then, is also a part of Christology, as is the world of human hoping and believing. Christian faith will differ from Marxist faith or capitalist faith, but as the act of risk and commitment, it remains human faith and so every bit as much a part of this world. The world, with its hopes and fears, its history and its future, is therefore also part of the context of Christology. All three of these contexts need further preliminary definition.

ii. Israel's story as context

Israel's story is the primary context that makes the Church's language about Christ intelligible. The people Israel have had a story to tell about who they are and where they come from. "A wandering Aramean was my father" (Deut. 26:5) is one way they began their tale. "We were Pharaoh's slaves in Egypt, and the LORD brought us out of Egypt with a mighty hand" (Deut. 6:21) is another version. It is the story of God's rescue of this people, of the covenant made between them, and of their continuing history with God in this covenant. That story is the context in which the

Church set what it had to say about Jesus, from the earliest evidence we have of its language and up to today.

Much of the language of the people Israel, of course, does not take the form of a story; the Jewish people have talked even more about the Torah and its bearing on matters of daily life. The Talmud is certainly not a narrative. Nevertheless, the Talmud (or oral Torah) makes repeated reference to the written Torah in which Israel's story is begun, and in so far as it is possible to interpret the rabbis as having been oriented to the Bible (as Michael Wyschogrod does in *The Body of Faith*), it is fair to say that Israel's story underlies and is presupposed by the whole halakhic tradition that comments upon it.

The important beginning and early stages of Israel's story that are the context of Christology are available to the Church in Israel's Scriptures. It can therefore be said that Israel's Scriptures are the original context of the Church's talk and reflection on the things concerning Jesus of Nazareth. In every stratum of the complex material that went into the final form of the Apostolic Writings, the Scriptures of Israel were, in a variety of ways, cited, referred to, or drawn upon in the early Church's various presentations of Christ. We shall have reason to raise questions about some of those ways; yet in all of them, the Scriptures of Israel provided the vocabulary and imagery with which, and above all the story within the framework of which, the Apostolic Writings tell of the things concerning Jesus of Nazareth.

A Christology for the Jewish-Christian reality needs to emphasize at this point that the context of the things concerning Jesus of Nazareth is *Israel's* Scriptures, not the Church's "Old Testament." The Church's "Old Testament" differs from Israel's Scriptures even when (as in some branches of the Church) the text is a reasonably accurate translation of them. The difference lies in the fact that the "Old Testament" is bound together with a "New Testament" for which it is thought to be a preparation and anticipation. The "Old Testament" points ahead to Christ as the fulfillment of all the hopes and promises contained in it and so as its total completion. If I were to claim that the "Old Testament" is the context of Christology, I would be saying nothing more or other than what the anti-Judaic church has said in developing a Christology that was the foundation of its traditional anti-Judaism. The "Old Testament" is certainly the context of the anti-Judaic Jesus of the anti-Judaic church.

It is quite otherwise if we claim that the context of Christology is provided by the Scriptures of Israel. Jesus is then set within Israel's story, and Israel's story is still unfolding. Staggeringly new chapters of that story have been written in the twentieth century of the Common Era, and the most important one, concerning the founding and development of the State of Israel, is only at an early stage. The Scriptures of the Jewish people, the story from and in which they have lived and still live to this day: that is the context for the Church's confession of and reflection on Jesus Christ. This is an important distinction, because what is at issue is a context of the living Scriptures of a living Israel that will direct our attention to the living reality of Jesus of Nazareth in an unfinished history.

iii. The ecumenical context

The second context that must be understood in order to understand Christological statements is that of the Church and its faith. I call this the ecumenical context because the ecumenical movement of this century is more a movement for the renewal of the Church than it is a drive for its reunion. The *oekumene* embraces the whole Church, in all its branches, all those who in fact confess Jesus as Lord and who know in some degree that renewal comes from the one so acknowledged. The *oekumene* lives from a Christological confession and engages in critical reflection on it in the hope of a renewal, of which a reunification of the churches is looked for as one of the fruits.

It is, further, a fact of the present life of the Church that this confession and critical reflection upon it cut right across the lines that divide the churches. If one is sufficiently concerned about the Church's Christology to read at all extensively in the current literature on the subject, one finds at once that one's reading is no respecter of ecclesiastical divisions. A survey of the index of current authors in almost any book on Christology today confirms the judgment that this subject is one that confronts the Church as a whole, and that particular concerns of Roman Catholics, Lutherans, Anglicans or Baptists are not the most important ones needing to be addressed. At least on the subject of contemporary Christology, the Church reflects as one, and the diversity that surely exists does not follow denominational distinctions.

Christology as the Church's confession of faith, and as its critical reflection on that confession and its implications, may indeed be enriched by attending to the special emphases that have developed within distinct denominations. The Eastern Orthodox, Roman Catholic, Lutheran, Reformed, Anglican, and the Radical Reformation churches all have something to contribute. Although none of these has been free of traditional Christian anti-Judaism, nevertheless all have served to uphold the Church and have served as the expression of the Church's faith. They are all candidates for critical analysis, but they are all worthy of respectful attention.

Above all, it is the Church as a worshiping community of faith that needs to be kept in view if one wishes to understand Christology. Christological assertions are confessions of faith before God and so are always speech-acts having the high level of personal investment characteristic of doxology. By the way in which it speaks of Jesus Christ, the Church is always defining itself before God. This self-involving element in Christology is fundamental to its meaning, and this is as true of its critical reflection as it is of its confession.

iv. The world as context

The Jewish-Christian reality is a visible part of the larger reality of creation, and the God of Israel to whom both the Jewish people and the Church bear witness is acknowledged by them as Creator and Lord of all. The central confession of the Church, that it is the Church of this God through Jesus Christ, reflects this wider context, which is therefore also essential to understanding its meaning.

Obvious though it may be, it often goes unnoticed that the language of Christology is only one or another natural language, be it English, German, Greek, or Russian. The vocabulary that the Church must draw upon in making its confession, or in reflecting critically upon it, is taken entirely from that of the natural language of its worldly context. "Father," "Son," "prophet," "priest," "king," "word," "flesh," even "incarnation" are all words that serve many purposes besides those of the Church's confession. Indeed, had they no other uses, they would be useless in this particular case. For Christology to be possible and understandable at all requires the context of natural languages and the world of which natural languages are so vital a part.

There is, consequently, no such thing, strictly speaking, as "religious language," but only natural language put to use for particular purposes by people who say of themselves that they are religious, or are so defined by others. To put it another way, so-called religious language is merely our natural language as it is used by Jews and Christians (and Muslims and others) in those circumstances that touch on their identity, or self-understanding, as Jews or Christians (or Muslims or others).

In the particular case of Christology, the rule holds as well: it remains a use of natural language by the Church, although this use is one in which none engage except the Church, since engaging in this use of language is precisely what defines membership in the Church. That does not mean that none but members of the Church can understand it. To pledge allegiance to a foreign country is something that I may not do as a citizen of the United States of America, but I can certainly understand what citizens of that country are doing when they make such a pledge. In so far as there is a technical vocabulary to Christology, it is only the use of some terms that are not widely used as the Church uses them, or used to use them. In every case, however, these are words drawn from the wider context of natural language. The words themselves come from that context of the world apart from which Christology would make no sense.

Finally, the world is the context of Christology at the deepest level of content. "God so loved the world" is the reason the Church gives for that event to which it bears witness in its confession of Jesus as Lord. In making a confession of where and how it stands before God, the Church points to where and how the world stands before God, knowingly or unknowingly. The Church takes seriously for itself the things concerning Jesus of Nazareth, because it is convinced that they matter to the whole world that belongs to the God of whom it speaks. Its Christological confession will always reveal that the Church's "God-language" is ever at the same time "world-language."

2. CHRISTOLOGY AS RESPONSE

i. *Christology as doxology*

Christology is a response, an answer, to a word previously addressed to the Church. That word, which has the definite form of the apostolic proclamation of the things concerning Jesus of Nazareth, addresses the Church with an offer of a gift of life in God's service, and therefore a total claim upon the life so given. As a response to this word, the Church offers its confession of faith, which is the primary form of its Christology.

Its confession of faith is of course a declaration of its trust in God and in what he has done and is doing in Jesus Christ, but it is also an acknowledgment, made in this trust, that God is who he has shown himself to be in the things concerning Jesus of Nazareth. Its Christology is therefore doxology, praise of God. It is an act of thanksgiving. This can be said not only of Christology as confession, but also of Christology as critical reflection, for that reflection is concerned with an amendment of life or a reform of behavior to bring the life and actions of the Church more into conformity with Christ. In as much as the church means "to show forth [God's] praise not only with our lips but in our lives, by giving up ourselves to [God's] service" (from the General Thanksgiving, *BCP*), so the critical examination of how it confesses Christ and the practical implications that follow from that confession are also acts of praise. Theology, of course, is not prayer. It takes a more argumentative form than is usual in prayer. Yet we may recall that Anselm's *Proslogion*, a highly sophisticated theological argument, was written precisely in the form of a prayer addressed to God. As critical reflection on praise, reflective Christology is at the least in the service of praise. In this sense, it too is doxological, even when it is pointing out the difference between a doxological and a dogmatic use of language and reminding the dogmatician (the theologian) that doxological assertions, like expressions of love are, as Emil Fackenheim said of rabbinic *midrashim*, to be taken always with the utmost seriousness, but never "literally."

ii. *Christology as confession*

In its primary form, Christology, the Church's speech concerning Jesus of Nazareth, is a confession of faith. The subject matter of this speech is Jesus Christ, but because it is a confession, it tells much more than information about Jesus. It does give a certain amount of information about Jesus, but it gives at the same time important information about the speaker. A confession of faith (or trust) lays bare a relationship between the speaker and the object of trust. The Church's confession of faith in Jesus Christ is also an acknowledgment of how the Church understands itself in the face of the God whom Jesus called Father. The place and role of Jesus in the Church's confession, as we shall see, is crucial, and yet it could also be said that that confession is really not *about* Jesus at all. Jesus, we shall argue, plays the indispensable role of catalytic agent for that which is central in the confession, namely, the laying bare of the speaker before God, the God of Israel, Maker of heaven and earth. The Church's confession of faith is an act of undressing, so to speak, of acknowledging that the Church stands before the One from whom nothing can be hidden, there being no place to hide. It is the last thing the Church can say. It can therefore only be spoken with an investment of the whole self.

iii. *Christology as ecclesial self-understanding*

The conclusion to which we are led by these reflections on Christology as confession is that Christology would seem to imply and reveal the Church's definition of itself. By the way in which the Church speaks of Jesus Christ, its self-definition can be detected. In other words, with each Christological title that the Church ascribes to Jesus, it commits itself to assigning a corresponding term to itself. If Jesus is master, then the Church is made up of his servants. If he is called Teacher, then Christians are his disciples. If Jesus is Lord, then the Church is his possession. If he is the Word of God, then the Church consists of hearers of the Word. The Church, in sum, would appear to have already committed itself to all that it will be able to say about itself when it has said all it is able to say of Jesus Christ.

The Church has ascribed more glorious and powerful titles to Christ than any of these, however. It has said of him that he is "God of [or from] God, light of [or from] light, very God of [or from] very God, of one substance with the Father." Those are the titles of the Council of Nicea. How were the Fathers of Nicea defining themselves when they spoke thus of Jesus? It could be argued that they defined themselves as worshipers, called to adore the one of whom they spoke.

There is, however, an ambiguity in the self-definition implied here, reminding us that language can conceal as well as reveal, and that critical reflection is needed in this matter. It could also be argued that the Nicean Fathers were defining themselves as the possessors of a definitive knowledge of one fully equal with a God whom they did not seem to have understood always as one who had set before them a crucified Jew as their sole way to God. Perhaps in calling Jesus "God" they thought they already knew what God was and were now saying that Jesus is that too. If they already knew (as did the authors of one out of many church confessions that could be cited here, and who surely thought they were being faithful to Nicea) that God was "everlasting, without body, parts or passions; of infinite power, wisdom and goodness" (Article I, The Anglican *Articles of Religion*), and if they said that Jesus was very God of this very God, then that made Jesus Christ similarly passionless and omnipotent. Would it not seem to be in order that the Church of this divine being should rule as his vicar on earth? Was this Jesus Christ then the mighty victor over all his enemies already, and should not his Church share already in that victory? Determining the implied ecclesiology in the Church's Christology turns out not to be a simple matter. Or we could also say because of the ecclesiological dimension to Christology, raising questions about how the titles given to Christ bear on the behavior of the Church provides a critical check on which titles to use and how to use them. Because Christology is a response, critical reflection upon it will always include critical reflection on the responders.

iv. Christology past and present

Reference to Nicea reminds us that any Christology, including one for the Jewish-Christian reality, has to reckon with a Christological tradition. The formulations of the councils of Nicea and Chalcedon have so major a place in that tradition that they have influenced all subsequent reflection on the things concerning Jesus of Nazareth. They warrant our attention and respect if for no other reason than that they have shaped for so long and for so many believers the Church's response to Christ and to God.

Yet the classical Christology of Nicea and Chalcedon, precisely as the Church's response, solidified and shaped a long history of Christian anti-Judaism, and also of pride and patriarchalism. It therefore stands in need of critical analysis and correction. The roots of the problem go back earlier than those ecumenical councils, but those councils fixed the course of Christological reflection for most of the Church's history to this day. Christology today has to reckon with this fact.

In developing what was to become classical Christology, the Fathers of Nicea and especially of Chalcedon gave careful attention to defining the relationships between Jesus and God, and between Jesus and his fellow human beings. The context which appears to have been uppermost in their minds was that provided by God as omnipotent Creator, and humanity as God's creatures. How Jesus was related to that God and to humanity was therefore the question that seems to have led to the formulations of the Council of

Chalcedon. The dogma formulated at that council, therefore, centered almost exclusively on the divinity and the humanity of Jesus Christ.

Certainly the relationship of Jesus to God and to humanity is a possible way in which to put the issues of Christology, and unquestionably they derive from the things concerning Jesus of Nazareth as these are presented in the Apostolic Writings. What is equally certain is that Chalcedon represents a remarkable narrowing of the rich diversity of these presentations. More importantly, the context was drawn far more narrowly than had seemed to have been necessary to the authors of those Writings. Israel had dropped out of the picture almost entirely. Israel was either taken for granted by the bishops at those councils, or it was only alluded to. Israel's story, as a result, no longer formed a controlling context, and as a result, it was not felt necessary to say that God is the God of Israel. Furthermore, Israel no longer provided a context for Jesus of Nazareth. The relationship of Jesus to the God of Israel and his relationship to his own people Israel do not seem to have been questions that the Council of Chalcedon felt it necessary to address. In their place were set the issues of the divinity and the humanity of Christ.

F. W. Marquardt has raised this question by pointing out that for the Church of the patristic period it was necessary to clarify the divinity of Christ, and that in the modern period it was necessary to clarify his humanity. Today (after Auschwitz), it is the Church's task to clarify the sociology of Jesus (Marquardt, "Was haltet ihr von Christos?"). The term "sociology" may be slightly misleading, but the point is right: Christ in context means Jesus as a Jew among Jews, brought up on Israel's story and understood in the framework of that story and in his solidarity with his people. When the intimacy of God with his people Israel and of Jesus with his people are ignored, the divinity and humanity ascribed to Jesus become abstracted from the context in which the apostolic witness presents him to us for our good. I would therefore correct Marquardt's provocative assertions by saying that the patristic Church asked after Christ's divinity, already a fearful distortion of the apostolic concern for his relationship to the God of Israel's story, and the modern Church asked after his humanity, a fatally distorting reduction of his relationship to his own people. The task incumbent on us today is therefore to attend to Christ in the actual context evident in the early apostolic witness to him.

Christology today will be, as it has always been, the response of the Church to the things concerning Jesus of Nazareth. In making that response today, the Church could rest on and repeat the Christology of the classical tradition *if* it were satisfied with the traditional conduct of the Church, including its anti-Judaism. I maintain that after Auschwitz, such a course is immoral and intolerable. That is not to say that the dogmas of the ecumenical councils are wrong and to be rejected. It is to say that while we may learn from them of errors that threatened the Church then and may do so again today, we cannot simply settle for the Christology of the past as adequate for the Church today. Nicea and Chalcedon should be listened to and respected, but if their words should be rehearsed, they will not be the last words of a Church making a living response today to its living Lord.

3. THE CONTINUING CONFRONTATION

i. Jesus Christ: the proclaimed proclaimer

Professor Willi Marxsen in his study *The Beginnings of Christology* argues persuasively that those beginnings "lie at the point where the relationship between Jesus and the believer becomes visible for the first time," and therefore that we are not forced by historical investigation to choose between the earliest Christian community and the historical Jesus (Marxsen, *Beginnings,* 37). Marxsen, a radical, post-Bultmannian German biblical scholar, thus comes out on the side of continuity, rather than discontinuity, between the Jesus who came preaching the approaching reign of God and the early proclamation of Jesus by the primitive Christian community. There is continuity between Jesus the proclaimer and the proclamation of the Church because in the earliest level of the Church's witness, "Jesus was always already the one who was proclaimed" (Marxsen, *Beginnings,* 79).

Marxsen's carefully argued thesis is that the earliest testimony to Jesus that can be detected by means of form-critical analysis of the gospel texts is itself a proclamation of Jesus as the one who with supreme urgency called men and women to a radical faith or trust in God. Even where explicit Christological titles are lacking, as for example in Matthew's Sermon on the Mount, Jesus is nonetheless presented as the one who confronts his hearers with the word of God's absolute offer of unlimited love, a love that lays a claim of unreserved commitment upon the hearer. In short, from the farthest back into the history of the Jesus-movement that the historian can probe, which means to the earliest possible testimony to Jesus, there was already being proclaimed the proclaimer of the reign of the God of love and justice.

If this analysis is right, then the so-called gap that an earlier period of biblical criticism thought to find between Jesus and the faith of the early Church turns out to be an illusion. Everything we have from the early Church in our sources has been clearly shown by form-critical analysis to be in the service of its preaching or proclamation. The one it proclaimed, however, is always presented as the one who confronted his first hearers with the love of God. He who proclaimed the nearness of the reign of God was then proclaimed as doing just that, and the purpose of this proclamation of Jesus is evidently to confront the reader with precisely that same love and the call to faith with which Jesus had confronted his first disciples.

Thus it is possible to say that between the Jesus who preached the reign of God and the Church that preached Jesus, there is only an apparent gap, which disappears when we notice more carefully that the Church preached the Jesus who preached the love of the Father.

ii. Jesus Christ yesterday

"Jesus Christ is the same yesterday and today and for ever" (Heb. 13:8). So said the author of the possibly quite early (if heavily edited) sermon that goes by the inaccurate title of "The Letter to the Hebrews." I take it that the Church has believed this to be true ever since. But what was Jesus Christ yesterday? The earliest yesterday available to the critical historian is the earliest testimony of the early Church. The nearest we can come as historians to Jesus is the witness that is transmitted with more or less editing by the authors of the Apostolic Writings. That witness points to an actual Jew, known to his disciples and to others as Jesus of Nazareth or as Jesus called the Anointed, who came preaching that the reign of Israel's God was about to break in, and who called his fellow Jews to repent and trust totally in their God. It is safe to say that nothing concerning Jesus was written down until some time after his death, and since it is by way of those writings that we have access to presumably early and orally transmitted memories of Jesus' message, we can see that the story of Jesus is told always with his end in view and because of what happened on Easter.

Nevertheless, it seems unlikely that the story of Jesus' death and of Easter would have had the impact they appear to have had, had there been no prior story. If Jesus had not had a following before going to Jerusalem, there would have been no disciples to be so shaken by his death and by Easter. Indeed, whatever else we shall want to say about it, the Easter event was the discovery that the Jesus of yesterday was, in spite of his death, still able today to confront his disciples with the present reality of God's love as God's claim upon them.

Jesus yesterday, then, as we can establish from the Apostolic Writings and particularly from the synoptic Gospels, was Jesus as we see him through the eyes of those who were confronted by him with God's radical claim upon them. This proclaimer of the immediacy of God's love—now, not tomorrow!—and the totality of its claim made upon them—turn around, follow me!—is the one they proclaimed. That is Jesus yesterday.

The witness to Jesus yesterday takes a wide variety of forms that we shall have to examine, but in each one the same Jesus comes through. Whether as wandering preacher or worker of healings and other wonders, he was for his disciples one who left them no alternative and no escape. Confrontation with Jesus meant for them a confrontation, as they had not experienced it before, with God's immediate and total claim upon them. We may presume that as Jews they surely knew about God's love and God's demand. As Israel, they knew Israel's story. Now the heart of that story of God's love for Israel and Israel's love for God became concentrated in the here and now. In Jesus they were confronted with that story in a new and intense way. In that confrontation was born a new or renewed faith in God, and out of it was born Christology, the Church's rehearsal of the things concerning Jesus of Nazareth.

This brief, introductory reconstruction of the beginning of the Jesus-movement is there to be read from the texts when examined by histori-cal-critical methods. It does not take eyes of faith to discover it. Whether historians find themselves similarly confronted and make a similar re-sponse as did the disciples is another matter. But thus far, the reconstruc-tion is on fairly firm historical grounds. If we were to try to go farther and ask about Jesus' own self-understanding or his own inner experience, we would have moved to the level of speculation. What went on between Jesus and the one he called Father is a matter of speculation. What is quite certain is what went on between Jesus and his disciples that led them to speak of Jesus' relationship to his Father as they did. That Jesus awakened in them a trust in God as a Father who loved the most unlova-ble is a matter that may be established historically. Christology can build, as indeed it grew originally, on that firm basis. It has no need to speculate about Jesus' so-called "*abba* experience" as Edward Schillebeeckx does in his book *Jesus.* That can be at best no more than a hypothetical construc-tion far too weak to support the Christology of the Church. What exper-iences Jesus had of his Father can be reconstructed from the evidence only hypothetically. What can be learned with some certainty from those same sources is the experiences his disciples claim to have had of this Fa-ther because of Jesus. That is, finally, all the Church needs to know.

iii. Jesus Christ today

The primary tense of Christology is the present. Were this not so, there would be no Christology. If Jesus Christ yesterday is the Jesus in whom his disciples were confronted with God's love and its claim upon them, then Jesus Christ today will be the living Je-sus with whom the disciples, beginning with Peter, were first con-fronted on Easter day, and who has confronted the Church again and again in word, sacrament, and in the least of his brothers and sisters down through the centuries. "Today," for the author of Hebrews and for the Church ever since, is the time after the death of Jesus, beginning with Easter and up to and including now—and above all now. The central claim that constitutes and is made by the Church, and out of which all Christology is developed, is that Jesus is today, in the present, the same as Jesus yesterday.

What is going on, how can we make sense of it, when we hear it said that a man, a Jew, who most certainly died a violent death at Gentile hands, *is* (present tense) the same today (after his death) as he was yesterday (before his death)? How are we to understand the unanimous proclamation of the early Church and the Church ever since, that Jesus lives? And how are we to understand the variety of other ways—and we shall have to examine with care how various they are—in which that proclamation is preserved for us: that Jesus appeared to Peter and then to others; that he is risen from the dead; that he is exalted to the right hand of the Father; that his tomb was empty? What lies behind that (to us today) strange notion "resurrection"?

One thing is clear: with the single term "resurrection," the Church has masked to itself and others the variety of ways in which the Apostolic Writings have preserved the conviction of the early Church that the Jesus Christ of yesterday is the Jesus Christ of today; that in spite of his death, who and what he was and was doing were believed by the Church—and are to this day believed by the Church—to be matters of the present, not merely of the past.

The single term "resurrection" may not have been the best one for the Church to have used to pull together the various ways in which the earliest witness expressed its conviction that Jesus had to be spoken of in the present tense as well as in the past. Although the Acts of the Apostles speaks of "the Twelve" as being "witnesses of [the Lord Jesus'] resurrection" (Acts 1:22), no verse in Acts nor any other text tells us a word about anyone seeing or being present at an event that could be called "the resurrection of Jesus." Rather, we are told of Jesus appearing to certain people or being seen by them—and then disappearing. We are told that he has been raised to the right hand of the Father. We are told of certain people having seen his tomb and that it was empty. We are not told that Peter or anyone else saw Jesus rise from the dead. The witness, in short, is to Jesus alive, either alive as one who appeared, briefly and somewhat ambiguously to certain people, or alive as present with God.

That Jesus lives or is alive would seem to be a better summary of the diverse witness of the early Church, if summary there must be. But "live" and "life" are rich words: the Oxford English Dictionary (*O.E.D.*) gives over six columns to the first and nine to the second. An important sense of "to live" is "to have life," which is to have the characteristics of life. These can be thought of in biological terms, but the *O.E.D.* gives priority to a definition in functional terms. This seems to capture the use of the apostolic witness: as Jesus in his preaching and actions confronted his hearers with the gift and claim of God's unlimited love, so Jesus proclaimed by his disciples confronted the hearers of his witnesses with the same gift and claim. Jesus made men and women into servants of God, after as well as before his death. He was alive.

We shall have to weigh carefully the pros and cons of such a functional interpretation of Easter, and compare these with those of the more traditional picture of a physical resurrection and an empty tomb. It should be stressed, however, that we shall end up, on either hand, with an interpretation made by the early Church. If we ask what is being interpreted, the nearest that we can come to a historically supportable answer is the faith of the early Church, beginning presumably with Peter: the conviction that Jesus was doing again, after his death, what he had done before—confronting his disciples with the God of Israel and the gift and claim of God's unbounded love. As the passage quoted from Hebrews put it, "Jesus Christ is the same yesterday and today and for ever."

iv. Confrontation and the future

We have discussed in a most preliminary manner the identity of the Jesus Christ of Easter with the Jesus Christ of the time up to his death. But we have claimed that the primary tense of the Church's Christological confession and reflection is the present. That means that the principal focus of Christology in the late twentieth century is with Jesus Christ in our own today near the end of this twentieth century. And the second tense is the future, so Christology today will ask about Jesus Christ today and then also tomorrow. Only when it is clear that these are the topics of primary concern to the Church will it be at all comprehensible why it should be so interested in what is supposed to have happened in the first third of the first century.

A Christology for today, a Christology after Auschwitz, will have to wrestle with its own origins. So much of the Church's anti-Judaic tradition and behavior stems from a certain reading of those origins and from an interpretation of the things concerning Jesus of Nazareth that marked the final shape of the Church's Gospels and other canonical writings. If it reevaluates its origins in order to correct unhistorical or ahistorical interpretations of Jesus, that is a small contribution to paying off the colossal debt that the Church owes the Jewish people. That, however, is not going to be reason enough to produce the Christology demanded by the Jewish-Christian reality. That reality calls on the Church to say where it stands right now and where it means to go tomorrow. It challenges the Church to answer responsibly whether it lives in its past, or whether it is able to repent, to turn around and begin afresh.

But just this was the challenge of Jesus Christ yesterday and in the today of Easter. The Church today—if its Christology is to be indeed the response of doxology, confession, and ecclesial self-understanding—will be driven in reflecting upon the things concerning Jesus of Nazareth by the question of whether these things are all over and settled in the past, or whether now and tomorrow come first. For the Church today facing tomorrow, does Jesus

Christ live, or does he only live in its past? Is the Church interested in the past of Jesus because it knows him as the one in whom it is brought face to face today with the God of Israel and therefore also into the presence of and solidarity with the Israel of God, the Jewish people of whom Jesus is one? Christology today, and that means a Christology for the Jewish-Christian reality, has to help the Church to think about this and to find a confession of Jesus Christ appropriate to him today and tomorrow.

4. THE SERVICE OF RECONCILIATION

i. *Paul's witness to reconciliation*

In a letter to the church in Corinth (2 Cor. 5:18–19), Paul summed up his gospel by saying that God "through Christ reconciled us to himself and gave us the ministry of reconciliation; that is, in Christ God was reconciling the world to himself, not counting their trespasses against them, and entrusting to us the message of reconcilation."

Krister Stendahl has warned us to be careful with Paul's use of personal pronouns. Who is the "us" that were reconciled to God? In the next verse, the object of reconciliation becomes "the world." (The second "us" refers evidently to Paul, or to Paul and his fellow missionaries, although of course every new convert would by that fact share in the ministry of reconciliation.)

The reference to "the world" is clarified by a passage from Paul's letter to the Romans (11:11–12) in which he used "the Gentiles" and "the world" synonymously. The first "us" of 2 Corinthians 5:18 would therefore refer to Paul's Gentile converts with whom, as a result of his ministry to them, he identified himself. That identification, however, does not remove the difference, which appears in v. 19, between "them" (i.e., you Gentiles) and "us" (Paul and his fellow apostles to the Gentiles).

Paul's gospel was the good news that the God of Israel had reached out to gather the Gentiles to himself in Christ. Paul's ministry was to make known to those Gentiles the good news of their reconciliation. His own calling as an apostle to the Gentiles, and his gospel concerning the Gentiles, as he understood them, were inseparable.

The reconciliation of the Gentiles to the God of Israel put them alongside the Israel of God. It therefore followed that "in Christ," that is, in the church of Christ, there was no more conflict between Jew and Gentile (Gal. 3:28). By baptism, all were what the Jews in the early Church had always been: sons of Abraham (v. 29). Thus was God's promise to Abraham, enshrined in the first book of the Torah (Gen. 17:5; cf. Rom. 4:17), that he would be the father of a multitude of *goyim*, enacted in Paul's ministry of reconciliation.

Paul also longed for a further reconciliation, one between the Church—made up of reconciled Gentiles and Jews—and the rest of the Jewish people. How could the Church of God and the Israel of God not be reconciled? Yet Paul could see this was not yet the case. It was his hope, perhaps even his expectation, that this was soon to happen. If we take his "in Christ" eschatologically, as an attempt to anticipate the total reconciliation of all creation in the ultimate realization of God's purposes, then all would be one, Christ would no longer have any further function, and God would be "all in all," or "everything to everyone" (1 Cor. 15:28).

It is to be noted that Paul's aching desire for reconciliation between the Church and the Jewish people (cf. Rom 9:1–3) was not shared by the Pauline disciple who wrote what we call the Epistle of Ephesians. This later writer was satisfied to rejoice in the reconciliation between Jews and Gentiles that existed within the Church (2:11–22). I am following here the argument of Peter von der Osten-Sacken (*Grundzüge*, 100–103) against the interpretation of M. Barth.

For Paul, then, reconciliation was at the center of his Christology and so of his ministry and message to the Gentiles. Reconciliation was God's purpose in Christ, and it was therefore the content and purpose of Paul's gospel. As reconciliation had created the Church, so reconciliation was to be the prime purpose of the Church.

ii. The Gospels' witness to reconciliation

The proclamation by the early Church of Jesus was of one who proclaimed that the reign of God was at hand. Those are his opening words as he is presented in what is broadly thought to be the first of our extant Gospels (Mark 1:15). The coming of God's reign is the recurring theme of parables and sayings attributed to him by the whole synoptic tradition, just as his acts of healing are signs of the new era already effective in his actions. The witness of this tradition is to a Jesus who both announced and confronted people with the immediacy of God's healing presence.

Although the word reconciliation occurs only once in this tradition (Matt. 5:24), reconciliation is a fair summary of what it presents as the consequence of the preaching and actions of Jesus. Sinners are reconciled to God with the result that they are reconciled to each other. The reign of God means the redemption of all creation, in which sin and all its consequences are overcome. The sick are healed, the disabled are returned to wholeness, the dead are restored to life. In the presence of Jesus, according to the gospel traditions, the reconciliation of creation to God began to take place.

The consequence for anyone confronted with the reign of God, according to the traditions lying behind our Gospels, is that reconciliation was made possible and necessary with one's fellow human beings. More specifically, the elder brother was to receive with rejoicing the repentant younger brother, righteous Israel was to take back and embrace its formerly errant but now repentant unrighteous ones. In the immediate face of the reign of God, all were the recipients of a total gift of God's immeasurable love. But that meant that each recipient had to see all others as being in the identical situation. Love of neighbor, service to the least of Jesus' brothers or sisters, was entailed, since all were loved freely by the one God. As a later writer put the point, "If any one says, 'I love God,' and hates his brother, he is a liar" (1 John 4:20). Before or in the presence of God, which is where the tradition tells us the disciples found themselves in the presence of Jesus, reconciliation took place with God and with the neighbor.

iii. Christ the divider

The testimony of the early Church has preserved a tradition of Jesus' solidarity with his own people. He is presented as having understood himself as being sent only to the lost sheep of the house of Israel (Matt. 15:24), and as having ordered his disciples to confine their mission solely to Israel (Matt. 10:5–6). The Jesus whom this witness presented as having so amazingly confronted them with the gift and claim of God's immediacy, and whom they proclaimed with the intent that their hearers and readers might be similarly confronted, was a Jesus deeply concerned for his own people. The apostle Paul, as we have noted, was one of the few authors of the Church's canonical writings to have certainly shared that concern.

Although Paul could write that Christ became a servant of the Jewish people (Rom. 15:8), it is only with care that one can detect the theme of Jesus' solidarity with, love for, and service to his people in our present Gospels, so heavily is it overshadowed by the countertheme of hostility. Evidently at a fairly early date, and at least before the passion narratives were constructed, a conflict would appear to have developed between the Jesus-movement, originally made up only of Jews but becoming increasingly Gentile in membership, and the rest of the Jewish people. In his letter to the Romans, Paul sensed the danger of such a conflict and tried to prevent it (Rom. 9–11). By the time of the final editing of our present Gospels, the hostility between the Church and the Jewish people was becoming intense. It can be felt in the polemics against the Pharisees in Matthew 23, for after the fall of Jerusalem and the destruction of the Temple, they or their successors had assumed the role of leadership of the Jewish people. It became especially dominant in the construction of the passion narratives, in which the death of Jesus at Roman hands is recounted in such a way as to place full responsibility for it on the Jewish leaders or even on the whole Jewish people.

The result was that Jesus the Jew from Nazareth was turned into an anti-Judaic Jesus, denouncing his people for their stubborn rejection of him and his message. The issue may more likely have been that the policies of the Pharisaic/rabbinic leadership, in their attempt to preserve the Jewish people after the disastrous war with Rome by teaching an all-encompassing application of Torah fidelity, conflicted with the practice of the increasingly Gentile young Church. Even before the war, it must have become evident to the Jewish leadership that this new movement was leading a fair number of Jews into disobedience to God's Torah, separation from their people, and acceptance of Gentile ways. Surely a leadership concerned for the survival of the Jewish people would have had no responsible alternative to resisting it.

Reconstruction of the origins of and early development of the conflict between the Church and the synagogue must be largely hypothetical, due to the nature and limited number of our sources, but if this is anywhere near how it came about and developed, it would suggest that the editors of the early traditions, who gave us our present Gospels, interpreted the conflict that ended in Jesus' death in the light of the conflict in which they were themselves engaged. But if that is somewhere near the truth, then neither Jesus himself nor his disciples' response to him may have had anything to do with the original conflict. If the issue was the Jesus-movement's acceptance of increasing numbers of Gentiles into its ranks, or even if the conflict began as a rivalry between the followers of two different *midrashim* (interpretations) of the Scriptures and two different conceptions of how Torah should be lived, which is another possibility, Jesus would seem to have been only a symbol of the conflict between the Church and the synagogue.

Regardless which hypothesis is thought to make better sense of the evidence, the fact remains that the Church came to believe, and to enshrine in the final form of the Gospels, its conviction that Jesus had been rejected by his own people. And the Jewish people, or its leaders, appear to have accepted eventually at least this much of the Church's conviction: since Jesus had been in conflict with his people (as the Church was teaching), the clearest way to reject the Church was to reject what it had to say about the things concerning Jesus of Nazareth (as we find in the talmudic Ben-Pandera legend—Jesus was the illegitimate son of Mary and a Roman soldier, Pandera—and the later parody of the Gospels, the *Toledot Yeshu*). The net effect was to have produced an almost Gentile Jesus for the Church, and an anti-Judaic one at that. One could hardly have expected the synagogue to know of any other Jesus than the one thrown at it by the Church. Confronted with such a Jesus— and the Church presented no other—the Jewish people saw in him what the Church saw: the root cause of division between them. If the disciples of this person were the enemies of Israel, as their actions proved them to be, then he was to be judged, along with and because of his disciples, by a sound Jewish principle: "By their fruits you will know them."

iv. The challenge of reconciliation

The long history of Christian anti-Judaism, with its resultant persecution and pogroms, cannot be undone. If the Church is to take up the service of reconciliation that follows from the solidarity of Jesus with his people preserved in the apostolic witness to him, it will need to repent of the witness of hostility that obscured this. It would then be in a position to develop a Christology for the Jewish-Christian reality, one that was built on the intimacy of both Jesus and the God he called Father with the people Israel. That might then lead the Church to recognize that it cannot be close to and serve either that Jesus or that God without being close to and serving the Jewish people. Nevertheless, this would still not annul the history of the past nineteen centuries.

The ministry of reconciliation that is at least possible for the Church today and tomorrow can never again be what it was in the early years of the Jesus-movement, and about this the Church needs to be clear. Were the Church to conform its presentation of Jesus to that of the early apostolic preaching, its "testified-to-Jesus" could not possibly confront a Jew today as the "witnessed-to-Jesus" of the apostles confronted Jews in their day. For a Jew in those early years to have heard the apostolic (and of course Jewish) witness to Jesus and therewith to believe oneself confronted by the gift and claim of God's unbounded love, and so to believe Jesus to be anointed of God, fully authorized by God to speak and act in the name of that love, raised not the slightest question about being a Jew or forsaking one's people. For Jews today, no matter how they respond to any witness to Jesus, to become a disciple of that person is to become a Christian and join the Church with its long, anti-Judaic history, and so to break one's ties with the Jewish people. The consequence of that history is that the service of reconciliation that challenges the Church today will have to begin with today. It cannot be a direct continuation of the reconciliation preached in Paul's letters or in the early witness to Jesus of Nazareth.

The service of reconciliation possible for the Church today will be shaped, for better or worse, by its Christology. If it can find a way to speak of the things concerning Jesus of Nazareth that is a response of joy to the discovery that in Jesus it is confronted anew by the gift and claim of God's love, and to a realization that Jesus came first of all to serve the Jewish people, it may find many ways in which it can follow him in a supportive service to Israel as Israel (see van Buren, *People Israel*, 333–343). It might then be able to confess Jesus as the Anointed, fully authorized by God to confront it in his name, without evincing the least concern to ask Jews to make a similar confession.

CHAPTER THREE

The Context of Jesus Christ: Israel

The fundamental context of the things concerning Jesus of Nazareth, according to the apostolic witness, was the covenant between God and Israel; their continuing context is Israel in its enduring covenant with God. Israel and its story is therefore the fundamental context for developing a Christology for the Jewish-Christian reality, that is, a Christology for the Church today.

1. WHY THE CONTEXT MATTERS

i. Words in context

If it is generally true, as we have argued, that in order to understand the meaning of words we need to know the context of their use, in the case of the things concerning Jesus of Nazareth the general truth is particularly evident. The very name Jesus (possibly *Yeshua* originally?), the village of Nazareth, and the title-become-name, "Christ," all point to a Jewish context. Repeated reference to Israel's Scriptures by the witnesses to him place those witnesses in the context of early Judaism and nowhere else. The coming "reign of God" and the title "Son of David" further specify the context somewhere within the spectrum of Jewish hope. There is a further specification of time provided by the existence of both synagogues and the Temple, not to speak of the names of specific political figures—Herod the Great, his son Herod Antipas, and Pontius Pilate—that occur in the witness.

No less important is what might be called the functional the-ological vocabulary of the witness. Words such as "repentance," "sin," "forgiveness," and "righteousness," as well as the use of such metaphors as the vineyard and its owner, and the sheep and their shepherd, have their particular meanings within Israel's sto-ry and they would be different if set in another context. More im-portant are the recurring references to Moses, Torah, and the Commandments. Conversely, there are distinctions, important to some other contexts, that are conspicuous by their absence in the apostolic witness. For example, there is no distinction between the realms of the sacred and the secular. Ritual and ethical purity are not distinguished. No line seems to exist between a religious and a political sphere. These are particular features of Israel's sto-ry, marking it again as the context of the witness to Jesus of Naza-reth. Unless we are aware of that context, the possibilities for misunderstanding that witness are great.

Were it not for the anti-Judaic tradition of the Church, the Jew-ish context of the early witness would be self-evident, for Jesus of Nazareth and all his disciples were Jews. All those to whom we owe the earliest witness to Jesus, whether beginning from Easter or before, were Jews. Their witness was that of Jews, was ad-dressed to their fellow Jews, and concerned a Jew. The strange fact that Gentiles were to use and also misuse the original Jewish message, with its Jewish vocabulary about Jesus, came later. If Gentiles are to use that vocabulary with fidelity to its original meaning, they will need to be familiar with its Jewish context.

The Church has always been concerned about the fidelity of its mes-sage to that of the original apostles on the premise that the apostles were chosen witnesses to the things concerning Jesus of Nazareth. For centur-ies, it was assumed that the texts of the Apostolic Writings recorded that witness faithfully. Only in relatively recent times, with the rise of histori-cal-critical studies, has it become relatively clear that the texts preserve the witness of the Church of the time of their composition, and that any presumably early witness has to be reconstructed from them. Much in the texts is the result of an editorial process, oral and written, which represents the understanding of the earlier witness by later authors and editors in their own contexts. It is therefore a historical question to be decided by historical methods whether the Apostolic Writings are faithful to the original witness. The results of historical-critical analysis of the Apostolic Writings open the question of the Church's canon or norm: how can the extant text be our norm, when it becomes evident that the text contains both the original apostolic witness to a Jewish Jesus and also later editing that presents us with an anti-Judaic Jesus? This is no small matter, for the Church's Christology, and therefore its behavior, still depend on how we deal with this diversity preserved in the Apostolic Writings as we have them.

The reason why the Church should be concerned that its Christological witness be in conformity with that of original apostolic witness is because that witness proved to be effective in producing the Church, and so made the Church's Christology possible in the first place. The concern for conformity or fidelity is the concern that the things concerning Jesus of Nazareth continue to work their way in the world.

ii. A story in context

The things concerning Jesus of Nazareth, according to the apostolic witness, do not consist of a list of items. They consist of a story. The witness took the form of a narrative. The Gospels each tell the story in a different way, but they each tell a story. Paul's gospel is less obviously a narrative, yet for him too there was a sequence, as can be seen in Romans 1:3–6, 5:6–11, or 8:3–4. In his generally nonnarrative style, Paul too told of something that had happened.

Something has happened. That is what Christology has to make clear. It can do so only if what has happened is set within its own context. That which took place was an event in a particular time and place and therefore within another history. The gospel does not begin, "Once upon a time . . ." It begins, "In the days of Herod the King . . .", or "John the baptizer appeared in the wilderness, preaching . . .", or "When the time had fully come, God sent forth his Son . . ." (Gal. 4:4). We are thrust immediately into the history of Israel when we hear the first words of the apostolic witness.

The author or editor of the Gospel according to Luke has done this vividly with the three psalm-like songs of his introduction, Mary's *Magnificat* (Luke 1:46–55), Zechariah's *Benedictus* (1:68–79), and Simeon's *Nunc Dimittis* (2:29–32). With these songs, Luke set the story of Jesus Christ that he wanted to tell within that of Israel. It can hardly be accidental that he chose the Psalms of Israel as his model for them.

The fundamental context of the story that the early witnesses tell of Jesus, however, is the covenant between God and Israel, with all the tensions inherent in that relationship. All of the Gospels place the preaching of John the Baptist, who is portrayed as standing in the line of Israel's prophets, at or near the beginning of their story. John preaches the approaching climax of the relationship, the coming of the LORD and the day of judgment. John's theme is the inescapable immediacy of the crisis and hence the need to repent, to return to the faithfulness that God requires of his covenant people. The note of urgency continues in the preaching of Jesus that God's reign is at hand. The story of Jesus thus brings the issue of Israel's covenant into the present: will God be Israel's God and will Israel be God's people, now, at this moment, with no excuses or delays? The Gospel witness to Jesus portrays him as one who had made that issue demanding and life-giving to those who heard and saw him. The Evangelists presented that story of Jesus as posing the same issue for their readers. They evidently meant their story of Jesus to have the same impact on their readers as they present Jesus as having had on his disciples, namely, that the covenant between God and Israel become an immediate issue, here and now.

iii. *The Scriptural story as context*

Because Israel's covenant with God was the context of the things concerning Jesus of Nazareth, the early witnesses and their later editors told his story in the terms of and with constant reference to the Scriptures, the repository of Israel's memory, charter, and hope.

At the time of those early witnesses, Israel was in the early stages of developing what would become the oral Torah, the Mishnah and Talmud. We hear of this oral tradition from Paul (Gal. 1:14) and in a Synoptic Gospel saying (Mark 7:3–5, Matt. 15:2–6), but this was relatively new at the time and Israel was not yet of one mind as to its value. Contrary opinions about the authority of this oral tradition were one important difference between Pharisees and Sadducees, the latter holding conservatively to only the written tradition, the Scriptures, the former giving high authority also to the oral tradition. We hear echoes of that controversy in a late text of the Apostolic Writings (e.g., Acts 23:6–8). In all probability, however, at the time of Jesus and of the early witness to him, the Scriptures were universally acknowledged by Israel as the definitive record of its charter, the storehouse of its sacred memories, and the expression of its hope.

Much work has been done in recent years on Second Temple Judaism (see *EJ*, 8, 625–42). Our summary is too brief to do justice to the many issues involved. Of special interest is the work of such Israeli scholars as Y. F. Baer, E. E. Urbach, and D. Flusser on the *hasidim* of the period, raising the possibility that Jesus should be counted among them (see *EJ*, 7, 1383–88).

The original witness to Jesus was made by Jews for whom Israel's Scriptures were the Word of God. Their response to Jesus was that of women and men whose lives and thinking were formed by those Scriptures. To understand their witness, therefore, one needs to know what they knew. Creation and its Creator, Abraham and Isaac, Exodus and Sinai, Moses and Aaron, David and Solomon and their Psalms and Wisdom, and above all the Torah, all these were in the tradition of those who first bore witness to Jesus Christ. So too were Amos and Hosea, and Isaiah and Jeremiah, and the prophetic tradition of a hope for the restoration of the house of David and the return of Israel's independence. To attempt to understand that witness apart from this context provided by Israel's Scriptures is to invite misunderstanding.

Israel's Scriptures, then, were sacred writings for the early witnesses as they were for Jesus as they present him. They were also that for the later authors and editors of the texts of the Apostolic Writings. In sum, the whole of the apostolic witness to Jesus presupposes those Scriptures as its context. Israel's Scriptures do not give us all of Israel's story. Israel has lived for over twenty-two centuries since the last of them were written. But in all those centuries, the Scriptures have remained canonical for Israel's continuing story as they were for the Jews who first bore witness to the things concerning Jesus of Nazareth. They will have to be the context also of any Christology that means to serve the Church today as that witness served the Church in its beginnings.

It matters that we have spoken consistently of the Scriptures of Israel, not of the Gentile Church's "Old Testament." With the Church's new title for those writings came an interpretation that changed their meaning. This change was in part due to the fact that in its struggles with Gnosticism, the Church handled badly the issue raised by Marcion and his followers. Marcion at least read the Scriptures as they had originally been intended. Jaroslav Pelikan (*Tradition,* 77–78) has made the astute observation that Marcion was probably the only Christian leader of his day to have recognized that the Scriptures were Israel's, unquestionably the Bible of the Jews. On that starting point, at least, Marcion was historically correct and theologically sound. His mistake was to conclude that the Church should have nothing to do with those Jewish writings. He had evidently missed completely the point of his beloved Apostle to the Gentiles, that that root was the foundation of the Church, that the Gentiles had been grafted onto the root of God's dealings with Israel, of which the Jewish Scriptures tell. The "orthodox" leaders, however, in rejecting Marcion's conclusion, rejected as well his sound starting point. They denied that the Scriptures were Israel's, promising, for example, an actual piece of real estate to an actual people, and turned them into the Church's Old Testament, with those promises spiritualized and allegorized so as to make them *directly and originally* promises to the Gentile Church. Thus, in winning the battle with Marcion, the Church lost the war with Gnosticism. Christian anti-Zionism is but a part of its present payments on the colossal debt to Gnosticism incurred in the second century.

iv. The subsequent context

Understanding the things concerning Jesus of Nazareth requires, finally, that we be aware of their subsequent context. To understand the context from Israel's beginnings, up to, and including the apostolic witness is not yet to see the whole picture. A Christology that took Israel's Scriptures and the Apostolic Writings as the whole context would be distorted, for it would have left out the history of the effects of that witness. The story of Jesus Christ did not come to an end with the Apostolic Writings. It has continued in its consequences, and this too has a bearing on a Christology for a Church that acknowledges the Jewish people today as the Israel of God.

The continuation of the things concerning Jesus of Nazareth has two sides, neither of which may be ignored. On the first and positive side, it has been the case that for countless Gentiles over centuries the story has done its work. That is to say, the witness of the early disciples to Jesus was to one who confronted them with the gift and claim of God's love, and who by so doing proved to them that he was fully authorized to represent that love. As that witness was proclaimed to others, the same confrontation took place and the same gift and claim were acknowledged. Moreover, this soon began to happen not just among Jews, within Israel, but also among Gentiles. A Gentile Church that knows the gift and claim of the love of the God of Israel is the final consequence of the positive continuation of the things concerning Jesus of Nazareth.

There is, however, also the negative side, which has been equally effective and which is also an unavoidable part of the context necessary to developing a Christology for the Jewish-Christian reality, the reality that the Church has acknowledged as its own since Vatican II. The things concerning Jesus of Nazareth have been told by the Church with concern to be faithful to the Gospels as it knew them in their edited or final form. But that final form obscures the witness to Jesus' solidarity with his people behind a picture of ever-deepening hostility. The witness to solidarity was not suppressed, but it surely was given a minor place behind the major theme of hostility.

The Jesus whom the Church has known best, consequently, has been the Jesus that comes through from the finished texts, and that Jesus is in conflict with his people. He denounces them and they plot against him, betray him, judge him and turn him over to the Romans, who only kill him at their insistence. An unavoidable part of the subsequent context of the things concerning Jesus of Nazareth, therefore, is that Jews came to be called "Christ killers" by Christians. The anti-Judaism of the Church's thought and behavior, with all the resultant persecutions, killings, and pogroms (and certainly not excluding Hitler's "Final Solution," built as it was on the background of centuries of that anti-Judaism) has to be taken into account if we would understand the full context of the things concerning Jesus of Nazareth.

This painful fact of the negative consequences of the witness to Jesus Christ should be a warning to any who undertake to develop a Christology for today: as it has been in the past, so it will be in the future. That is to say, an important part of the meaning of what the Church says about Jesus Christ today will be determined by what consequences follow from it tomorrow. A responsible Church will therefore think long and hard about the likely and the possible future consequences of how it takes up today, in the context of the Jewish-Christian reality which it has come to recognize, the things concerning Jesus of Nazareth.

2. WHY ISRAEL'S STORY COMES FIRST

i. Jesus and Israel

The things concerning Jesus of Nazareth have a complex context. It includes the time, place, and people of his birth, together with their tradition and their long history in their covenant with God. It includes also a recital of where and how these things have been understood, honored, and preached through many centuries and up to today. And it encompasses each act done in his name, whether for good or for bad. We have seen Israel in its covenant with God to be the fundamental context of the early presentation of Jesus. One could also call that context the covenant seen as immediate and urgent. Or, if one keeps Israel's whole witness in mind, one could call his context simply God, as in "I will be your God and you will be my people."

If "God" were to be thought of apart from Israel, or apart from the covenant, then it would be misleading to call his context "God" or to concern oneself with the relationship between Jesus and such a "God." To ask about "the divinity of Jesus," as a question apart from the context of the covenant between God and Israel, is to talk of some other Jesus than that of the apostolic witness, namely a Jesus out of context and so an incomprehensible Jesus. Note that it is Jesus who becomes incomprehensible, not just the concept of divinity. Indeed, the more definite the concept of divinity becomes as one undetermined by the covenant, the more incomprehensible becomes the figure of Jesus when the concept is predicated of him.

We have been considering the context of what we are presuming to have been an early witness to Jesus, considering the subject from the outside, so to speak, but we shall see our conclusion confirmed by looking at the matter from the inside. That is to say, if we consider how that same witness to Jesus presents him as speaking and acting, we shall see reinforced the intimacy between Jesus and Israel. It takes the form of his concern for his people, and especially for the weakest, the lowest, the least lovable or acceptable of his fellow Jews.

In speaking of Jesus' words, actions, and attitude, I am referring to the Jesus of the early witness, the testified-to-Jesus. In *Jesus and Judaism*, E. P. Sanders shows how cautious one should be in claiming historical knowledge of the man Jesus of Nazareth about whom the testimony was given. For the purposes of Christology, I believe I may leave open the question of how much we may know of the Jesus discoverable by historians. I see no historical grounds whatsoever for doubting that he existed and said and did things related to what the testimony says. The work of critical scholarship, however, suggests that if we try to say what Jesus must have said or done or thought, in order to account for the witness of the disciples, we remain to an important extent in the realm of more or less probable conjecture. When I speak of Jesus' concern for his fellow Jews, then, I am speaking of the concern we can know about, namely that which is preserved in the historically determinable witness, not of a necessarily somewhat conjectural concern of the historical Jesus. (What I wrote about Jesus' concern for his people in *People Israel,* chapter 8, and especially pp. 244–46, might be criticized for not making this distinction sufficiently clear.) I should add that it seems highly unlikely, and in no way contrary to that concern, that Jesus never disagreed with other Jews about anything. He was, after all, a Jew.

The evidence is not vast but it is clear: the extant texts of the Gospels preserve a witness to a Jesus deeply concerned for Israel, the Jewish people, and for them before all others. I have chosen to call this witness "early," because it seems to me unlikely that the increasingly Gentile Church of the time of the Evangelists would have invented it. (Nevertheless, we cannot be certain of its origin, for there remains the unlikely but possible hypothesis that it could have arisen in a Jewish-Christian community that found the Gentile mission objectionable.) This witness has Jesus say of himself, "I was sent only to the lost sheep of the house of Israel" (Matt. 15:24), and it has him ordering his disciples, "Go nowhere to the Gentiles . . . but go instead to the lost sheep of the house of Israel" (Matt. 10:5f). It portrays him lamenting over Jerusalem, "How often have I yearned to gather your children, as a hen gathers her brood under her wings" (Matt. 23:37, Luke 13:34). It presents him responding to a Gentile woman's plea for help by saying, "It is not right to take the children's bread and throw it to the dogs" (Mark 7:27, Matt. 15:26). It is clear that this witness wanted to present Jesus in the closest solidarity with his own people. He was preached as sent to Israel, concerned for Israel, calling Israel to immediate faithfulness to God. The testimony presents him as the good shepherd, looking for the lost sheep of the house of Israel (lapsed, assimilated, alienated, or unrighteous Jews) and concerned to bring them back into the fold. The owner of the fold was coming, so the task was urgent. In the tradition of Israel's prophets, the Jesus of the early witness was dedicated to Israel's renewal, now presented with utmost urgency in the face of the coming reign of God.

ii. Israel's unfinished story

The testimony to Jesus presents him as not expecting a future in the ordinary sense of the word. He expected only the coming of the reign of God, which would replace this era in which what we call history takes place. In that sense, the preaching of Jesus as presented is timeless or ahistorical. For quite different, noneschatological reasons, the rabbis of postbiblical Israel were also ahistorical in their teaching. Neither the early witness to Jesus nor the later rabbis paid any attention to what we call historical development. In fact, however, history has gone on. Israel has continued and developed. So has the covenant between God and Israel; at least, so we must trust if we believe in Israel's election at all. Israel's story did not end with the last book of Scriptures, it did not end with a coming of the reign of God, and it has not ended to this day. Israel's story continues, and both horrifying and exciting new chapters have been added to it in the twentieth century.

This continuing story of Israel is also part of the context that the Church has to take into account in speaking of the things concerning Jesus of Nazareth, for he has had much to do with Israel's unfinished history. In his name, much of Israel's unfinished story has had to be told as a tale of pain and suffering. In his name, many of Israel have died. If Jesus lives, he lives in this context of the continuing, living covenant between his people and his Father, the God of Israel, in which his Church has played so negative a role in his name.

In recent years, the Church has come at least to glimpse this context. It has finally, after nineteen centuries of blindness, come to see the covenant as a living reality. It has done so in part because of coming finally to recognize the self-contradiction in which it had been living as an anti-Judaic Church of the God of Israel. But it has come to its senses in part because it has been confronted with living Israel in a new way. A new stage, a fresh chapter in Israel's story, has begun with the founding of the State of Israel. Israel, in a way that would have surprised the rabbis of the Talmud, has "returned to history," to use Emil Fackenheim's phrase. The Church, in a way utterly unforeseen by the apostolic witness to Jesus, has had to see the covenant in history in a new way. This new reality, of the covenant having once more to be worked out in political and social history, is a challenge to the Jewish people, but it is also a challenge to the Church. Christology can no longer be worked out ahistorically if Israel is back on the plane of history. The State of Israel is also part of its context. By having acknowledged that Israel's covenant is alive today, the Church has committed itself to including the reality of the State of Israel as part of the context within which it speaks of the things concerning Jesus of Nazareth.

The argument for this conclusion can be put concisely. The Church has acknowledged the covenant as eternal. It follows that it recognizes the Jewish people today as the people of the covenant, the Israel of God. But Israel in its covenant is the fundamental context of Jesus Christ. If Jesus lives today, and if the Church is to speak of him in the present tense, as it must if it is to have any Christology worthy of the name, then the Jewish people today remain his context and the Church will have to speak of him in the context of his people. An important manifestation of this people being their State, however, that State—in all its ambiguity (see van Buren, *People Israel,* 187–89)—becomes an unavoidable part of the present context for the Church's confession of and reflection upon the things concerning Jesus of Nazareth. Christology today has to take the State of Israel into account, in all its secularity, as part of the Jewish history and reality, and if it fails to do so, it will fail as a Christology for a Church that has acknowledged the Jewish people as the Israel of God.

I would point out that F. W. Marquardt came by a somewhat different route to a similar conclusion in a study which he completed in 1966 but published only recently: *Die Gegenwart des Auferstandenen bei Seinem Volk Israel* ("The Presence of the Risen One with His People Israel"). Marquardt's study raises the question whether we should say that the risen Jesus is present now with his people (and how does "present" work in this sentence?), or whether we have said enough if we say what we can give some account of, namely that his people are the context for our Christology. Perhaps we have said all we can if we insist on speaking and understanding him always in the closest association with his people, for what else could we be saying if we also said that the risen one is present with them?

A further and painful point is worth making. As it has long been impious on Quranic grounds to speak of a risen Christ *crucified,* so now it is equally impious for Muslims to speak of the Jewish *State.* That is a problem first of all for Islam, not for the Church. But it is also a problem for us because it is a pressing problem for Israel, being a problem for its Muslim neighbors. It is interesting that, in this alien framework, Jesus and his people come together for us once more.

iii. The Church (and Christology) as one sequence of a sequence

The story of Jesus of Nazareth is itself a sequence, following upon the early part of Israel's story that is told in the Scriptures. It is, however, only one sequence of that early story. There are others, including some that were as short as that of the story of the Qumran community. The longest of the others is the rest of Israel's story, on through the period of formative Judaism under the rabbis and up to the present, including the founding of the State of Israel. But one sequence of the story of biblical Israel is the story of Jesus of Nazareth. From it has followed the Gentile Church, including its Christology.

The story of the Church, which follows from and is itself a part of the story of Jesus of Nazareth, is also complex. It includes the remarkable fact of Gentiles responding to the things concerning Jesus of Nazareth as did those Jews who were the first to tell of them. It includes the countless words and acts of love and mercy performed by those Gentiles in his name and to the honor of the God of Israel. It includes also the no less remarkable fact of the long history, not yet fully behind us, of Christian anti-Judaism: Gentiles who came to know of the love of the God of Israel turning against the Israel from whom it had first heard of that love. It includes other consequences of the history of a pride that so seriously corrupted the Church's attempt to lead the powers of this world into the service of God by using a power other than that of the love from which it lived. It includes also a patriarchalism with which the Church is only now beginning to deal. The sequence of the things concerning Jesus of Nazareth, therefore, includes both good and bad.

The sequence to the things concerning Jesus of Nazareth that is the Church, however—including all that is good and all that is bad—depends upon Israel's story, as does the story of Jesus itself. That is why Israel's story has to come first in reflecting on the context of Jesus and of Christology. There would have been no story of Jesus had there not been first of all the story that Israel told, the story of creation and of Abraham, of Moses and Sinai, of the election of this people and its long life in its covenant with God. If the Church in its Christology is to speak of a living Jesus Christ, then it will need to speak of him in a living context. That living context will of course include the living Church, but it will begin with living Israel, for that is the foundational context for all that the Church has to say about itself and about the things concerning Jesus of Nazareth. This rule has not been sufficiently observed in the history of the Church's Christology, for only in the twentieth century has the Church come to recognize living Israel as a reality of which it must speak in order to make sense of itself. Now that it has come to this recognition, it has no coherent alternative but to see living Israel as the fundamental context for its Christology. It has no coherent alternative to developing a Christology for the actual situation of which it has newly become aware and which we have been calling the Jewish-Christian reality.

3. THE LIVING CONTEXT OF ISRAEL

i. The Church's acknowledgment of Israel's continuing covenant

Beginning with the Declaration *Nostra Aetate* of the Second Vatican Council, the Church has gone on record with increasing clarity and in all its major branches (see van Buren, *Discerning*, 174–85, for evidence, and now the further collection of church documents in Croner, *Relations*) as acknowledging that the Jewish people today are the heirs of and continue in God's eternal covenant with them. The Jewish people today, according to this teaching, are the Israel of God. The ancient covenant between God and Israel, in other words, continues today, ever new and alive in the ambiguous contemporary life of the Jewish people.

Not since the Apostle to the Gentiles insisted on this point has the Church seen this so clearly. It constitutes a reversal of the tradition (already established by the second century C.E.) at a point so central to the Church's understanding of itself and God, as well as of Israel, that it cannot fail to have major consequences for Christology.

This reversal is a fact. It has happened. It may be that it took place with little awareness of the extent of its consequences, but it has happened. Whenever the Church speaks of or reflects on *any* subject that matters to it (and not just those concerning the Jews), and does so coherently, its agenda will now have to include Israel today, the living Jewish people. It will not do to refer only to ancient Israel. That may have been logically in order before the reversal, when the Church was coherently anti-Judaic. If, as it now claims, it is not anti-Judaic, if it acknowledges that the covenant is eternal, then all of postbiblical Israel, and especially Israel today, has to be of as much concern as ancient Israel was for the Church before. The logic of this is clear: if Israel in the ancient covenant was essential to the ancient Church's understanding of Christ (and the Church acknowledged this in its rejection of Marcionism), and if the covenant is believed by the present Church to continue in force to this day, then Israel in the ancient-and-still-in-force covenant is essential to the present Church's understanding of him. The whole history of the whole covenant, not just the biblical beginnings of it, becomes the context in which the Church will have to express in its Christology how it understands itself before the God of this covenant.

The consequence of the reversal only barely begun by the Second Vatican Council is, therefore, that the Church will gradually have to follow Israel's lead back into history, or else abandon all pretense to theological coherence. It will have to think through the things concerning Jesus of Nazareth in the context of what has been going on between God and Israel over the past twenty centuries while the Church was looking to another world and reciting a Christology primarily in the past tense. It will have to turn its eyes to a living history, that of the Jewish people, and begin to translate Christology into the present tense. Israel's continuing covenant requires these changes.

ii. The Covenant in movement

The anti-Judaic Church derived its conception of the covenant primarily from its "New Testament," read as the fulfillment of its "Old Testament." The Old Covenant served to foreshadow or prefigure the New, which was therefore definitive and decisive. The result was a concept of covenant as grace. The focus was almost exclusively on the unmerited gift of divine favor.

The covenant of grace in which Israel has lived and still lives, however, has always been two-sided. With grace comes responsibility. With the gift there comes a task. This dual character of the relationship between the God of Israel and the Israel of God is there to be seen in the early, Jewish witness to Jesus, as it is in Israel's Scriptures, in such parables as that of the Last Judgment (Matt. 25:31–46), or that of the talents (Matt. 25:14–30). It is there in Matthew's Sermon on the Mount and in Mark's story of the rich young man (Mark 10:17–22). It is there in all those passages in the Gospels that the Church has had to bend or twist or ignore in order to maintain its traditional anti-Judaic theory that set the gospel in opposition to the Torah.

Israel's awareness of its responsibility in the covenant was undoubtedly heightened through the teaching of the rabbis, and it was brought to a new peak by the crisis leading to the founding of the Jewish State (cf. van Buren, *People Israel,* 121, 295–301). The State would never have existed had all Jews lived by the rabbinic maxim, "All is in the hands of heaven except the fear of heaven." The Zionists had to have the courage to take responsibility for the future of the covenant into their own hands, thus making a highly creative confirmation of, or change in, its terms.

A living covenant means a covenant in history, and history is the story of change. But this living covenant, subject to change as it must be because it is lived in history, is the only one there is. It is the covenant as it is lived between the living God and his living people Israel. This covenant is the fundamental context of the living things concerning Jesus of Nazareth. If Jesus lives, in whatever sense, he lives in this context. The latest stage of this living covenant—the State of Israel—therefore cannot be irrelevant for the Church's Christology, unless the Church chooses to return to its anti-Judaic past. At the least, it suggests that Christology should not be developed as a story only of grace and sheer gift. With grace will be linked responsibility, and with the gift there will be a task. A deeper appreciation of mutuality in the divine-human relationship will be called for than has characterized the Christological tradition of the anti-Judaic church.

iii. Christology as a present task

We have argued that, because the Church in developing its Christology has to take Israel in its covenant into account, and because the State of Israel is the most recent fruit of that covenant, the Church should therefore take the State of Israel into account in developing a Christology for today. From this it follows that the task before us is to develop a Christology that will be covenantal and historical in ways that were not imaginable for the Church before it acknowledged the continuing covenant between God and the Jewish people.

The first consequence is that Christology will have to be covenantal in the sense in which the Church has recognized Israel's continuing existence as covenantal. In the light of the founding of the State of Israel, that means, as argued above, that Christology will not be presented as a matter of grace alone. Faith and works, to use traditional terms, may not be set up as alternatives. We shall have to question any presentation of Jesus, for example, as a man who could never have been mistaken because he was the incarnate Word of God, and we shall have to explore a presentation of himself taking, and calling his disciples to, full human responsibility in the cause of God.

The second and more complex consequence is that Christology will have to be historical in a new way. If the history of the covenant since the first century of the Common Era is taken into account, a Christology for the Jewish-Christian reality will need to handle critically the eschatology of the first century and of the apostolic witness to the things concerning Jesus of Nazareth, for the evident reason that the reign of God, as that testimony presents it, was not in fact at hand at the time and has not yet arrived after nineteen centuries. A historical Christology will have to analyze critically the tradition of speaking of the things concerning Jesus of Nazareth as a once-for-all event, as well as talk of a realized eschatology or of the fulfillment of all God's promises to Israel. Obviously, the displacement or supersessionist theology of the tradition will be excluded: Israel in its covenant continues and is alive to this day. Whatever is to be said of what God accomplished in Jesus Christ, it will have to make room for over nineteen centuries of Jewish life in the covenant and now the existence of the Jewish State, not just the existence of the Church. It will also have to make room for Auschwitz.

iv. Jesus and Auschwitz

In his book *To Mend the World*, Emil Fackenheim posed three hypothetical questions about Jesus for Christians to answer, questions to which the usual answers from traditional Christology would be not only irrelevant to the post-Holocaust world but immoral to maintain. The questions are: (1) "Where would Jesus of Nazareth have been in Nazi-occupied Europe?" (Fackenheim, *To Mend*, 280). (2) In the light of Auschwitz, "has Good Friday overwhelmed Easter? Is the Good News of the Overcoming itself overcome?" (Fackenheim, *To Mend*, 286). (3) "Could Jesus of Nazareth have been made into a *Muselmann*?" (Fackenheim, *To Mend*, 286). The questions deserve a response, although they pose no new issues. As we shall see, they do not provide leads for a Christology for the Jewish-Christian reality, but they do throw light on the massive apostasy of the Church during the Hitler era from its traditional faith.

1. "Where would Jesus of Nazareth have been in Nazi-occupied Europe?" Our answer and that of the tradition would be the same: as a Jew, he would in all likelihood have been with his fellow Jews, in or on his way to the death camps. It is necessary to add

that only a few of his disciples were there where he surely would
have been. A Christology after Auschwitz will only be authentic if
it is so confessed as to make it unambiguously clear that any future
"Aryan legislation" would leave its confessor no alternative but to
resist those laws and to stand by the Jewish people. The tiny number who did resist could do so on the basis of traditional Christology, but they were few.

2. In the light of Auschwitz, "has Good Friday overwhelmed
Easter? Is the Good News of the Overcoming itself overcome?"
The witnesses to Easter of the early apostolic communities appear
to have been acutely aware of the tentative and ambiguous character of Easter. They declared it to be a victory for God and in
some way a victory for Jesus, but they did not declare it to be already a victory for the rest of the world, only the ground for assurance that God's victory would ultimately be a victory for his
creation. A full quarter of a century after Easter, Paul could speak
of the whole creation groaning in agonizing labor pains for a redemption not yet come. The Church of succeeding centuries has
not been so cautious. A Christology after Auschwitz will only be
authentic if it is so confessed as to make it unambiguously clear
that its confessors know that death and its many servants still exercise tremendous power over this post-Easter world. This too is
not new in its essentials.

3. Finally, "could Jesus of Nazareth have been made into a *Muselmann?*" *Muselmann* was death camp jargon for a person so worn
down by starvation, beatings, physical and mental exhaustion as
to be no longer a person. A survivor, quoted by Fackenheim, described them as "non-men who march and labor in silence, the
divine spark dead within them, already too empty to suffer. One
hesitates to call them living: one hesitates to call their death
death, in the face of which they have no fear, as they are too tired
to understand" (Fackenheim, *To Mend*, 99–100). (How this unfortunate term—simply the German for "Muslim"—came to be
used, I do not know; it says something about the depth of racism
and intolerance of European Christendom that Hitler exploited
so well.)

I do not see how it could be maintained, even on traditional lines, that Jesus of Nazareth could not possibly have become such. A Christology after Auschwitz will only be authentic if it is so confessed as to make it unambiguously clear that its confessors believe that God's authorization of Jesus to speak and act in his name in no way exempted Jesus from the human condition. Only so could he really be a fully human expression of God's unbounded love, the love of a God willing and able to enter into and share all the suffering and weakness of his creation. One might hope for Jesus, hypothetically imagined under these conditions, as for any other of God's creatures, that he would have so trusted in God as not to be turned into such a nonperson. That was indeed the case of many, who went to their deaths with human dignity in a situation satanically designed to deprive them of all dignity. But if that may be hoped for in the case of Jesus, an authentic Christology after Auschwitz will have to make it unambiguously clear that the hope is based on the fact that some did not let the camps dehumanize them, and *not* on any supposed evil-proof nature of Jesus' humanity resulting from his divine authorization. There is all the difference between a Word that only "put on" flesh and a Word that *became* flesh, as the bishops at Chalcedon meant to make clear.

Fackenheim's questions, then, underscore dramatically the Jewish humanity of Jesus and help us to see that these features of the Christological tradition proved to be too weak to guide the Church's behavior in the face of the most deadly challenge to have confronted the Jewish people in many centuries. For the Church today, however, Christology will need to take into account not just the fact of, but the full context of Jesus the Jew.

4. JESUS AS ISRAEL'S GIFT TO AND CLAIM UPON THE CHURCH

i. Jesus the Jew

Jesus the Jew is presented, by the apostolic witness to him, as one of his people to such a degree that his story recapitulates theirs, as in Matthew's story of his flight into and return from Egypt. His life was a Jewish life, lived as one of his people. His death was an all-too-typically Jewish death of the time: he was killed by Gentiles. When he died, there was one less Jew in the world.

To a Gentile Church estranged from the Jewish people, Jesus can only be a stranger. With his own people he was intimate, as is clear from the witness of his Jewish disciples. As a Jew, he was also intimate with the God of his people, for that God is intimate with that people. It should be noted that Jews have often found the intimacy of their God with them to be a strain and a burden. They have also concluded that God was, in spite of the intimacy, all too often absent, sometimes when his presence was most needed. This is the context in which a Christology for the Jewish-Christian reality will need to reflect upon his disciples' witness to the intimacy between Jesus of Nazareth and the God he is presented as having called by the familiar name *abba*, Father.

The relationship between Jesus and his Father that the witness presents was a Jewish affair. It was the relationship between a Jew and the God of the Jews. It was therefore also a struggle bordering, most deferentially, on a quarrel. Abraham's polite but persistent bargaining with God over the fate of the Sodomites (Gen. 18:23–33), Jacob's wrestling match on the banks of the Jabbok (Gen. 32:22–32), and Jeremiah's lament over his calling and very existence (Jer. 20:7–18) are in the background of the stories of the temptation of Jesus in the wilderness and his prayer in the garden of Gethsemane. These stories were presumably the creations of their authors, there having been present no witnesses of the events as described, but they were the constructions of authors who had not forgotten and apparently wanted their readers to realize that Jesus was a Jew.

As a Jew, Jesus may have been intimate with God, but it would have been the intimacy of a Jew. It would have been a relationship that we could characterize as personal, and it would never have led to any confusion as to who was the Jew and who was God. We can only speculate about what went on in Jesus' own soul, but we can know how the early witness presents him. It presents him as we could expect Jews to present a Jew wholly devoted to God. It presents him as one whose will was to do God's will. His cause was nothing but the cause of God. In this sense and in no other, he had no will of his own and no cause of his own to defend. In other words, he was strong-willed and stubborn in the cause of God. In short, he was a Jew.

ii. Israel's gift

On the face of it, it sounds preposterous to say that Jesus of Nazareth is Israel's gift to the Gentile Church. The Church would certainly want to say that he was and is God's gift, and of course Jesus came out of Israel, but the anti-Judaic Church has seen Jesus as expelled by Israel, not given. For its part, Israel has never conceived of Jesus as its gift to the Church. Taking him to have been (on the human, historical level) more or less what the Church said he was, a Jew who turned against his people, Israel has tended to regard him as an apostate and a blasphemer (although some half a dozen modern Jewish scholars, beginning with Klausner, have begun, in Leo Baeck's words, to "take note of what is [their] own" (cited by Lapide, *Hebrew,* 193). At best, he might be seen by Jews as Jewish property stolen by, but hardly as their gift to, the Church.

The Church's conviction that Jesus is God's gift to it, however, needs further specification. If the conviction is sound, then what needs to be added is that Jesus is the gift of the God of Israel to the Gentile Church, reconciling it to himself. The God who makes this gift is the God of the covenant. The gift, then, comes from one already bound to Israel. As God is one, so his being bound to Israel and his giving of this gift cannot be unrelated. Israel knows that God is implicated in and affected by what Israel does, as sayings of its rabbis make clear (for examples, see van Buren, *People Israel,* 174, 213–14).

But if God is implicated in what Israel does, so Israel is implicated in what God does. If one partner of the covenant acts in a certain manner, that defines the responsive action of the other. The call to holiness, righteousness, and an *imitatio Dei* on Israel's part are all argued by the rabbis on this basis.

It follows, then, that if God has given Jesus as his gift to the Church, Israel too is implicated in that gift. Willy-nilly, Israel was associated with God as the giver of its son Jesus to the Gentiles, and it is his giver to this day. Gentile Christians will have to continue to come to know Jews of their day if they have any hope of coming to know the Jew Jesus as the Jew he was and is.

Does that in fact follow? Is is not possible to come to know Rabbi Akiva without knowing actual, living Jews? The answer to that is best discovered when a Christian makes the experiment of trying to study the Talmud with the aid only of books, and then studies it together with a Jewish student of the Talmud. From such an experiment one soon learns the advantage of learning about Jews and Judaism from and with Jews.

There is, of course, another sense in which the things concerning Jesus of Nazareth is Israel's gift to the Church. The witness to them, and the whole vocabulary used in that witness, were Israel's. Not only Jesus but every one of this followers and disciples, so far as we know, were Jews. Apart from them, the Church would know nothing at all of Jesus and so would not even exist.

On this solid historical ground we can confront a somewhat later witness with what we have been calling the early witness. The author of the Prologue of the Gospel of the Johannine community wrote of Jesus as the Word of God (John 1:11), that "he came to his own [home] and his own [people] received him not." That, fortunately for the Gentile Church, is flatly contradicted by the apostolic witness, including the witness on which the Johannine community depended. Were not Mary and Joseph his own people? Were not Peter and Andrew, and James and John, his own people? Were not the others whose names appear in the witness, not to speak of the multitudes of Jews who, we are told, received him gladly, his own people? No, the author of the Prologue is wrong. He came to and was received by a large number of his own, a number large enough to have borne a witness to the things concerning Jesus of Nazareth from which the Gentile Church has lived ever since. That witness, entirely Jewish and entirely from Jews, is certainly Israel's gift to the Church. The Church owes to Israel its whole story of the things concerning Jesus of Nazareth.

iii. Israel's claim

If Jesus the Jew is Israel's gift to the Church, then he is Israel's claim upon the Church. The Church is in debt to Israel for the whole Scriptural story into which it has been drawn. It owes to Israel the things concerning Jesus of Nazareth by which it has been confronted with the gift and claim of God's love. Jews provided the earliest gospel, and the Jew Paul and other Jews brought it to the Gentiles. The Church thus owes its whole existence to Israel.

The love of God with which the Church is confronted in Jesus is surely a gift, but it is also a claim. How could it not be a claim and a command, coming as it does from the one who gave his Torah to Israel? The claim of God's love with which the Church is confronted in the witness to Jesus is that it follow Jesus in his dedication to the cause of God. Since God's love knows no limits and no barriers, since it embraces his whole creation, and especially the poor, the weak, the dispossessed, and the oppressed, so its claim upon the Church is that it love all that God loves.

But God's love for Israel is the special love which is told of and celebrated in the story of Israel that is the context of the things concerning Jesus of Nazareth. In accepting the gift of God's love, the Church is therefore claimed especially to love Israel, God's beloved. In following Jesus, it is called to care for the least of his brothers and sisters, which must surely begin with, although not end at, the least of his Jewish brothers and sisters. How could it love God and not love the Israel whom God loves?

In following Jesus, the Church follows one who "became a servant to the Jewish people" (Rom. 15:8). It will therefore be claimed for this service. What the Church owes to the Jewish people, therefore, is that it be faithful disciples of Jesus Christ, the Jew who served his people. That is Israel's claim upon the Church, sealed by Jesus Christ.

The Church will never be free of its debt to Israel, because it will never be free of Israel. And that, in turn, is because Israel is and remains the context of Jesus Christ. To acknowledge the claim of God's love, with which the Church is confronted in the witness to Christ, is therefore always to acknowledge the legitimate claim of Israel. No Jew need repeat that claim today, since it is repeated to the Church again and again, whenever it rehearses the things concerning Jesus of Nazareth, by his reality as a Jew. It comes as his call to follow him in his service to his people.

The Context of Jesus Christ: The Church

The proximate context of Jesus Christ is the Church, the communion of those who acknowledge themselves as loved and claimed through him by the God of Israel. In his presence they discover the presence of that God, and they find themselves, in standing before him, to be standing before that God. The Church's Christology is its ever-new effort to confess this ever-new discovery and to understand its implications.

1. THE CHURCH AS THE CONTEXT OF JESUS CHRIST

i. Where Jesus Christ is met

Jesus Christ is met within the framework of the Church. That is in no way a boast which the Church might make. It is, rather, a claim the truth of which is determined by the workings of our language. I may meet a stranger anywhere, but if I can say that I have met a particular individual, I shall ordinarily know his name. In order to meet someone, I need to know at least that person's name. That is simply a grammatical remark on one use of the verb "to meet."

Jesus Christ may perhaps be met by all sorts of people in all sorts of contexts, but if this were the case, they would not be able to say that it was he whom they had met, unless they were in some sense within the framework of the Church. That is, they would at least have had to know his name and so to have come within hearing distance of the community in which that name is remembered. Apart from that community, therefore, it is unclear what it might mean for someone to say that they had met Jesus Christ. In a strict sense, the concept of an "anonymous Christian" is incoherent.

Within the Church, then, the name of Jesus is remembered and rehearsed. The Church recognizes his name and recalls the confrontation that he initiated between his disciples and the God of Israel. It recalls that confrontation by rehearsing the testimony of the early disciples to it. In doing so, it finds itself, from time to time, similarly confronted. That is, from time to time, the recollection of Jesus has the same effect within the Church that the person of Jesus is testified to have had upon those who heard and saw and followed him as his first disciples.

The Church, however, does not spend its whole time together in this act of recollection. It is, for the most part and for most of the time, scattered in a great variety of circumstances. In so far as it has met Jesus Christ in its acts of recollection, it is also able from time to time to meet Jesus Christ in the least of his brothers and sisters. If this happens, it will be with the same effect of confrontation with the God of Israel that occurs when it meets him in the Church's acts of recollection, or else it would not have grounds to say that it had met him. Indeed, with the same reservation, we can say that it may meet him in any place.

One hears frequently today in certain circles of "knowing Jesus Christ as your personal Lord and Savior." Without questioning the validity and importance of that to which this phrase refers, I would suggest that it is a misleading abbreviation of what is at stake in meeting Jesus Christ. According to the early witness, a relationship with Jesus Christ that stopped with him would not be authentic and so could be neither with a Lord nor a Savior. The relationship with him that is salvific is the one that brings a person before the God of Israel whom he called Father, and who is, as Israel's, also the world's Lord and Savior.

ii. In word and sacrament

The proximate context of Jesus Christ is the Church because there is where he is met as the one chosen by the God of Israel to confront Gentiles with the gift and claim of that God's unlimited love. When this occurs, it is ordinarily in the Church's word and sacrament. I say *when* this occurs, for "the Spirit blows where it wills" (John 3:8) and there is no human guarantee of this occurrence. And I say *ordinarily,* for it may occur in many other ways. It is the experience of the Church from its beginnings and to this day, however, that in its taking up and presenting in its own words the apostolic witness to Jesus, and in its taking up and making its own the meal that Jesus shared with his disciples, it is again and again confronted and claimed by the love of the God of Israel. In these acts of recollection, Jesus is effectively present to his Church. They are the way in which, ordinarily, he is met.

Before taking a preliminary look at these acts, it is well to recall that both are acts of recollection and therefore stand as structured examples of what can take place in far less formal acts. Any way in which the primitive witness to Christ is taken up and repeated, be it from a simple reading of it as it is found in the Apostolic Writings, or as it has been rehearsed with reasonable faithfulness in other writings that the Church has produced down through the centuries, may be the occasion in which Jesus is effectively recalled. Or the witness may come in the form of words spoken by some member of the Church, or in an act of love or forgiveness done in the name of Christ. In each case, as with the more formal preaching of the word or the celebration of the Eucharist or Lord's Supper, if the intent is to present Christ to others, the presentation may be effective. The proof will always be in the result: either Jesus will come alive for hearers or he will not, and this can only be judged on the basis of the fruit: by whether the hearers find themselves confronted by the gift and claim of the God of Israel whom Jesus called Father.

The apostolic preaching of the things concerning Jesus of Nazareth would seem to have been the foundation of the early Christian communities. So it was evidently in the churches founded by Paul, as his references make abundantly clear: "Faith comes from what is heard, and what is heard comes by the preaching of Christ" (Rom. 10:17); he spoke of the gospel that he preached to the Galatians (Gal. 1:6–9), and of having portrayed publically to them Jesus Christ as crucified (Gal. 3:1). The author of Acts presents the apostles preaching from the beginning the things concerning Jesus of Nazareth.

Preaching has continued to this day to be a fundamental feature of the Church's corporate activity and an indispensable part of its corporate worship. When it has been omitted or done without care, not to speak of its being done without fear and trembling, the Church has been deprived of its foremost way of meeting Jesus Christ anew and so of being confronted anew with the gift and claim of the God of Israel.

The second and no less vital way in which the Church meets Christ is in the reenactment of the Lord's Supper, which it does in thanksgiving and so calls it Eucharist (from the Greek for "thanksgiving"). Developed from the meals that Jesus was remembered as having shared with his disciples, and then from the disciples' discovery of his presence when they continued the practice after his death (see the Emmaus story of Luke 24:13–35), the Eucharist has provided from its beginning the basic form of corporate worship whenever the Church gathered. Like preaching, the Eucharist is an act that recalls the presence of Jesus, and when it does so, the Church is once again brought into the presence of the Holy One of Israel. In these two acts of recollection, the Church discovers again and again the authorization of Jesus to confront it with the gifts and claim of God's gracious and unlimited love. In these two acts, it is met by the one who brings it into the presence of God.

iii. In the neighbor

Those who have met Christ in word and sacrament may also meet him in their neighbor. The neighbor is by no means confined to the Church. The neighbor may be anyone, just so long as that one is there. The Church is there in the person of the one who, already having met Christ, may be met by him again in the neighbor.

The grounds for this possible meeting are presented in the witness to Jesus, particularly in the parable of the Good Samaritan, as himself having become for others their neighbor. The parable confronts us with one who proved himself to be a neighbor to one left half-dead by the side of the road. The hearer or reader is left to identify personally with that one who has been rescued by the neighbor, and then challenged to go and do likewise.

The parable is presented in response to the question, who is my neighbor? The command lies there already in the Torah: we are to love the neighbor because God loves the neighbor, especially the poor, weak or oppressed neighbor. When the hearer of the parable is confronted by one who manifests God's love for the neighbor as a love that reaches also the hearer, then that hearer is permitted and invited to accept that love and so the challenge to love the neighbor whom God loves. To ask who the neighbor is, is to fail to accept that love at all: the question implies a distinction, as if that love were for some particular person who qualifies as my neighbor, but not for others. The parable cuts through this evasive question by confronting the hearer with a figure, Jesus, who himself made no such fine distinction. His love for all the unlovable—the lepers, the lame, the handicapped, the disreputable—is what confronts the hearer. To accept that love is to go and do likewise.

This does not mean that the neighbor becomes Jesus or that Jesus becomes the neighbor. When I meet and love the neighbor I meet and love only the neighbor. But that neighbor, the early witness tells us, is the one loved by Jesus because of the love of God for that person. By loving and serving only the neighbor, and with no thought of loving and serving anyone else—as the striking ending of the parable of the Last Judgement in Matthew 25:31–46 (see particularly vv. 35–40) emphasizes—one will have loved and served the one who set himself in solidarity with the afflicted neighbor. One will have met Jesus.

iv. In Israel

Those who have met Christ in word and sacrament may also meet him in Israel, namely, in the persons of the Jewish people. They are, after all, the blood brothers and sisters of Jesus of Nazareth, and they have first claim on the Church's attention when it hears that it is to love and serve the least of his brothers or sisters. The Church will have failed to hear the witness to Jesus clearly if its love and service were to stop with the Jews, but it would show that it had failed to hear it at all if its love and service did not begin with them. "Truly, I say to you, as you did it to one of the least of these my brethren, you did it to me" (Matt. 25:40). According to this witness, to meet in love any of Israel is therefore to meet Jesus Christ, especially if one has no idea that this is the case and thinks only to meet and to serve the Jew in whatever is needed.

It is a proper reading of this witness to Jesus to see that the Church is challenged to meet and serve all those who are hungry, thirsty, estranged, naked, sick, or imprisoned. In them it will meet him, especially when it is not aware of this, when it serves them only in order to serve them, and when it loves them only because they need love. But this concern for the wretched of the earth could not possibly be well directed were it to bypass precisely those among whom Jesus taught and among whom this witness was first presented. They are, after all, his people and the people of the God whose love and claim upon the Church is effectively presented by the witness to him. The Church is given in them the most concrete evidence it has that the things of Jesus of Nazareth take place in this world. That evidence is nowhere more concrete than where the people of Jesus are in their own land, not "The Holy Land" of Christian pilgrimage, but the Land of Israel precisely as the land of the Jewish State. The world in which the things of Jesus of Nazareth took and are taking place includes Israel as their ultimate context and now the Church as their proximate context. In belonging to him, Christ's Church belongs close to and supportive of his people and of their State. There its members may meet and serve him again.

2. WHERE GOD IS MET THROUGH JESUS CHRIST

i. Other ways than through Jesus Christ in which God is met

In making its confession that it is precisely through Jesus Christ that it has met and hopes to meet again the God of Israel, the Creator of heaven and earth, the Church would do well to adopt a humility that the early witness ascribes to Jesus himself (cf. Phil. 2:3–8). In speaking of what it knows, it would do well not to speak of what it does not know. What it knows is what has happened to it: Jesus Christ, and he alone, has confronted the Church with God in his holy love and righteousness. The Son has been chosen and has chosen to reveal the Father to them (Matt. 11:27; Luke 10:22). He has been the way to the Father (John 14:6) for those who were without hope and without God in the world (Eph. 2:12). So be it, and let the Church rejoice in this and give unstinting praise and thanksgiving to God for such a gift.

Whether and how God has related himself to and allowed himself to be met and known by the rest of his creation is something that simply has not been revealed to the Church, for it forms no part of the primitive witness to Jesus as this can be determined from the texts of the Apostolic Writings. What we do find in those writings is the witness to the reality of that meeting with God that the Church was convinced had taken place in its having met Jesus of Nazareth, a witness that is eschatologically colored, and therefore intensely insisted upon. We find it further colored, especially in the writings produced by the Johannine community, by a history of conflict in which that reality had been called into question. (For a reconstruction of this process, see Brown, *Beloved Disciple*.) That community insisted most forcefully that through Jesus of Nazareth and by no other means, both before and after his death, its members had been met by the gracious God of Israel whom Jesus called Father.

From our experience of modern advertising, we should be familiar with the pattern: "No one knows what it is to drive a car until they drive this car." "You haven't lived until you try so and so." The enthusiasm of conviction often leads to a negation of all alternatives. That is characteristic of the language of praise or doxology. When doxological language is taken over unchanged into doctrine, however, it becomes dangerous. Words that are appropriate for praising God can become denials of what God may have done or be doing for the other, concerning which the Church in fact has no information whatsoever. Are we to con-

clude from the understandable enthusiasm with which the early
disciples sang of God's gift of love, that God had ceased to love
the rest of his creation and above all his firstborn son, Israel? Is
the answer to Abraham's deferential but daring question to God,
"Shall not the Judge of all the earth do right?" (Gen. 18:25), to be
in the negative? In the fully authorized things concerning Jesus of
Nazareth, has God rejected his people? God forbid, was Paul's
answer.

We see no other conclusion consistent with the gospel of the
early witness to Jesus Christ than that the Church simply does not
know how else God may be met apart from Jesus Christ and his
context, Israel. It does have the most solid grounds for believing
that Israel, the people of God's loving election, had met God long
before the coming of Christ, and that it has gone on being met by
God apart from Christ ever since. Indeed, in Israel's case, the
Church will have to insist that God *can* be met apart from Jesus
Christ, for otherwise it would not know that it was the God of Israel whom it had met in him. It can therefore coherently only
leave the matter open as far as other peoples are concerned, and
this in no way detracts from the fullness of the God of Israel's gracious meeting with the Church through Jesus Christ.

ii. Meeting God through Jesus Christ

It is just this meeting, however, that calls the Church again and
again into life. The witness of the early Jesus-movement makes
clear that the movement began because of Jesus. In some no-long-
er-clear connection with the preaching of John the Baptist, Jesus
began his work as an itinerant preacher and healer, announcing
and acting upon the immediacy of God's reign and the need to
turn around and start living by the reality that was at hand. But no
sooner do we hear of Jesus than we hear also of his disciples.
Something happened between him and them. In him, as their witness presents it, they discovered themselves to have been found
by the gracious but righteous God of Israel. His call to them is
presented as literally lifting them right out of their former lives
and recreating them as Jesus' disciples (Mark 1:16– 20). He spoke
and it came to be. The people who heard him stand in amazement

before the evident authority with which he speaks of the things of God. The demons, those spiritual powers who derange God's creatures and so are evil, are nevertheless spirits and so are able to recognize him (Mark 1:23–24). What the witness to him makes clear is that, in the conflict between the things of God and the things of the world, Jesus stands unqualifiedly on the side of God.

The witness of his disciples emphasize that he and he alone stands with God. His disciples find that, before him, they are with the world. "Depart from me, for I am a sinful man," is the reaction of Simon (Luke 5:8), already cast as the spokesman of the apostles before he is called and renamed Peter. No departure is possible, however, for "sinners" stands as the title for just those to whom Jesus is presented as coming. He ate with them, he kept company with them. They and not the righteous were the ones he sought out. Standing with sinners, with those deranged by demons, and with the sick and dying, the disciples presented their witness to Jesus as one in whom the forgiving, liberating, healing and life-giving God of Israel comes to their aid.

If in him they found themselves to have been met by the One before whom they knew themselves as sinners, it is yet more pronounced in their witness that in meeting him they had met the source of their life. From him they heard "words of eternal life" as they had never heard them (John 6:58). We owe to the Johannine community the clearest articulation of this witness. Jesus is presented as saying it for the disciples: "He who has seen me has seen the Father" (John 14:9), and it is brought to its ultimate expression when the apostle Thomas exclaims in the face of the risen Jesus, "My Lord and my God" (John 20:28). As a witness of the early and entirely Jewish community, this could not have meant that the Jew Jesus was God, the God of the Jews. It could indeed mean, however, that directly and specifically in their meeting with Jesus of Nazareth, they had met their God, the God of Israel.

It is important to add at this point, however, that Jesus is presented in the apostolic witness as having been sent to Israel's sick, the healthy having no need of a physician (Mark 2:17; Matt. 9:12–13; Luke 5:31–32).

That means that the witness to Jesus includes also this further witness concerning a healthy, righteous Israel, the ones who (so Jesus is presented as saying) had no need of him presumably because they already knew and served their God.

iii. They see only Jesus

We miss the force of this witness, especially that of the Johannine community, if we do not notice that these amazing claims were made by the early disciples precisely about Jesus the Jew from Nazareth. It insists that it was in meeting this man that they had met God. That calls for reflection.

It is essential to remember that all of these disciples—during the lifetime of Jesus and also on Easter and for a few years after— were Jews. What they present as having happened to them, they present as having happened face to face with this man, a fellow Jew, and then again in hearing from other fellow Jews about this particular Jew. They would, in all probability, have had some awareness of the Word of their God because of the good work of the Sages and Pharisees and their widespread institution, the synagogue. From their rabbis, from the readings from the Scriptures in the synagogue, and from each other, and because it was embedded in the literature of their people and its history, they would have heard the Word of their God to Israel. As noted above, the apostolic witness reminds us of a healthy, righteous Israel as well as of those "lost sheep" to whom Jesus is presented as having been sent. But any Christian or Jew today can well imagine that this Word might not have had much of an impact on many of them. So it is, often, in the Church and in the synagogue today. The Word comes across only as a word, or as so many words.

With Jesus, the witness makes clear, it was different, radically different. With Jesus, so they testify, the *Word* of God became the word of *God*, "words of eternal life." The Johannine community was so impressed with this feature of the early witness that it presents Jesus himself as that Word, now evidently become (John 1:14) the flesh and blood of the Jew Jesus of Nazareth. In hearing him, in being met by this man, they had heard and been confronted by God's own address. It was therefore necessary, they thought, to hold on to this man, in all his earthly Jewish reality, to "gnaw" (John 6:54) on his physical, human, Jewish actuality as a dog gnaws nosily on a bone (on this verb, see Hoskyns and Davies, *Fourth Gospel*, 297). No greater misunderstanding of this witness could be imagined than the theory that this man had been divinized—that what had happened in his all-too-human presence (namely, the discovery of God's presence) should be understood as a transformation of his human reality by another, divine reality, such that the flesh that the Word had happened as had ceased being Jewish flesh and had become something ethereal.

Is the patristic interpretation an adequate defense against such a misunderstanding? But of course, the Church fathers, unlike his apostles and disciples who left us this witness, were not Jews! The bishops at the Council of Chalcedon certainly wanted to protect the Church from a docetic dilution of Jesus' full humanity, but one must ask whether they could ever have done so by relying on a single category, "nature," which they felt free to apply both to human beings and to God. Had any Jews been invited to that council even in the status as "observers," surely a warning would have been sounded. The Church has always gotten itself into trouble when it has presumed to talk about the relationship between the Jew Jesus and the God of Israel without consulting any Jews.

But the early witnesses were Jews. For them there could be no confusion between the Jew Jesus and the God of the Jewish people. Brought up on the intimacy of their God and their people, they had no need of such a confusion in order to say what mattered to them most: in the presence of this Jew, the LORD, the God of Israel, Creator of heaven and earth, had met them so starkly in love and with such an unqualified claim, making the covenant so gloriously and fearfully a matter of here and now, that they could say no less than, "My Lord and my God!" Gentiles, who have to cope with their own ambiguities, may ever have trouble understanding this peculiarly Jewish ambiguity. It may be asked whether the Gentile fathers of an anti-Judaic Church could ever have understood it, and then whether a modern Gentile Church could come to understand it by purging itself of its anti-Judaism.

An interesting variation on the Johannine community's version of the apostolic witness is to be found in the story of the Transfiguration (Mark 9:2–8, with parallels in Matt. 17:2–8 and Luke 9:28–36). Following a mystical apparition of Jesus shining as the sun in the presence of Moses and Elijah, the vision evaporates and the disciples "no longer saw any one with them but Jesus only" (Mark 9:8). That "Jesus only" fits exactly with the "highest" christological claims of the Johannine community. The genuine meeting with the God of Israel—the God of Abraham, Isaac, and Jacob—and the God and Father of Jesus of Nazareth, which the early witnesses to Jesus claim had happened to them, happened in their meeting with the Jew Jesus and in the early apostolic witness to him. So the Church has claimed to this day. When it claims to have met God, it knows that in this event it has met "only Jesus." If it has seen the Father, it is because it has seen only, but then really seen, it would want to say, the Jew of Nazareth.

iv. They worship only God

We come now to a crucial issue in Christian faith and so in Christology, and one on which the teaching and practice of the Church has been less than clear. "God," Paul wrote to his beloved Philippian community (Phil. 2:9–11), "has highly exalted [Jesus] and bestowed on him the name which is above every name, that at the name of Jesus every knee should bow . . . and every tongue confess that Jesus Christ is Lord, to the glory of God the Father." Paul wrote this (either quoting or enlarging upon an early Christian hymn) about the humble Jew of Nazareth, the slave in whose name he felt impelled to preach humility. This humble one had had bestowed upon him, just as had Israel itself, the name that is above every name, that is, the name of God himself. "The name of God" refers to God's own presence. As God had chosen to dwell with Israel, so he had chosen to dwell with this son of Israel. To be an enemy of Israel was to be an enemy of God, the rabbis taught, and so to be an enemy of this son of Israel as Pilate (and "the rulers of this era," I Cor. 2:8; cf. Eph. 6:12) was, was to be at war with God. As the presence (name) of the God of Israel and Israel in the flesh are eternally inseparable, so the name (presence) of the God of Israel and this Israelite are eternally inseparable. They are certainly distinguishable ("Why do you call me good? No one is good but God alone"–Mark 10:18), but they are inseparable.

The consequence is that, at the name of this Jew in all his human Jewishness just as in the presence of the Israel of God, the Gentile world is to know that it is in the presence of the concrete effects of God's involvement in his creation for its good. It should therefore bow, and bow low. When Israel passes by, the world should recognize the breath of God blowing into his creation. When this Israelite passes by, it is the same. And so the Gentile world should confess that Jesus, the Jew from Nazareth, bears the very presence (= name) of God, as do his people. If the world should ask where God is, let it begin by looking to see where Israel is, and therefore where also this Israelite is. In Greek grammar an "is" is appropriate here; in Hebrew, none would be needed: just Israel and the God of Israel side by side; just Jesus for the Gentiles and the God of Israel side by side.

But now the decisive point: this confession of the closest proximity of the Israel of God and the God of Israel, and now of the Israelite of God for the Gentiles, and the God of Israel who will also be the God of the Gentiles, is by no means intended to glorify either Israel or this Israelite. Far be it from Israel to want that; and the early Jewish witness to Jesus, including unambiguously this hymn to the humble one, could hardly have wanted that. No, this is all to the glory of God the Father and to his glory alone. The Church's Christology will make this clear, or it will stand in conflict with this early hymn about Jesus of Philippians 2.

The line can so easily be overstepped, especially in doxological contexts, yet it is important that the line be clear. The "higher" the Church's Christology, the nearer it is to the witness of the early Church, if "high" means to stress that God in all his humble majesty is precisely the One whom the Church meets in Jesus of

Nazareth. He and his Father are really one in this event. But if this be expressed so as to make it appear that it is to the glory of Jesus, then the church gives to him a glory other than that bestowed upon him by God. Instead of Jesus as the one whose glory lies precisely in his staggering humility before his God in order that his God may be the God of the Gentile Church, it turns him into the God-man of the anti-Judaic, proud, and patriarchal Church of the past.

3. WHERE WOMEN AND MEN ARE PRESENT TO GOD THROUGH JESUS CHRIST

i. *Other ways of being present to God*

What is it to be present to God? I use this phrase to speak of the human side of the event or situation more usually called the presence of God. It is at least theoretically conceivable that God could be present to most people most of the time without any of them being aware of it.

I am doubtful if any sense can be given to the idea of God being present everywhere and all the time, for that rules out all possibility of absence. A presence that excludes even the possibility of absence must also exclude all coming and going. It can therefore only be an impersonal presence and thus tell us nothing at all about the personal God of Israel and the Father of Jesus Christ. Theologically, the concept of omnipresence appears to be incoherent. It could only have entered the vocabulary of an anti-Judaic Church that had forgotten that its God was the quite personal God of Israel.

In order to avoid the impossible task of trying to speak of that which God may be doing, but of which we have no awareness, it seems wiser to turn to the human side of what from time to time is remembered and hoped for as being in God's presence. I have been referring to it by speaking of being present to God. It means to be open to God's presence, should he come. It means being at God's disposal. It means living as a creature aware from time to time that one is a creature and that one belongs to one's Creator at all times and in all circumstances. It is a stance described in some detail in Matthew's Sermon on the Mount, in 1 Corinthians 13, and in the hymn of Philippians 2. The Church's clearest picture of it is the early witness to Jesus. The picture of that humble Jew is the Church's best image of what it is to be present to God, and hence the best image possible to creatures of "the invisible God" (Col. 1:15)

In speaking of what it knows, the Church, once more, would do well not to speak of what it does not know. What it does know is what has happened to it: Jesus Christ, and he alone, has confronted the Church so as to make it present to God. He has been the way to the Father (John 14:6) for those who were without hope and without God in the world (Eph. 2:12). So be it, and let the Church rejoice in this and give unstinting praise and thanksgiving to God for such a gift.

What the church does not know is whether and how others may have found themselves, apart from Jesus and Israel, present to God. Again, in the case of Israel, the Church must believe that God's people have been present to him again and again, even if not at all times. Had not Abraham, Jacob, and, above all, Moses and all the people at Sinai, been present to God, there would have been no Jesus of Nazareth through whom he could have effected his presence to the Church. And if that presence, as God's *Shekhinah*, has not been with Israel since then, grounds for confidence in the fidelity of God would be undermined. At least Israel, the Church must confess, has been present to God apart from Jesus Christ, above all in its ancient and continuing practice of the study of Torah to this day, and in the daily life of obeying the *mitzvot*, the commandments.

As to the rest of the world, the Church cannot know and had therefore best not say. Because Israel stands as a massive exception to what the Church knows from its own life, it would seem wise for the Church at least to be open and receptive to the possibility that there may be many ways in which women and men can be and are present to God, including ways that are not those generally thought of as religious.

ii. Present to God through Jesus Christ

What the early witness to Jesus claims is that, in the presence of Jesus, the disciples found themselves in the presence of God. They do not say Jesus is God. They say that where he is, God is. God's love reached them, disclosing them to themselves as sinners, but as forgiven sinners; unprofitable, but unprofitable servants; lost sheep who had been found and lovingly brought back to their fold. They bore witness to Jesus as one anointed by God, authorized by God to speak and act in God's name and as God's love, and their witness is their testimony to their conviction that that authorization had proved to be effective in their case and in the case of so many who had come within the range of that healing love.

Beginning with Easter, the disciples discovered that Jesus' authorization continued to be effective in their witness to him. And the Church has ever since lived from the fact that in taking up the apostolic witness to him and making it its own, Jesus by becoming present in the Church's word and sacrament, continues to make women and men present to God. They discover themselves as forgiven sinners, unprofitable servants, and recovered lost sheep. In short, Christ proclaimed by the Church continues the work of Christ the proclaimer of God's radical and unlimited love. In his name, the healing and reconciling love of the God of Israel continued to be effective, also among Gentiles. Paul was able to sum it up by saying that "neither death nor life . . . nor anything else in all creation, will be able to separate us from the love of God in Christ Jesus our Lord" (Rom. 8:38–39).

The Church is the proximate context of Jesus Christ because it is the community of those who have discovered themselves to be present to God in being present to Christ. Their witness to this and their reflection upon it is the Church's Christology.

iii. Only before Jesus

It is a fundamental feature of the testimony of the early witnesses that they are all about, and only about, Jesus. They present him without a visible support system: his friends think him mad (Mark 3:21); he has no credentials (Mark 11:28); his disciples do not understand him and are afraid (Mark 10:32). Jesus stands alone in this witness, and it is simply he himself, in both his words and his actions, that make up the things concerning Jesus of Nazareth that they claim had had such an effect upon them and others. Even in the Emmaus story of Luke (Luke 24:13–35), which indicates (v. 17) that at least Luke's community had a whole *midrash* (interpretation) of the Scriptures to support its witness, it is revealing that it is Jesus himself who provides his disciples with this *midrash*.

Paul's gospel seems to have been consistent with this, for in a letter to the church in Corinth he reminded his readers (1 Cor. 2:2) that he had "determined to know nothing among you except Jesus Christ and him crucified." The author of Acts strikes the same note with his story of Peter and the lame beggar, to whom Peter has only the name of Jesus to offer. Jesus is neither a moral model nor a metaphysical principle. He is that Jew in whose presence strange things happened, and so the preaching of the disciples took the form of presenting just that Jesus. They told his story, which became our Gospels. They recalled his words as best they could. They told the parables he had told. They recounted his deeds of healing. Evidently, they wanted their hearers and readers to be confronted by one thing and by one thing only: Jesus Christ, the Jew from Nazareth. They therefore thought that there was for them only one thing needed, that they ask only for that which the Gospel of John has some diaspora Jews ask of Philip: "Sir, we wish to see Jesus" (John 12:21).

iv. Present only to God

Once more we arrive at a crucial issue for Christology and so for the faith and life of the Church. Let me first put the issue crudely: Is the Church and its faith about Jesus, or about God? That is too crude a question to warrant an answer, for it should be clear that the Church and its faith center in Jesus *and* God (cf. Milet, *Dieu*). Yet the question is designed to spur our thinking about the dynamics of faith and the function of the figure of Jesus within it.

A faith in Jesus Christ that is consistent with the apostolic witness means trust that Jesus was and is God's anointed, that this Jew is indeed authorized to speak and act in the name of the God of Abraham, Isaac, and Jacob, that in being present to him the Church is indeed present to the God of Israel. The Jesus of the early witness wishes to be a means to this end, even in the witness of the Johannine community. That witness has Jesus cry out, "He who believes in me, believes *not* in me but in him who sent me" (John 12:44)! It also has Jesus insisting that he seeks not his own glory but the glory of God alone (John 7:18). For Christian faith, according to the apostolic witness, Jesus is an effective means to God's end.

The early witness presents a Jesus who gave the glory to God, a Jesus who refused every title, even being called good, as we have seen. He is also presented as leading others to praise God, not himself, for the healing which he effected (Mark 2:12). He orders the healed demoniac of Gerasene to "Go home to your friends, and tell them how much the Lord has done for you, and how he has had mercy on you" (Mark 5:19), an order that the man immediately disobeys by going and proclaiming "how much *Jesus* had done for him" (v. 20). There lies the challenge to Christology in two verses: to say that fully in the presence of Jesus the Church is in the presence of God, and so to give thanks for this which Jesus accomplishes, that we give our thanks to God alone, as we have been ordered to do. The balance seems caught perfectly in the ending of the hymn of Philippians 2: Jesus is to be confessed as Lord so that it is clear that this is being done to the glory of God the Father alone.

Is then the Church's faith, faith in Jesus or faith in God? The answer to which the apostolic witness leads us is that the Church is to trust in this man as the one whom God has set before the Church as his way to awaken its whole trust in God. So trusting, the Church will be following the lead that the witness to Jesus provides.

4. WHERE GOD'S CLAIM IS ACKNOWLEDGED THROUGH JESUS CHRIST

i. The claim of one making no claim for himself

The church is the context of Jesus Christ because, and in so far as, it acknowledges the claim of God's love that comes through the witness to Christ. In doing so, the Church becomes the fruit of Christ's continuing work and therefore united with him as his disciples and as servants of the God of Israel. It acknowledges God's claim as the witness to Jesus presents him as having done: without making any claim for himself.

Jesus is proclaimed in the apostolic witness as one who proclaimed the coming of the reign of God, which is the immediacy of God's love in action. That love in action is announced as an absolutely free gift, unearned and unearnable, coming to good and bad, rich and poor, the righteous and sinners. It knows no limits and it comes without qualification. "Fear not, little flock, for it is your Father's good pleasure to *give* you the kingdom" (Luke 12:32).

God's love, according to this witness, precisely as a free gift, lays a claim upon those who receive it. How could it be otherwise in the context of Israel? How could it be other then covenantal love when it is proclaimed by a Jew to Jews, and by one authorized—so the Church must believe—to speak and act in the name of the God of Sinai? Israel's acknowledgment of the commandments lies behind this proclamation of love, and, as the Talmud makes clear, so does the Jewish understanding of the call to an *imitatio Dei.* To hear that one is loved by this God is to hear the command, spread throughout the proclamation of Jesus that his disciples proclaimed, "Go and do thou likewise." (Luke 10:37)

Go and do thou likewise. Like what? Like the God whose love reaches the unlovely and the unlovable, the unjust as much as the just, and especially the poor, the sick, and the oppressed. As God's love knows no limits, so one who is loved is commanded to love without limit, not stopping at even seventy times seven. The command reaches all God's creation, including one's enemies. The command is not to like one's enemies but to love them, to intend their well-being as God's creatures, and to pray for them. The claim is as revolutionary as the love that grounds it. The command is to go all the way in imitation of this God who goes all the way (Matt 5:44–48). A Christology to which this commandment was not integral would be a mockery of the apostolic witness to Jesus Christ.

The one who proclaims this commandment and lays this claim upon his hearers, however, is one who is presented as having made absolutely no claims for himself. This is an essential feature of the witness. He wanted no titles, they tell us, and he would not be a king or ruler. He seems to have distanced himself from the resistance movement that was to lead the nation into a disastrous war of liberation a generation and a half later. He is not presented in the early witness as starting a movement of his own, either one united around his own person or one in his own cause. He had no cause of his own and he made no claims for himself.

The later, more developed witness qualifies what has just been said. Knowing that beginning with Easter there arose a movement, the Jesus-movement, around the witness of the early disciples, the Church could hardly think of itself as other than started by Jesus, as indeed it was in a certain fashion. The assertion that Jesus founded the Church must stand without historical support, however, if it is made as an insertion about an intentional act of the "historical Jesus," since uncertain inference from—and in part in conflict with—the earliest witness is its only foundation. What founded the Church historically was the efficacy of the witness to Jesus as one who founded nothing and had no cause of his own. His authority for his Church rests entirely on his authorization by the One he called Father, not on any supposed claim which he made for himself. The Johannine community expressed this with clarity in having Jesus say, "I can do nothing on my own authority; as I hear I judge; and my judgment is just, because I seek not my own will but the will of him who sent me. If I bear witness to myself, my testimony is not true; there is another who bears witness to me, and I know that the testimony which he bears to me is true" (John 5:30–32).

ii. One whose cause is God's

The witness to Jesus Christ is to one who had no cause of his own because his whole cause was God's. His radical claim is not presented as being on his own behalf because it is solely God's claim that he announces. The witness is consistent and clear on this: the Jesus they proclaimed was totally, unreservedly dedicated to the cause of God. "Not my will, but thine be done" stands over every story, saying, and action reported from beginning to end. So he lived, so he taught, and so he died. His cause was the cause of God.

Others have believed that they served the cause of God, and others have had followers who presented them as having served that cause. Moses comes immediately to mind, and then Israel's lesser prophets. There is no so-called objective way in which it can be decided if their cause was God's, or only God's. The decision will be made, in the case of Jesus as with those of the prophets, as a decision of faith. That is to say, either one hears their cause as the cause of God, as the cause of that which one takes to be ultimate, or one does not. One hears their claim as ultimate and unconditioned, or one does not. It is evident that the witness to be found in the Apostolic Writings was made by men and women who understood the cause of Jesus and heard his claim as the cause and claim of the God of Israel, Maker of heaven and earth. To share in that understanding and hearing is to be a Christian, and the Church of Jesus Christ is constituted by just this understanding and hearing to this day.

Perhaps it is in this connection that we may understand that strange bit of the apostolic witness that speaks of a sin against the Holy Spirit and says that it is the one sin that will not be forgiven (Mark 3:28–29; Matt. 12:31–32; Luke 12:10). In the witness of the Apostolic Writings, the Holy Spirit is the Spirit of God who speaks through the prophets, and also the Spirit of Jesus Christ. The sin against the Holy Spirit may be the failure to hear the witness to Jesus as the witness to God's claim. If one will not hear God's claim and command as God's, the authors of this witness may have been saying, one has placed oneself outside of the realm of God's forgiveness. How faithful or fruitful a witness this is to Jesus may be left open. If God's love reaches also to his enemies, one might be excused for concluding that it must surely be able to include blasphemers, not to speak of doubters. If, on the other hand, we take the saying (with Geza Vermes) to mean that all sins against human beings, Jesus included, will be forgiven, but not sins against God, the same conclusion would seem to be in order.

iii. A Church with no cause of its own

The Church as the context of Jesus Christ is the Church that acknowledges itself as loved and claimed through him by the God of Israel, the Church that, in standing before him, finds itself to be standing before that God. Because he had no cause of his own but only God's, and because he made no claim for himself but only for God, such a Church could have no cause of its own nor advance any claim on its own behalf. If it were to say that it is the Church of Jesus Christ, that could not be a boast, but only the admission by a slave of its Master's name. Because its Master was one who made no claims for himself and had no cause of his own, the Church can only say with the Apostle to the Gentiles, "If I must boast. I will boast of the things that show my weakness" (2 Cor. 11:30). And why is this? Because it will be able to say, with the same apostle, "For what we preach is not ourselves, but Jesus Christ as Lord, with ourselves as your slaves for Jesus' sake" (2 Cor. 4:5), and also, "You are Christ's, and Christ is God's" (1 Cor. 3:23).

It follows that the Christology of such a Church will be so formulated as in no way to sound like a claim on its own behalf. The Christology of the anti-Judaic Church sometimes did sound like such a claim. Not only figuratively but sometimes literally, it used the cross as a hammer with which to beat others (mostly, but not only, Jews) into submission or death. It preached an imperial Christ, vested in the robes of the Caesars, and one who made all manner of claims for himself. Quite consistently, it preached itself as the imperial Church, commissioned to exercise Christ's monarchy as his vicar on earth. It can only be said that such a Church may well be the context of such a Christ, but that this Christ is not the Christ of the apostolic witness. Such a Church proves by its Christology, and consequently and inevitably by its behavior, that it is abandoning the apostolic succession.

iv. The humility of love—God's, Christ's, and the Church's

The Church that is faithful to the witness of the apostles will preach another Jesus than that. It will join them in preaching the one who preached the humble love of God, a love willing to get on its hands and knees to go hunting in the dirt in search of that which is lost and trampled on. To proclaim such a one, however, is to set before itself as well as any hearer one whose behavior and message were integrated, one who humbled himself and took the form of a slave, being obedient to God's call even to the point of death (Phil. 2:7–8). That is in no way a contradiction to his being in the form of God (Phil. 2:6); it is, rather, its confirmation. That is to say, the humility of Jesus reflects the humility of God, and from the humility of Jesus Christ the Church learns of the humility of God.

The humble God, made known to the Church by the humble Christ, can be faithfully served only by a humble Church. Obedience to such a God will therefore set the Church walking in harmony with the Israel of God. What the Church is to learn from Jesus Christ, and from the apostolic witness to him, is what Israel had heard long before and was reminded of by one of its prophets: "He has told you, O man, what is good, and what the LORD requires of you: only to do justice and to love goodness, and to walk humbly with your God" (Micah 6:8). To walk with that God can only be done in humility (or with modesty), for such are the ways of the God of Israel and the Father of Jesus Christ.

Humility before God should not be confused with or thought to imply bowing down to humiliation imposed by others. The Church has not always made this distinction clear, either to itself or to others, thus providing Nietzsche grounds for his aphorism, "A worm, when stepped on, curls up into itself, lest it be stepped on again: Christian humility."

5. CHRISTOLOGY AS UNFINISHED

i. For the Church

The Church's Christology is and must remain unfinished. With its Christology, the Church speaks of the things concerning Jesus of Nazareth. Those things, however, are still going on. They are not completed. Indeed, they could not be spoken of as completed unless they had come to an end. But then Christology would no longer be a matter of the present tense, but wholly of the past. That would mean that there was no more Church to speak of him. Therefore the Church, so long as it endures, will always have an unfinished, an intentionally and explicitly incomplete, Christology, and it will thank God for this incompleteness because it is a sign that the Church is still alive.

The Church's Christology is incomplete in part because the Church itself, God knows, is unfinished. Even the Church is well aware that it has not come to that fullness, the wholeness to which the witness to Jesus sees it as having been called. It has certainly not reached that conformity to Christ to which it has been called. In a word, Jesus Christ is far from finished with his Church, and the Church's Christology should make that clear.

The Church's Christology is unfinished, to go to the root of the matter, because God himself is not yet finished with what he set out to do in Jesus of Nazareth. That means that every Christological predicate, every title or function assigned to Jesus, needs, so to speak, a date assigned to it. If I am right about the priority of the present tense in Christology, then Christology will need to be thoroughly diachronic, with every claim made about Jesus set in the particular social, political, economic and cultural circumstances of the present of the Church that came in its day to say what it did about the things concerning Jesus of Nazareth. Such a procedure would place in brackets the whole of the Church's classical Christological tradition.

In this connection, the reiterated "greater things" that are to come, to which the Johannine community testified (John 1:50, 5:20, 14:12), bear pondering. The Church's Christological tradition shows little or no awareness that an actual historical future appears in all probability to lie ahead of us, and that it is the future of God and of his Christ. The only future in which the tradition has shown an interest has been that of the *eschaton*, the End, even as it saw the passing of centuries. A Christology that is fit to serve a Church that has confessed the eternity of the covenant between God and the Jewish people will need to be radically more historical than that. The reason for this is that God has given the Church, not to speak of Israel, a long history in which the things concerning Jesus of Nazareth have continued to unfold. For such a Church with such a history, classical Christology will never be the last word.

ii. For the Church with Israel

The Church's Christology is and must remain unfinished, secondly, because it is evident that God is not yet finished with what he intends in the matter of the relationship between the Church and the Jewish people. That relationship is grounded in Jesus Christ, the chosen instrument from among the chosen people, through whom many Gentiles would be chosen to come to the knowledge and service of the God of Israel. Since the relationship between the Church and the Jewish people is incomplete, Christology can only be unfinished: the Church will be able and need to say more and other things tomorrow concerning Jesus of Nazareth than it can say today. What it says today will therefore have to be open to amendment.

Reconciliation, we saw, lies at the heart of the things concerning Jesus of Nazareth. Reconciliation became an urgent concern as the Church moved from the first stage of its history to the second (on the periodization of the Church's history, see van Buren, *People Israel* 171–72). We may call the first stage that of *the Church within Israel*. Whether its beginning be defined by the calling of the first disciples, or perhaps more soundly with the Easter faith of Peter and the others, the Church was a gathering of Jews, a movement that had no sense of being other than Israel, called to be Israel in anticipation of the coming reign of the God of Israel.

The second stage began to develop with the entry of Gentiles into this Jewish movement, and the reconciliation of Jews and Gentiles within it was a matter of utmost concern. Its occurrence is celebrated above all in the document called Ephesians, but its author seems to have been utterly unaware of its fearful cost: the developing hostility between this Church, made up of Jews and ever more Gentiles, and the great body of the Jewish people, the Israel of God. The Apostle to the Gentiles is the only one, in those early days, whom we can be sure saw the danger and agonized over it. The bulk of the evidence shows the Church entering without hesitation or doubt into the second stage of its history, which we may call that of *the church against Israel.* In this second stage, which began during the second half of the first century and whose course was clearly set before its end, the Church became the anti-Judaic Church and developed its anti-Judaic Christology. The second stage was to last many times longer than the first.

As Israel's loss of Jerusalem in the war with Rome marked the transition from the Church within Israel to the Church against Israel, so Israel's regaining of Jerusalem as the capital of the Jewish State may have signaled what could turn out to be a third stage in the history of the Church, of which the Declaration *Nostra Aetate* of the Second Vatican Council could count as the beginning. We may call the third stage that of *the Church with Israel.* As with the first transition, the second appears to be a gradual change, and we are today far too close to it to see clearly what the third stage will look like, or whether we have named it accurately. Obviously *A Theology of the Jewish-Christian Reality* is intended as a contribution to the Church's understanding for the third stage of its life, offered in the hope that I have named it correctly. If I have, then the Church is entering a new stage of its life, in which reconciliation may begin to be realized between the Church of God and the Israel of God. For such a stage the Church will need a Christology appropriate to its new situation, a Christology for the Jewish-Christian reality, for it will no longer be able to speak of the things concerning Jesus of Nazareth as it did when it understood itself as the Church against Israel. It will have to learn to hear the witness to Christ that comes from its first stage and, without letting that be drowned out or twisted by the witness that comes from the beginning of its second stage, build upon it its present understanding of Jesus Christ. This is the new task which we are exploring in the present volume. Christ in context means Christ in his Church today. That calls for a new Christology developed out of the new context of the Church with, not against, Israel.

iii. For the Church and Israel with the world

We can at this stage only indicate what will have to be a subject for our fourth part: the Church of God and the Israel of God need to recognize that more has been placed on their agendas than their relationship to each other, for they are the Church and the Israel of the Judge (that is, the one who decides, the one who settles disputes) of all the world, to use the terms ascribed to Abraham (Gen. 18:25). There is more to God's concern for reconciliation than the relations between the Church and the Jewish people. Therefore there is more to Christology than the Jewish-Christian reality. Since the service of reconciliation, which the Church and the Jewish people together owe to the rest of the world, is far from finished, the Church's Christology will have to be unfinished, open to new things that may become possible and necessary to say concerning Jesus of Nazareth. It is a judgment based on the order of what has been shown to the Church and the order of the Church's history to this point, that the Church will not be able to develop a Christology for the wider reality of the world until it has first developed a Christology for the Jewish-Christian reality. This judgment is confirmed for the author by his perception that, in order to see the dimensions of that prior task (in this third part), it was necessary first to develop a Christian theology of the people Israel (see van Buren, *People Israel*).

iv. Unfinished Christology: the necessity and limits of Christocentrism

Christology may be unfinished but it remains at the center of what the Church has to say. The Church has not just its origin but the grounds of its present life in the things concerning Jesus of Nazareth. Christ and the Church's relationship to him is simply the center of the Church's whole existence. A Church in which Jesus Christ is not at the center is inconceivable. That would be a contradiction in terms, for the Church is the Church of Christ or it is nothing.

Christ is the Church's center, but he is so by the will of God. As Paul put it addressing the Church of Corinth, "You are Christ's, and Christ is God's" (1 Cor. 3:23). Christ is the Church's center because that is how God has chosen to create and sustain his Gentile Church. If Christocentrism means that Christ is the Church's way to the Father, the one in whose presence alone it is made present to God, then there can be no question of its necessity.

We have seen, however, that Christology is and must be unfinished. The final reason for saying this lies in the word of the Apostle to the Gentiles, that, in the end, when Christ's work is done, he will "be subjected to him who put all things under him, that God may be everything to every one [or all in all]" (1 Cor. 15:28). If that is how it is to be at the last, then perhaps we should say that God is the limit of Christocentrism. And that is to say that for this time, for the Church in its present situation and for the foreseeable future, Christ is necessarily at the center. The necessity is temporal, however, as are all things pertaining to the Church. In God's future things may be different, but in the Church's present, in its here and now, Christ is its center by the will of God. Christocentrism is therefore necessary because of the God of Israel who is its limit; it will therefore be a Christocentrism that clearly gives the glory to God the Father.

CHAPTER FIVE

Christ Risen: Easter

*The Church exists in the trust that it is following God's lead in affirming
the Jew Jesus as God's living way of being present to it. Easter is the ambiguous event in which the Church recognizes both God's refusal to abandon his cause, which Jesus made his own, and the cross as evidence of the
seriousness of the conflict between that cause and the misuse of human
power.*

1. CHRISTIAN FAITH AS EASTER FAITH

i. The confirmation of God and his covenant

The beginning of what we know as the Church of Jesus Christ
lies in the covenantal event of Easter, and it is fundamental for the
Church and its Christology that this event be understood as covenantal. Traditionally, Easter has been understood as God's confirmation of Jesus. Luke applied Psalm 16:10 to the event: "Thou
shall not let thy Holy One see corruption" (Acts 13:35). Paul
wrote that Jesus had been "designated Son of God in power according to the spirit of holiness by his resurrection from the
dead" (Rom. 1:4). It is clear that the apostolic witness to Jesus
arose from the Easter conviction that God had confirmed Jesus
"by raising him from the dead." The Jesus so confirmed, however, is the same Jesus whom his disciples understood to have been
authorized by God to call them as Jews into a renewal of the cov-

enant. This was the Jesus presented as sent only to "the lost sheep of the house of Israel," who had longed to gather Israel together into the total service of God. To confirm this Jesus entailed a confirmation of the cause for which he lived, which was no other than the cause of the God of Israel. If God had confirmed Jesus, Jesus *in context,* then God had first of all confirmed his own cause. But God's own cause, "according to the Scriptures," is the covenant, the whole story of God and his people which began with Abraham, was confirmed and renewed under Moses, and then reaffirmed with King David. God's self-confirmation in raising Jesus must therefore be seen as a confirmation of his covenant with Israel and of Israel in its covenant partnership with God.

The Jesus confirmed on Easter, in short, is Jesus in the context of the story within whose terms he is reported to have lived and taught and acted, not a Jesus in isolation. The classical Christological tradition in its own way also meant to set Jesus in context, but it chose the universal context of all humanity, even all of creation. The relationship between him and the total human situation was stressed, but his more immediate relationship to his people and their history was almost ignored. That jump from the historical to the cosmological is too quick for an event that was claimed to be "according to the Scriptures." Moreover, it passes too quickly from Israel (as Jesus' primary and immediate context) to the church. The issue is whether Israel is the fundamental context for understanding Easter, or whether the later Church may be substituted in its place. More sharply put, is Easter to be preached by the Church according to the Scriptures, or is it to be preached according to the life and doctrine of the Church? If the Church means to preach the risen Jesus of Nazareth, and not some new and different one, then it will want to insist that his confirmation by the Father is at once the confirmation of God's cause and covenantal purpose.

ii. *No other faith*

To believe in and therefore to preach the risen Jesus of Nazareth is to trust in and confess the present reality of Jesus of Nazareth's bringing the Church into the presence of God. Easter faith is simply Christian faith, and the Church knows no other. To believe that God has exalted, or confirmed, or raised Jesus from the dead (and we shall take more careful note of the variety of ways in which the apostolic witness expresses this basic trust) is primarily a belief in God, the trust that God has confirmed Jesus in his devotion to the call and purpose of God. It is the trust that God has indeed authorized Jesus to continue to confront the Church with God's own love and demand, after and in spite of Jesus' death on a cross. Easter, with its responding trust of the disciples, is therefore the beginning of the Church; trust that God's authorization of Jesus continues to this day to re-present God's love and claim is what keeps the Church alive. This is what lies behind the assertion of the Apostle to the Gentiles, that "if Christ has not been raised, then our preaching is in vain and your faith is in vain" (1 Cor. 15:14). There can be Jewish faith without Easter, but for the Gentile Church, as for the original Jewish Church within Israel, there is no Christian faith but Easter faith.

The point seems so evident on purely historical grounds that it should not call for emphasis, were it not for the fact that one of the champions in the attempt to rid the Church of its traditional anti-Judaism has come to argue in recent years that the root of that traditional sickness lies precisely in the Church's faith that God raised Jesus from the dead. The resurrection of Jesus, so A. Roy Eckardt has argued (Eckardt, "Heart," 306), establishes the triumph of the Church over Israel. It must therefore be denied if the Church is ever to recover from the anti-Judaism of its past.

What is to be denied, so the argument goes, is that there was a resuscitation of the dead Jesus. The resurrection was a fact or it was nothing. Either the dead Jesus began to breathe and walk and talk again, or else he remains dead and there was no resurrection. (We shall see in the next subsection how strange an interpretation this is of the ways in which the various apostolic witnesses speak of the event of Easter.)

It is difficult to know what to say to this argument, since it rests on a commitment to a particular and questionable philosophical conception of what a fact is. One gets the impression that, to Eckardt, the only event worthy of the name is one that can be recorded by photographic and electronic means. Surely the sort of resuscitation that Eckardt seems to have in mind would not of itself establish the claim of Easter faith. That claim concerns the present, continuing, post–crucifixion effectiveness of Jesus to confront persons with the reality of God's love and God's claim upon their lives. If this claim were invalid, it could hardly matter whether Jesus of Nazareth started breathing and talking again after his death.

On the other hand, the claim that is essential for and that expresses Easter faith does not need to specify the physical means whereby God confirmed Jesus in his function of confronting persons with God's love and claim. The fact of Easter that matters absolutely for the Church is that Jesus once more proved effective in standing for God and God's cause, that, in the cause in and for which he had lived before, he was alive again.

Finally, this claim of Easter faith cannot be itself the root of the Church's anti-Judaism. That root we have seen to consist of the subtle and not-so-subtle transformation of the original witness to Jesus as a Jew committed to the renewal of his people in their covenant with God, into a witness to an anti-Judaic Jesus in deepest conflict with his people. If Easter faith concerns this one who, as Paul wrote, became a servant of the Jewish people (Rom. 15:8), if the event of Easter is preached, as Paul claimed he had both learned and practiced, "in accordance with the Scriptures" (1 Cor. 15:3–4), then it undercuts the anti-Judaism which developed in the Church. That development was due not to the Church's conviction that God had confirmed God's authorization of Jesus of Nazareth on Easter, but to a reinterpretation of the cause of the crucifixion. If the conflict between the covenantal cause of God with which Jesus confronted his disciples, and the misuse of human power which Pilate exercised to rid himself of this disturber of the *Pax Romana*, be replaced by a conflict between Jesus and his own people, a foundation for anti-Judaism is already in place even without a resurrection from the dead. Indeed, resurrection only stands in the way of anti-Judaism, since it underscores the continuity of the risen one with the Jew from Nazareth. For the cause of anti-Judaism, far better a mythic and spiritualized endorsement of this new anti-Judaic Christ than so Jewish a claim as the resurrection of a Jew killed by the Romans! I am therefore pleased to note in a last-minute addition, that Professor Eckardt's last word on the subject (Eckardt, *J&C*, 156) leaves open the possibility of a "non-eschatological, non-triumphalist teaching of the Resurrection" to which perhaps this chapter may be a contribution.

iii. God's act and the Church's act

The event of Easter was a covenantal act in the primary sense that it consisted of two sides: it was at once an act of God and an act of the Church, and both acts were constitutive of one event. This seems to me to be, however novel, nonetheless the fundamental conclusion to be drawn from the peculiar character of the witness to the appearances of the risen Christ to his disciples. It has often been noted that every account of an appearance of the risen Christ, beginning with Peter and concluding apparently with Paul, was to a person who thereby became a believer. There is no reference to an appearance of any sort to anyone who was not thereafter a member of the Church. From this feature of the witness, contrary conclusions have been drawn. It has seemed to some that the appearances were of such an objective and self-authenticating nature that belief was no longer optional. The resurrection, certainly including the appearances of the one raised, was a pure act of God; the recipients of the act were purely recipients. Or, on the contrary, it has seemed to others that the appearances were the subjective experience of believers, so that it could be said that Jesus rose into the *kerygma,* the preached faith of the disciples. Each of these conclusions misses the covenantal character of Easter: it was at once an act of God and an act of the disciples, of the nascent Church. Without a doubt the witness to Easter, consistent with the witness to Sinai, insisted on the priority of God's initiative but, as in the case of Sinai, the action of those who bore witness to it was constitutive of the event.

Easter—the exaltation or raising of Jesus of Nazareth, his confirmation even as the crucified one as authorized by God to act and speak in God's name and to confront those with whom he came in contact with the love and judgment of God—was first of all an act of God. We say "first of all" because the witness of the apostolic communities is consistent in affirming this event as God's act. God raised him up. God exalted him. God set him at God's right hand. God has given him the name that is above every name, God's own name of *kurios,* Lord. To this the disciples can add their *amen*, but it is always an addition, not the originating act. Only God could authorize a human being to speak and act for him, and only God could confirm this authorization as valid and continuing after the crucifixion. Easter was first of all the act of God.

But Easter was also an act of the Church. The *amen* of the disciples was constitutive of the event, for without it there would have been no Church, no continuing confrontation with God brought about by Jesus, and so no gospel of Easter. Apart from their *amen*, their "So be it!," "it" would not have been. For the God who acted first of all is no other than the God of Sinai, the God of the covenant, whose way with his creation has ever been to invite his creatures to cooperate with him in serving his cause. To have acted without such an invitation, to have acted in sovereign isolation, "over our heads" so to speak, would not have been characteristic of the ways of the God to whom Israel, and so also Jesus, bore witness.

It is therefore entirely appropriate that none were witnesses of the resurrection who were not by that very fact "believers," women and men made by this event into members of the Church-coming-to-be. The event of Easter which is, as we shall see, possibly misleadingly designated by the word "resurrection," was a dual confirmation of Jesus as God's authorized agent. He was confirmed by God and he was confirmed by those who saw and believed, as also by those who came to believe on the basis of the word of those first witnesses (John 20:29). To present the Easter event without the active response of the disciples is to present it other than did its early witnesses. It is to ignore the clearly covenantal character of Easter.

iv. Jesus lives as Emmanuel

Emmanuel, God with us: that is the central claim of Easter faith. For the first disciples, presumably all Jews, this would have meant that they discovered as of Easter that the immediacy of their God (the God of Israel) and the intensity of God's love for his people and his claim upon them in the service of God's cause (with which

Jesus of Nazareth had confronted them in person in Galilee) returned with renewed power. For the Gentiles who were drawn by the preaching of some of these Jews, it would have meant a more radical discovery: they had been drawn into the knowledge and love of Israel's God and had a place along with Israel in the service of God's cause. For both, the figure who made that cause, and so God himself, present and alive for them was the same Jesus of Nazareth, "the same yesterday and today and for ever" (Heb. 13:8). Now as before, in his presence they discovered God with them and themselves before God. That discovery, beginning on Easter and continuing ever since, is what made and makes the Church. It is the discovery called Christian faith, which finds its characteristic expression in its weekly celebration on the first day of the week, the day of the Easter event.

2. THE EVENT OF EASTER

i. *The diversity of the witness*

On the basis of these preliminary reflections, we are now in a position to consider the witness to the event of Easter as this is presented to us in the Apostolic Writings. And the feature of that witness that strikes us at once is its diversity. Were the first appearances of the risen Christ in Jerusalem or in Galilee? Was the first appearance to Peter or to one or more women disciples? If the appearances were of one whom the disciples had known so intimately, why is there so much emphasis on their failure to recognize him at once? If the appearances were of a bodily Jesus, how is it that he appeared and disappeared in so unbodily a fashion? If the appearances were the initial occasion of the response of faith, how can some witnesses simply omit them, as though Jesus had been raised from death directly to the presence of God, as if the resurrection, so-called, consisted in fact of an unseen ascension to the Father? And finally, where does the tradition of the empty tomb, evidently arising in and possibly peculiar to the Jerusalem community, fit into the witness, and what are we to make of it? These questions arise from the diversity of the witness to the Easter event, a diversity that warns against any simple image of the event of which they speak.

The earliest *written* testimony concerning Easter is generally held to be that found in 1 Corinthians 15:3–8. Here Paul says that the tradition that he had received was that Jesus "died for our sins," "was buried," and "was raised on the third day," and all this "in accordance with the Scriptures." Then he says that Christ appeared to Cephas (Peter), to "the twelve," to "more than five hundred brethren at one time," then to James, then to "all the apostles," and "last of all," to Paul himself. Dead, buried, raised, and then the appearances, beginning with Peter.

The empty tomb tradition is not mentioned specifically, yet Paul does tell us later in the chapter that resurrection involves a transformation from the perishable to the imperishable, from the mortal to the immortal, and it could be argued that he implies that the dead body could no more have been found after the resurrection than the seed that is sown once the plant appears.

Mark's Gospel, generally taken to be the first written, concludes with the story of certain women (depending on which text is followed) coming to the tomb in which Jesus had been buried and finding, not Jesus, but a young man in white who tells him that Jesus is risen and that they are to tell "his disciples and Peter" that he is "going before you to Galilee; there you will see him." The women flee in fear. No accounts of appearances are given, only the promise of one in Galilee.

The author of the Gospel according to Matthew appears to have filled out the details of the Markan account. The owner of the tomb who arranged for the burial is further identified as a disciple of Jesus (Matt. 27:57); the story of "the chief priests and the Pharisees" (a coalition difficult to imagine) setting a guard at the tomb is added; the tomb door is opened by a great earthquake in the presence of Mary Magdalene "and the other Mary" (Matt. 28:2); in response to the words of the young man, the women depart with joy as well as fear, and Jesus appears to them and himself tells them to tell the disciples that they will see him in Galilee

(Matt. 28:8–10). Finally, Jesus does appear to them in Galilee, and "they worshiped him, but some doubted" (Matt. 28:17). The appearance to the two women and the doubt of some disciples are interesting additions to (or at least differences from) the Markan account.

The Johannine account has Mary Magdalene going alone to the tomb, finding the stone removed, and running at once to tell Peter that "they have taken the Lord out of the tomb and we do not know where they have laid him." Then Peter and the beloved disciple race to the tomb, with the latter waiting to let Peter enter first, but it is said only of the beloved disciple that "he saw [i.e., the empty tomb] and believed" (John 20:1–8). Then follows the appearance to Mary Magdalene who recognizes Jesus only when he speaks her name. That evening Jesus appears to the disciples in a room with the doors shut, and a second time a week later when Thomas is with them. Finally, in the added chapter 21, Jesus appears to the disciples in Galilee on the shore of the sea, and again he is not immediately recognized. This time he eats a breakfast of bread and fish with them, and the author reminds us that this was "the third time that Jesus was revealed to the disciples after he was raised from the dead" (John 21:12–14). The appearance to Mary, the rivalry between Peter and the beloved disciple, and appearances both in Jerusalem and in Galilee are to be noted.

The so-called Epistle to the Hebrews presents us with a quite different picture. Here in a sense there is no Easter, for "when [Jesus] had made purification for sins, he sat down at the right hand of the Majesty on high" (Heb. 1:3, cf. 12:2). In place of an empty tomb and/or appearances, following a most realistically defined death, Jesus simply "passed through the heavens" (Heb. 4:14) in order to begin there before the Father his true ministry as a great high priest. For the author, this seems to have been the meaning of the more traditional sounding praise of God "who brought our Lord Jesus again from the dead" (Heb. 13:20), but he assigns "the resurrection of the dead" to the class of "elementary doctrines" which he wanted his hearers or readers to leave behind in order to go on to more mature matters (Heb. 6:2).

Finally, Luke combines many of these points and sets them all in or about Jerusalem and in his own chronological order. The women discover the empty tomb (Luke 24:1–12); two disciples suddenly come to recognize the risen Jesus at the breaking of the bread at Emmaus, after hours of exegetical conversation, and return to Jerusalem only to discover that Jesus had already appeared to Peter (Luke 24:13–35). Whereupon Jesus appears to the gathered disciples (although some of them "supposed they saw a spirit"), and in their presence eats some broiled fish (Luke 24:36–43). Other appearances are mentioned, spread over a period of "forty days," and then Jesus ascends into the heavens (Acts 1:3, 9).

From this diverse material one is led to suspect that the early traditions concerning Easter may not have been all the same and included among them at the least: the discovery of the empty tomb by Mary Magdalene and one or two other women; a first appearance to Mary Magdalene or Peter and perhaps several to a number of disciples in Galilee according to one tradition, in Jerusalem according to another; the element of doubt or failure to recognize Jesus; as well as an ascension through or to the heavens, perhaps without reference to either an empty tomb or to appearances. In Paul's case we have his word that he himself had seen the risen Christ, and this would seem to have happened some time, perhaps several years, after Easter.

One further point is to be noted. In all their diversity, these witnesses are given as confessions of faith and as praise to God. They are themselves acts of trust in what God has done. They tell us in a variety of ways that God has done a new and mysterious thing, and that they as witnesses have been caught up in this event. They use the Jewish language of resurrection, but none of them claims to have seen a resurrection; what they speak of are the diverse consequences of what they came to call a resurrection: that the tomb was empty, that Jesus appeared, that he was alive, that he was "at the right hand" of God.

What, then, shall we say was the event of Easter? Any answer to this question will reveal the speaker's understanding of God and self. The answer of the Church, that God raised Jesus from the dead, entails the judgment that God's full authorization of Jesus to speak and act in his name has been affirmed and continues as a living reality, and the further confession that the crucified Jesus does in fact confront the Church today with the presence of God. The cross has not canceled that authorization nor led to a cessation of that confrontation. Jesus of Nazareth lives in confirmation of the covenantal cause of God and to his glory.

ii. The ambiguity of the witness

The judgment and confession with which the Church has answered the question about Easter can in no way remove the ambiguity of the witness to that event. The Church really has no solid answer to the question, hypothetical or otherwise, of Paul's Corinthian congregation, "How are the dead raised? With what kind of body do they come?" (1 Cor. 15:35). Paul's speculations on the subject are only that, an attempt of a first century Jew to speak of the event of Easter with the Jewish language of resurrection. Some parts of the witness of the Apostolic Writings seem to contradict Paul by presenting the risen Jesus as having a physical body quite up to eating fish. Other parts present the risen one as appearing and disappearing in a quite unphysical manner and suggest that the risen one was not at all so obviously recognizable as Jesus of Nazareth. Yet others tell us that Jesus has been raised to the presence of God, in or through the heavens. The how and the what on this level have to go unanswered.

It is therefore necessary to answer cautiously the quiet modern question, whether we should say that the event of Easter was a historical fact. It depends on the rules for speaking of historical facts. In our present linguistic circumstances, we might say that the Church should not claim it to be a historical fact, precisely because the Church wants to say that it was first of all an act of God—and history, by the rules generally accepted by modern historians, excludes acts of God. Bultmann was only following those rules in concluding that a modern historian cannot go behind the rise of Easter faith as the root event of Easter. For the same reason, God's covenant with Israel and his gift of Torah at Sinai could not be called historical facts. On the other hand, the Church's commitment to the importance of that election and that covenant, with their historical manifestation in the continuing life of the Jewish people, lead it to hesitate to deny that they are realities having historical consequences. So also with Easter: it has to do with the continuing impact within history of the Jesus of Nazareth who was certainly a figure in history. There is no reason, however, why the Church cannot admit that any definition of the event of Easter, adequate for its needs and purposes, will not fit within the categories of a historical investigation that excludes speaking of God's history with his creation.

iii. Ambiguity and certainty

The witness to Easter may be ambiguous in many important respects, but that does not mean that the Church must be uncertain in its Easter faith. The reason for this is that the faith of the Church is no more a response to the how and what of Easter than was the faith of the original disciples. Easter faith, which we have argued is the only Christian faith there has ever been, is a response to the confrontation with God that Jesus effected after his death, whether today or on the first day of the week after his crucifixion. Either Jesus becomes present for the Church from time to time in the witness to his words and deeds as these are mediated primarily by the Gospels and the proclamation of the Church or in the rehearsal of his last meal with his disciples, or he does not. Either the Gentile Church hears from him God's invitation into Israel's story (and therefore understands him "in accordance with the Scriptures") and in his presence finds itself standing before God, or it ceases to be the Church. If Jesus of Nazareth is not alive for his Church today and doing for it what he did for his disciples in Galilee and then anew beginning on Easter, then no matter what we think happened on that first Easter, its effects would have ceased to be a living reality for the Church and the Church would therefore have ceased to be a living Church.

God's raising up of the crucified Jesus to the Church's Lord and its way to the Father is often called an "eschatological event." By this it is usually meant that this event was a forerunner of God's own future for his creation, the first fruits of a promised harvest. Within the terms of first century Jewish eschatology that may be, but it raises difficulties for contemporary Christians who live in a world as far removed from that world as do contemporary Jews. It has, more importantly, the unfortunate consequences of detracting from the significance of the long history of the Jewish people and the church since the first century. It therefore seems to me a better response to both Easter and the many centuries which have followed it for the church to confess what it must, and to be silent on what is not yet clear. What Easter faith means for the Church is an assurance that the God of Israel has drawn it into the strange story that began with Abraham. What it tells us about God's future is not so clear. The "how" and "what" of my own future is certainly not made clear other than that, since death was not the end of Jesus' story, and since I have been drawn into that story and so into God's story with Israel, my death will not be the end of my involvement in that story. God remains God and he will not withdraw from his loving contest with his refractory creation. That is the good news of Easter which is for the Church beyond doubt.

iv. The empty tomb

For contemporary Christians, the empty tomb seems to be a primary focus of uncertainty. This is unfortunate, because it puts the issue of Easter faith in the distant past. The empty tomb tradition is certainly ambiguous, as the Gospel of Matthew revealed by adding the story that the body might have been stolen. Yet the tradition of the empty tomb appears to be as solid as any other part of the Easter traditions. In its stark negativity, it forces no theory upon us as to the "what" or "how" of the Easter event. It is as compatible with the witness of Hebrews to a Jesus raised to the Father without appearances as it is to those of the most bodily sorts of appearances. It offers no answer of any sort to questions about "how the dead are raised or with what sort of body they

come." It says only that the dead Jesus was not found, that whatever it was that now concerns the Church, it is not a dead Jesus. Of
itself it will not lead to faith in the living Jesus and the God he
serves. It forces no issues. It is, however, a powerful sign of the
mystery of one who once lived, died, and lives again. It is perfectly
possible to believe that the tomb was in fact empty and not be a
Christian; the body could have been stolen. It is also possible to
doubt the historical validity of the empty tomb tradition and still
share the Easter faith, being convinced that Jesus lives today to
the glory of God the Father. But it seems to me better for the
Church to continue to tell the story of the women who found the
tomb empty and fled in fear, as a reminder that Easter faith depends on a living present, not on a dead past. To forget this would
be to forget that the Church's response to Easter has been from
the beginning an act of praise and worship.

3. GOD'S PERSISTENCE

i. *The faithfulness of God*

The God whose cause Jesus made his own and proclaimed in
word and deed is a God who does not give up on that cause. He,
the Shepherd of Israel (Isa. 40:11, Jer. 31:10, Ezek. 34:12, Ps.
80:1), will not abandon even one lost sheep. The central message
of the Easter proclamation about God is precisely that of Jesus
himself as the Gospels present it and which Paul expressed in his
assertion, "that neither death nor life . . . nor anything else in all
creation, will be able to separate us from the love of God in Christ
Jesus our Lord" (Rom. 8:38–39). The issue is God's faithfulness
to his own cause.

The conviction that God will never reject his people Israel is
therefore reinforced by the message of Easter; God did not abandon the crucified Jesus but raised him up on the third day to continue his service to the cause of God. Easter is a covenantal act
between God and the Church because it is first of all a covenantal
act between God and Jesus: "he will not let his holy one see corruption" (Acts 1:27, Ps. 16:10). And it is a covenantal act between

God and Jesus because, according to the witness of his disciples, Jesus served and revealed no other God than the God of the covenant between himself and his people Israel. If the Jews can be for the Church the enduring sign and witness to God, then the Church as the fruit of Easter could be for the Jews a support for their trust in God's faithfulness to his covenant with them. That could only be true, of course, of a Church that knew that it was no other than the Jew Jesus, crucified in solidarity with his people, whom God raised from the dead, and so a Church that knew itself grounded in that one covenant.

The apostolic witness to the risen Christ and its witness to the life and teaching of Jesus are therefore fully coherent when both are seen to be primarily witnesses to God, for what is maintained concerning the God of the Easter event is what is presented in the teaching and actions of Jesus. God will not let any "lost sheep" count as finally lost. In his persistence in reaching out to raise up those who seemed most removed (sinners, tax collectors, prostitutes), Jesus, as his disciples remembered him, was acting as he was remembered to have said God acted. His own behavior was itself a parable of the God of his parables, his own life an *imitatio Dei*. Just so, the God of Easter was preached as persisting in his faithfulness to the crucified one, in raising him for the further service of reaching out to those even further from God—Gentiles who were "alienated from the commonwealth of Israel, strangers to the covenants of promise, having no hope and without God in the world" (Eph. 3:12). The God of Easter, who is the God preached by Jesus, is the God of an eternal covenant with Israel, and this God is a persistent God

ii. God's victory?

Easter is evidence of God's persistence in his covenant purpose. Is it God's victory? Paul wrote once about a victory, but he put that in the future, "when the trumpet will sound, and the dead will be raise imperishable, and we shall be changed" (1 Cor. 15:52). "*Then*," he wrote, "shall come to pass the saying that is written, 'Death is swallowed up in victory' " (1 Cor. 15:54). Paul, no more than Isaiah (whom he quotes), did not presume to place the victory anywhere short of God's ultimate future. Easter anticipates that future, it invites hope in that future, but it is not itself the victory, the future for which Israel and the Church hope.

Easter invites us to trust that God is persistent, not that he is victorious, and this applies to Jesus as well. If Easter was and is a cause for joy as well as fear, then it invites us to consider what counts as a victory and what as a success, whether for God or for his servant Jesus. The apostolic witness claims that Jesus was vindicated by this event, reaffirmed by God and affirmed by the Church as God's faithful son, given God's name and authority as one fully authorized to represent God's cause. But he is so affirmed as the crucified one. His horrible death is not annulled. When he cried out from the cross, he was heard but he was not rescued. Roman might won the day, not Jesus, as it was to win again in crushing the Jewish rebellion some forty years later and again sixty-five years after that.

Moreover, the cause of God that Jesus served, to draw all Israel into a renewal before God, unfulfilled in Jesus' lifetime, was not realized on Easter. The risen one was not even returned to the land of the living to bring to fruition the work he had begun. Jesus' failure was not reversed by the event of Easter. Surely these things have to be said clearly if the Church's more positive assessment of Easter is not to ring hollow, in its own ears and not just in those of others. *"Christus Victor?"* The Feast of Christ the King? How can such titles not make for misunderstanding and worse, unless it be made clear that this "victor" was by any normal judgment a failure and that this "king" can only rule in humility as a crucified slave?

What may the Church say, then, of the cause of God that Jesus made his own? Is failure the last word? The event of Easter and its consequences call for a complex answer. The death of every Jew at Gentile hands must surely be seen as a setback for God's covenantal cause, be it the Jew from Nazareth or any and every Jew shot or gassed by Hitler's loyal subjects. But beginning on Easter and then from the witness of the apostles, possibly large numbers of

Israel began to respond to the cause of renewal that Jesus is presented as having preached. There was, we may say, a modest beginning of a success for God's cause. But then a new dimension began to materialize. What could at most have been an extended implication of the cause that Jesus had preached began to become the chief consequence of Easter. The covenantal cause of Israel's renewal, which had always had the wider world in view, now came to include the new birth of dead Gentiles through the preaching of Jesus' Jewish disciples. Thus was God's cause given a new, additional dimension.

With its eyes solely on this new dimension, the Church, looking only to itself, has spoken of victory, "this wonderful conversion of the world [i.e., all the world he knew of] to the Christian faith," in the words of Aquinas (*Gentiles,* I.6). The power and prestige of the Church were part of this victory, and these, being obligated to the powers and imperial interests that had brought Jesus to his death, seem hardly fit subjects for celebration. The Church has every reason to thank God for raising Jesus from the dead, but it has no grounds for viewing itself as triumphant—unless it forgets that the new dimension of God's cause that has given it life is intimately related to the continuing original dimensions of the cause that Jesus himself had served: God's covenantal concern for Israel. This calls for further reflection.

iii. God's cause

How the Church is to speak of Easter depends on how it understands the relationship between the new dimension of God's cause that followed upon Easter, and the original dimension of that cause that Jesus of Nazareth made his own. The issue is the continuity and discontinuity of Easter, whether and to what extent the risen one is the crucified one, and whether and to what extent the cause of the risen one remains the cause of the crucified one. For our answers to these questions, we are indebted to the apostolic witness through which we have our original access to both the crucified and the risen one.

The cause of the crucified one was the cause of the God of Israel: the renewal of the covenant and so of God's covenant partner Israel, for the sake of God's whole creation. The apostolic witness presents Jesus as one totally given over to this cause, even standing himself as its presence, in full immediacy: the kingdom, the full coherence of creation with its creator, was at hand: "if I by the finger of God cast out demons, then the kingdom of God is come upon you" (Luke 11:20). In this immediacy he sought out the lost sheep in the house of Israel, eating with sinners, calling them to repentance and restoration in his Father's house. Of course there were crumbs for the Gentiles, and many would come from east and west to feast of God's plenty, but unquestionably, renewal was to begin with Israel. For this renewal he lived and in his unswerving devotion to it, he ran afoul of the occupying power and died.

The cause of the risen one could be no other, if "Jesus Christ is the same yesterday and today," if the one proclaimed in the Easter Gospel is no other than Christ crucified. Luke's numbers in Acts may be somewhat exaggerated, but it seems that the cause of renewal, as it had during Jesus's ministry in Galilee, enjoyed some modest success in the period shortly after Easter. Yet that success was overshadowed and overtaken by the astounding harvest reaped in the mission among the Gentiles. It was as though the renewed disciples gathered by the Easter event had, for the purposes of the renewal of the world, taken up the role that Israel was to have played. These few Jews served as Israel's remnant, carrying through on behalf of all Israel the task assigned to Israel in God's covenantal purpose, and certainly Paul saw himself as part of just such a remnant (Rom. 11:1–5).

There was, however, a danger in this new development, the danger of misunderstanding Israel's remnant concept. Rather than seeing the remnant as the means whereby all Israel and God's whole purpose with Israel is carried forward, Israel's peculiar way of renewing itself "by subtraction," as Rosenzweig put it (*Star*, 404), one might come to see the remnant as the only part of Israel that matters, as a part that then displaces the whole. What happened in fact was even worse than this, for it was those made alive through the work of the remnant, which was only serving Israel's cause, who came to boast that they had replaced Israel, forgetting their dependence on the root that supported them (Rom. 11:18). In support of such boasting, it was fitting that an anti-Judaic Jesus be invented, and of course from that point on the increasingly anti-Judaic Church could play no further role in the central task of God's cause of the renewal of Israel. Instead, that was begun anew with remarkable success by the rabbis of Javneh. For the new development of God's cause among the Gentiles to be seen again in its relationship to God's cause with Israel— that is to say, for the witness to Christ risen to conform to the witness to him crucified, or in short, for the Church's faith in Jesus Christ today to become truly the same as its faith in him yesterday–the Church would have to rediscover its dependent relationship to the Jewish people, those to whom Jesus became a servant "in order to confirm the promises given to the patriarchs, and in order that the Gentiles might glorify God for his mercy" (Rom. 15:8,9).

iv. The course of the covenant

To speak of the success of God's cause then assumes that we are in a position to make a summary judgment on God's way with his creation, which we clearly are not. The reason is simply that the course of the covenant is not finished; the story is still going on and we do not know its outcome. Certainly there have been wonderful results along the way. One could mention only the renewal of the Jewish people under the Tannaitic and Amoraic rabbis, and the centuries of continued study of Torah and lives given to faithful service to God and his commandments. Every Sabbath greeted and observed bears witness to positive movement in the course of God's cause. Or one could think of so many pagan lives turned around and given to the service of God and the neighbor, the forgiveness practiced, the love shown, the mercy exercised, all in the name of him who has made God and God's cause a present reality for them. Certainly there have been many important positive steps along the way of God's covenant.

Unhappily, there have also been so many false and backward steps. The Church should leave to Jews the counting of theirs, but the Church should surely recognize at least some of its own errors: its hostility to God's Israel would be one, of which the evil consequences have been myriad. The list is too long to recite, but the sum of it hardly permits a judgment of success about God's will being done on earth.

The course of the covenant is not only a mixed one; it stands today in great uncertainty. Can anyone say with assurance that the recent experiment of an increased Jewish responsibility in the covenant, which is one of the things that the State of Israel represents, is going to be a successful step ahead in the course of God's ways with his creation? The toll of continuous hostile relations with its neighbors is rising and the cost in increasing nationalistic chauvinism is all too evident. As for the Church as it gropes for a footing amid the increasing secularism of the West and the newly acquired self-confidence of the nations of Africa and Asia, can anyone say for sure that it will count more for God's cause than against it in the future? The history of God's cause is not over, so judgments of success—and also of failure—had best be avoided.

In speaking of Easter then, the Church has insufficient grounds for talk of victory, triumph, or success. It has every ground, however, to rejoice that the God of Israel, Sinai, and Easter is a persistent God who does not give up on his cause and does not ultimately abandon those to whom he entrusts that cause. This is the God whom Jesus called Father, and this is the God that raised the crucified one. This is the God who, in spite of all the tensions of his conflict with them, sustains Israel, the Church, and the whole creation.

4. GOD'S CONFLICT

i. *The revelation of conflict*

In every presentation of a situation in which there is a conflict between God and this world or any part of it (themselves included), the witnesses to Jesus present him as standing on the side of God. There are sides because there is a conflict. Israel's story of creation in Genesis 1–11, as we have seen (van Buren, *People Isra-el*, 86–152), reflects its Exodus/Sinai conviction that the way of the world is not God's way, and that to be called into God's way is to be called into his conflict with the world. The witness to Jesus is to one who so unswervingly followed the way of God that he end-ed on the cross, a victim of the conflict between the world and God's cause.

Israel's Scriptures bear witness to the conflict between God and his creation primarily through the story of God's conflict with Is-rael itself. This is because Israel has been called by God to his side in the larger conflict. Israel's election to be God's witness in his conflict with the world sets Israel in a tension both with God and the world. The more it accepts its calling to God's side, the great-er its tensions with the world; the more it resists that calling, the greater its tensions with God. This is the result of being a part of the world which is in conflict with God, but also being called to the side of God in God's longing for the world's reconciliation with himself.

This double tension is revealed to the Gentile Church in the story concerning Jesus of Nazareth. That story was told in the conviction that Jesus had so faithfully accepted his Israelite call-ing to the side of God that there was no conflict between him and God. The story certainly tells of a tension: the temptation stories, the story of Jesus in the Garden of Gethsemane, and above all the witness of the Epistle to the Hebrews make clear the element of struggle. The tension, however, is surmounted so that conflict does not arise. The other dimension of conflict, however, be-comes all the stronger, and the story of Jesus comes to a climax in his challenge of the authorities that leads almost immediately to his arrest, conviction, and execution as an enemy of the Roman empire. Presented as being totally on the side of God, Jesus dies in total conflict with the world.

ii. The political character of God's conflict

The conflict with the world into which Israel and its son Jesus were called is basically political in character because the issue con-cerns power, and power in the world is political. Israel's conflict was with the political powers surrounding it, be they Pharaoh, the king of Egypt, or the rulers of Assyria and Babylonia. When the conflict became internal, Israel's prophets stood on God's side against Israel's kings and ruling class. As we shall argue in chapter 7, no demonstration could have been more political than that of Jesus in the Temple area at the time of the annual tax returns, which led to his execution as a rebel against the authority of the Roman empire.

If the event of Easter was the God of Israel's reaffirmation of Jesus the crucified one, then the implication is that God has not given up in his conflict with the political powers of the world. However, this must not be misunderstood. Never do we hear in Israel's story or in that concerning Jesus that political power is inherently evil. Nowhere are we told that there should not be kings or the officers and soldiers employed by kings to carry out policy. Caesar has his place and his rights, we are told, and even that Caesar and every other ruler exercise power by God's design. God's conflict with the rulers of this world is not because they are rulers, but because they rule unjustly. It is the misuse of human power that gives rise to conflict with God. "The governing authorities . . . that exist are instituted by God," Paul could say (Rom. 13:1), and the Johannine community could say that it was "from above" that Pilate had power to decide the case of Jesus (John 19:11). But when the governing authority becomes the beast, the whore of Babylon, no longer serving justly (cf. Revelation 13–18 and Karl Barth's provocative interpretation of Romans 13 and Revelation 13 in *Rechtfertigung*), then it stands in radical conflict with the God who instituted it. Easter affirms the reality of that conflict.

It is clear from the witness to the event of Easter that God's power, although in conflict with the misuse of human power, is of a different order. It is certainly power. Israel's witness to God and that of the Apostolic Writings agree in ascribing power to God, power that concerns how things are managed in this world. That is why there can be genuine conflict with human political power when it is unjust. But God's power does not meet political power on its own terms. God's power will always seem to be weakness when measured on the scale of misused human power. It works through suffering and love and forgiveness, avoiding the sword whenever possible. Yet it is power that is at stake, how it is to be defined and used. Power in the service of the poor and the weak and in the cause of justice is the power of God that makes for human justice and reconciliation. In this specific sense, God's power is according to the Spirit, and Jesus was designated Son of God in power by the Spirit of holiness (Rom. 1:3). It would therefore seem more faithful to the biblical story if we were to say that God's power is worldly power according to the Spirit, than to call it something so potentially misleading as "spiritual power."

iii. Easter and politics

The apostolic witness to Easter is insistent that the risen one is no other than the crucified one. But crucifixion was unquestionably the official form of public execution for political crimes, primarily for rebellion against the political power of the Roman empire. To proclaim Jesus alive, therefore, was a profoundly political act. It was to affirm God's reaffirmation of one who died in conflict with the misuse of political power and so to affirm God's cause in the just use of human power. That was the "spiritual" import of Easter faith.

Easter, then, was "spiritual" in the precise sense of being an event of God's persistence in directing and enticing his creation towards his own purposes for its own good. It was spiritual in the precise sense of being part of God's worldly concern for this world. It was spiritual in being a piece of this world directed in the service of God's spirit. To call it spiritual in some other sense— perhaps in the sense of being immaterial, unworldly, not a part of the history in which this world has to do with God—would be to see it quite otherwise.

Yet just this has happened in the history of the Church, with the result that it is common for Christians today to think of "religion" and "politics" as antithetical terms, areas of existence and points of reference that can have nothing to do with each other. So Easter and the cross itself are extracted from the political world in which they happened, and the seriousness of God's conflict with this world and the misuse of human power is diminished. With that conflict no longer centered in the heart of human activity—the exercise of power and the workings of the political ordering of human affairs—its focus was reduced to that of human sin conceived of primarily as individual failures on the personal level. So conceived, Jesus is seen to have died only for the personal sins of the individual. He is no longer a victim of God's conflict with the injustices of the Roman Empire, and he is risen only into the personal faith of the individual believer in his or her personal salvation, no longer the living evidence of God's persistence in pushing his cause for the sake of a better ordering, and therefore unavoidably a better political ordering, of his creation. A Church so oriented will of course take personal sins seriously, but it will be all too free to do so in blindness to the massive sin of the misuse of human power which manifests itself primarily in the social, political, and economic order (and here we give credit to the Liberation theologians for seeing this so clearly). One may say, then, that the blindness of the Church generally to the evil of Hitler and his Nazi movement was the direct consequence of its misunderstanding of the apostolic witness to the event of Easter. If Easter was not a worldly victory, as it clearly was not, then let it become a spiritual victory. The world can go its own way. Thus is God's conflict with this world restricted to the private and the power of God for making this world right reduced to the realm of personal development and fulfillment. This new "privatized gospel" may serve the cause of a Church wishing to gain a hearing in a bourgeois culture. It can hardly serve the cause of God in the service of which Jesus was crucified and in confirmation of which he was raised.

CHAPTER SIX

Jesus of Nazareth: The Presence of God

According to the apostolic witness, Jesus appeared as the representative of God's future already present with his people. The witness to him is therefore a testimony to God's loving involvement first with Israel and then with the Gentiles, a covenantal presence manifested in Jesus' fidelity to the commandments and his call to follow him in a creative, covenantal response to the immediacy of God by recognizing and responding to the proximity of the neighbor.

1. JESUS AND GOD'S FUTURE

i. Early Christian eschatology as problem and possibility

According to the apostolic witness as we hear it in the synoptic Gospels, Jesus appeared in Galilee as the herald of the immediacy of God's reign on earth. "The time is fulfilled, and the reign of God is at hand! Turn back [to God] and believe the good news" (Mark 1:15). This "good news" has a context in which alone it makes sense, and that context is the Jewish eschatological hope of the first century. It was the hope that God would come to the rescue of occupied Israel, restoring Jewish sovereignty and, in its more extended form, at the same time bring to an end the reign of disease and death over this world. It was a hope that the old— and still present!—era would come to an end and a new era of world history would be inaugurated. The "good news" was that this transformation was about to take place. The early witness to Jesus was to one who not only announced this event but also manifested the first signs of its impending arrival: "If I by the finger of God cast out devils, then the reign of God has come upon you" (Luke 11:20).

This hope, the essential context of the message and work of Jesus as the Gospels present them, poses enormous problems that should be faced. In the first place, no such transformation of the world has taken place. The Roman occupation continued. Disease and death are as much with us as they have ever been. Further, it is a view of reality and of the movement of history that is difficult for people influenced by the Enlightenment to accept. In earlier times such a view may have been more possible, as so relatively recent a theologian as Luther illustrates, yet from an early period in the history of the Church, one can see evidence that the eschatology of the early Christians has seemed to need interpretation. Catastrophic change is of course a possibility we can entertain. The threat of nuclear or less dramatic disaster is real. Such catastrophies, however, are far removed from the arrival of the reign of God hoped for by the witnesses to Jesus. That hope is unavoidably central to the message of Jesus which they presented, but it is also quite unworkable for most of the Church today.

Throughout its history the Church has tried in various ways to adapt the gospel witness to Jesus to the conception of history that each age has been able to entertain. It has stressed that Jesus gave no timetable for the coming of God's reign and has thus been able to say that it is still coming, a strategy that rather blunts the message. It has redefined the reign of God as a spiritual and interior matter (ignoring the clearly external and political dimensions so evident in the Gospels), thereby making it possible to think that God's reign has already begun. By an opposite move, the reign or "kingdom" of God has been removed to an "other world," "heaven." Some have even tried to think of the Church as the "kingdom," spreading through the world by the preaching of the gospel. Whatever else may be said of these moves, none of them can be said to be consistent with the early Christian eschatology in which the witness to Jesus is presented. They are evidence for the unworkability of that perspective, and not just for post-Enlightenment minds.

On the other hand, that perspective is not without its possibilities. The apostolic witness to Jesus presents him not only as the representative of God's future, but as one who claims that that future is *now.* So near is the reign of God, so near is God, that the only wise or even prudent course is to start from this moment to live in God's immediate presence. Jesus and his message stand so thoroughly within the perspective of early Jewish eschatology that they may be said to be beyond it. Precisely because the witness to him presents him as the herald of God's immediacy, the mechanics and timetable of God's reign need matter no more to the Church than they did to him. In the sense in which Jesus is presented as teaching it, the reign of God did not come and so was not "at hand." Nevertheless, the issue which he posed as herald of God's reign remains: who are we right now before God, and what shall we do right now before God? That "right now before God" was the issue then, and it remains so now.

An honest response to the gap between the eschatology of the witness to Jesus (and presumably of Jesus himself) and the continuing history of the "old" era to this day is to admit that, in so far as this witness presented Jesus as a herald of God's future as *future,* it made the mistake of many of that time and culture, against which Jesus is presented also as having warned: trying to discern a divine timetable. But as a herald of that future as God's *present,* Jesus poses today just the issue that he posed then in proclaiming God's reign at hand. The language of the future is ineradicably a part of that proclamation and so we shall continue to use it, but its use, its function, was to focus on the present. The moral, social, political, and personal immediacy of God was and remains the matter at stake in the apostolic witness to the preaching of the coming reign of God.

ii. The presence of God's future with Israel

The issue of God's future as God's presence was posed by Jesus not only in his words but in all he did, according to the apostolic witness. "He went about doing good and healing all that were oppressed by the devil, for God was with him" (Acts 10:38). As the herald of God's presence, he acted in God's cause and therefore in the service of Israel (Rom. 15:8). His food was to do the will of God (John 4:34), and that will was for the good of suffering men, women, and children, beginning first of all with Israel. His disciples therefore bore witness to him as bringing God's wholeness, health, and forgiveness in both word and deed, beginning first of all with his people Israel.

The witness to Jesus makes clear that he was the herald of God's future become present to *all* Israel. It was a marked feature of that witness that he sought out especially those on the fringes of his people—the sinners, the "lost sheep," those most in need of restoration. He came in God's name to do God's business of making his people whole. That included making the sick and dying well and alive, the halt and the lame to walk, the lepers clean, the outsiders (tax collectors, prostitutes), insiders, sinners forgiven. But he was also in the synagogues and was said to have been on good terms with some of the Pharisees. All Israel was his concern and the God whose future became present in words of forgiveness and acts of healing was present to his whole people.

God was present to his whole people in Jesus' words of forgiveness and reconciliation. That presence was covenantal, and so what Jesus is presented as speaking to Israel is covenantal: God does not simply forgive his people, nor does he establish reconciliation simply from his side—forgiveness and reconciliation are two-sided matters. God forgives, but then he expects Israelites to forgive each other: "Forgive us our sins as we forgive those who sin against us" (Matt. 6:12–15).

If we read "son of man" as a translation of a Hebrew or Aramaic original *"ben adam,"* meaning any human being, then we are told that it is a misunderstanding of the covenant to think that only God can forgive sins (Mark 2:5–12). God expects his covenant partners to share with him in forgiving. Indeed, if Israel initiates forgiveness, God lets that decision stand; it is valid also for God (Matt. 16:19, 18:18). Therefore Jesus is presented as calling his disciples to do exactly what he had done: to forgive everyone for their offenses.

God's covenantal presence with his people is also presented in the witness to Jesus' acts of compassionate healing. Where he found Israel suffering, he moved to relieve the distress. "He went about doing good and healing . . . for God was with him." When God is present with his people, good happens and healing takes place. So, as the apostolic witness tells his story, God's herald simply acted as one totally given over to the service of God and fully enabled to share God's healing presence with his people. Indeed, not just with his people but then also with those few Gentiles who are reported to have turned to this one Jew in the hope and trust that here, at any rate, the love of the God who had covenanted himself to Israel could also reach them. Or to put it another way, when Gentiles drew near to this one Jew (and so near to Israel) trusting in God's covenantal fidelity to them, they too found themselves touched by the healing power of God. This too is part of the apostolic witness to the present power of God's future with his people that had confronted them in Jesus of Nazareth.

iii. God's claim on Israel and the Church

The future of God that Jesus announced as present, since it was the presence of God, entailed judgment. To judge in Israel's tradition is to put things right. The book of Judges is a series of stories of men and women raised up by God to put things right in Israel. God himself as the supreme judge was to come to put things right in Israel, between Israel and the world, and in the world itself. But that implies that things are not right: not right within Israel, not right between Israel and the world, and not right with the world. Confronted with the Righteous One, the world's unrighteousness stands out. The apostolic witness makes this clear in the reaction to Jesus not only of the demons, but also of Peter: "Depart from me, for I am a sinful man" (Luke 5:8). As Israel's prophets had depicted the Day of the LORD, the time of God's putting things right, as a day of judgment, so the witness to Jesus presents him as the presence of God's judgment. Before him, men and women discovered themselves in dire need of being made right.

This discovery of the need to be made right, according to the witnesses, happened first of all and primarily in Israel. It was a Jewish discovery, as its very vocabulary reveals. It was a matter of sinners standing before God, or sinners in need of forgiveness, of sinners having to turn back ("repent") to God. Those are terms in Israel's vocabulary, the fruit of its covenantal life, and no Gentile would have understood them without first learning from Israel how to use them. So Israel, or rather some of Israel, discovered in Jesus' presence its need to become the Israel that God wanted.

God's judgment, his putting things right with Israel, implies God's claim upon his people. He has called them to holiness, to a quite special existence in his covenant with them and their covenant with him. The witness to Jesus sets him before us as the one through whom God laid his claim on his people anew or with renewed force, calling them to be his people alone and to love him as their only God. If Israel would be Israel, then, the witness claims, it would take sides with Jesus, since Jesus is on the side of God.

This claim was laid upon all Israel, but it fell especially on unrighteous Israel. There was of course also a righteous Israel, as the witness makes clear, the ones to whom Jesus apparently felt no need to go. The ones to whom he is said to have been committed were the ones whose company he sought, the unrighteous, those farthest from the covenant. They were the ones who needed a physician.

God's claim, however, touches all of Israel, and if there be any who do not acknowledge it, who think they are already in the right, then they too need to be reminded of Israel's prophetic understanding that no creature can abide the day of his coming (Mal. 3:2). Self-satisfaction, where it is found, is only a sign of another piece of Israel that needs to be put right. All Israel is included in its covenant with God, and so all Israel needs continually to turn back to God.

It came to pass that not many in Israel ever heard the message of Jesus or were confronted in him with the presence of God's immediacy. By the time that most of them would have even heard of

Jesus, they would have heard of him in the words of Gentiles. The message of *re*newal which some in Israel heard became increasingly a message heard by Gentiles of a gift of a whole *new* life for them. That life would have had to be new for them, for it came as a word of judgment, of God's having put them right.

God's claim upon the Gentiles, however, was and would have to have been a judgment not only upon them as a world that knew not God, but also as nations that conspire together against the LORD and his anointed (Ps. 2:1-2). The Gentiles needed to be put right not only with respect to the God of Israel but also with respect to the Israel of God. If Jesus was to be God's herald of his present future, then by drawing near to Jesus the Gentiles would of necessity be drawn near to him in the company he keeps. As God's anointed, then, Jesus binds the nations of the world to the nation of Jesus—the nation of the covenant, the Jewish people.

In this last sentence, I have followed the language of the confessional declaration of the Rhineland Synod of the German Evangelical Church of 10 January 1980, with one change. I have said, "as God's anointed," in place of the Synod's "as the Messiah of Israel." I make this change in order to avoid the implication that Jesus fulfilled what the Jewish people have taken to be an essential expectation of their Messiah: the rescue of the Jewish people from oppression by Gentiles. The Church has surely proved over the centuries that it has the least right of any institution to dare to make such a claim. What it may and must say, however, is that Jesus in his Jewish solidarity with his people can draw the Gentile Church to himself only in that solidarity of his and therefore always also to his people. "His people," of course, would have to mean all Jews without distinction, not just "religious Jews," since it would have to include the company he kept. He confronts the Church with God's judgment by putting it right with the Jewish people as it actually is, or he proves to be a failure as the herald of the presence of God's future.

It is a matter of historical record that, after a modest start in the second third of the first century, this binding of the nations of the world to the people of the covenant (a function essential to the role of an authentic herald of God's future become present) did not in fact happen. When we add to this the further historical fact that this binding is only beginning to happen (also on a modest scale) in the last third of the twentieth century, the Church would do well to exercise caution in speaking of the presence of God's future or of Jesus as the authentic herald of its presence. The Church may and should hope and pray—and above all *work*—that this will turn out to be true. If it does become true, then and not until then will come to pass the comment which the Gospel of Luke (4:18–21) ascribes to Jesus upon having read a passage from Isaiah 61:1–2:

"The Spirit of the LORD is upon me, because he has anointed me to preach good news to the poor. He has sent me to proclaim release to the captives and recovering of sight to the blind, to set at liberty those who are oppressed, to proclaim the acceptable year of the LORD."
    And he [Jesus] closed the book. . . .And he began to say to them, "Today this scripture is fulfilled in your hearing."

iv. Israel, the Church, and God's future

The most serious problem that early Christian eschatology has posed for the Church is not its incompatibility with its own experience of historical continuity, but that it has helped the Church to ignore Israel's historical continuity. Had the coming of Jesus marked the transformation from an old to a new era or marked the beginning of the end of history, there would be little reason to take succeeding history seriously. Everything would have already been brought to its consummation, so what happened thereafter could only be the unfolding of what was settled then and there. That Israel should endure, that the covenant between God and Israel should develop, that God's history should continue to include Israel and now also contain the Church, was ignored. The price has been the Church's anti-Judaism and incalculable suffering of Jews at the hands of Christians and, more recently, of pagans deeply influenced by and able to feed on the Church's long tradition of anti-Judaism. That the name of Jesus should have become a bone of contention between his people and those who claimed to be his disciples is the ultimate irony and the soundest possible argument for the utter failure of his mission. The fruit from this tree has been far from satisfactory. The Church needs to rethink what it is to do about the eschatology of early Christianity and presumably of Jesus himself.

In beginning this rethinking, two leads may be helpful. The first lies in that note of the early witness itself that warns us against making historical timetables of God's concern for his creation. The usual interpretation of this warning, however—that we are not capable of thinking God's thoughts—is not enough. It may be that God has no timetable at all, that God meant what is clearly implied in the covenant with Israel: the future is not simply in God's hands. It is also in the hands of Israel, and of the Church so long as it stands alongside Israel. It is not just that we do not know the schedule of God's future. It may be that God's future can consist of nothing other than the series of presents which we add on to the past. If God is indeed a living God, then it may be well to conclude that we should stop talking of God's future altogether and speak only of his present. What are we to do now? That was the question put to John the Baptist and then to Jesus, and the witness to him may be advising us that that is the only proper question for us. Certainly Israel's rabbis seem to have come to something like this conclusion in developing the halakhic tradition. The Church needs to meditate seriously on the structure and character of the Talmud.

The second lead is also present in the apostolic tradition. It is found in Paul's last comment about "the end" in 1 Corinthians 15:28, that Christ will also be subject to God, "that God may be everything to everyone," a thought that may lie behind the total absence of any christological reference in the great eschatological summary in Romans 11:25–36. The Church's Christology, like that of the Apostle to the Gentiles (see Romans 11:36), should be in every way to the glory of God alone. Every attempt to divide the honors between God and Jesus tempts the Church to give more honor to the Church than to Israel. Better that the Church not thus depart from the mind of Jesus as his witnesses present it:

"Why do you call me good? There is none good but God" (Mark 10:18).

Following these two leads, the course for the Church's Christology lies in attending less to early Christian eschatology and taking with utmost seriousness the present that we have. This seems to be not far from what the early witness presents Jesus as doing, and it then means that all of history should be taken seriously. It would also free the Church to take with greater seriousness the attention that Jesus as a faithful Jew gave to the commandments of the Torah that define the covenant between God and Israel.

2. JESUS AND TORAH: GOD'S COMMITMENT TO ISRAEL AND CREATION

i. *Jesus and the commandments*

The faithfulness of Jesus to God's commandments, his obedience to Torah as the inevitable form of obedience to God, is manifest in the witness to him. I shall not repeat what I developed at length in *People Israel* (230–39) but only rehearse the conclusions here: (1) The evidence from the Gospels is what one would expect: Jesus is never once depicted as breaking any commandment. On the contrary, he was himself, and called all who would listen to him to be, obedient from the heart to Torah as the express will of God. (2) According to Paul's witness, God had made Jesus to be the completion of the whole Torah by bringing also the Gentiles into the obedience of faithfulness, thus both confirming and initiating God's covenantal intent, promised to Abraham, of bringing the nations into his service. (3) As a result, the Gentiles are now released from the servitude that the eternal Torah exerts over a recalcitrant world not yet graced with God's covenant, and are invited to follow Jesus in his obedience to God. What needs to be further developed here, however, is that the apostolic witness sets Jesus before the Church as the living evidence that God's commitment to his whole creation is covenantal.

The Church has traditionally seen the commandments, and Torah generally, as a demand, a burden. This is especially true of those parts of the Church under the influence of Augustine and then Luther. What this view fails to account for is the saying in Matthew, "Take my yoke upon you and learn from me, for my yoke is easy and my burden is light" (Matt. 11:29–30). "His yoke" would refer to the Torah, of course as he interpreted it, for the Torah was the yoke that God had given to Israel. A yoke, people of an urban industrial culture need to be told, is a means of making it more comfortable and therefore efficient to pull a load. So Jesus, along with Israel, saw the commandments as God's gift of a guide for living that is easy and effective, as compared to having to try to figure out everything for oneself. God's Torah was his gift to Israel, and Jesus, fully obedient to Torah, saw it as a gift, a help, an easing yoke, making the so-called burden of the commandments light, and so a joy to carry.

God's commandments, however, are more than a way for human beings to walk. They are the evidence of God's commitment to those to whom they are given, signs that God cares about how his creatures walk. Moreover, God's commitment is not just to the fact of our walking; it reaches to the details of human life: eating and drinking, the handling of money, treatment of others, even to the numbering of every hair of the head. The covenant and its commandments show not just that God is committed to how Israel lives its life; they show the detailed nature of that commitment. Jesus, by living, teaching, and acting as a loyal son of the covenant, revealed to his disciples the immediacy, the extent, and the reality of God's involvement in creaturely affairs.

ii. The will of God

An important theme in the apostolic witness to Jesus is his unswerving obedience to the will of God. His will was to do the will of his Father: "Not my will but yours be done" (Luke 22:42). Indeed, he is presented as knowing God's will, both as an interpreter of Torah and also as one in intimate contact with God in prayer. So he is said to have taught with authority, not having to "check his sources," as we might say. Jesus is presented as living in a dual relationship to God's will. He both obeys it and stands for it.

Jesus is presented as so thoroughly and consistently obedient to God that it seemed to some later commentators that they shared a single will, as though Jesus of Nazareth had no will of his own. This idea was rejected by "orthodox" thinkers because it made him less than a complete human being. More seriously, such a theory undercuts its own starting point in the apostolic witness: the testimony to his obedience would make no sense if we could not also say that he *willed* to obey God's will. Unity, as contrasted with oneness of will, presupposes two wills that might not have been as one. The idea of only a single divine will at work departs completely from the covenantal context in which alone Jesus may be understood. As the obedient son of his Father, Jesus lived as and with Israel, and so covenantly faithful to, and thus able to stand for, God.

There is no need, and indeed no way, to show that Jesus was in point of historical fact the only Jew to have lived in perfect obedience to God. I see no reason to change what I wrote on this matter some years ago: "The apostolic witnesses made no attempt to account for Jesus' obedience. Rather, they stood in awe before this obedience, which was authenticated for them by the Easter event. There is no external criterion by which we might see whether Jesus was in fact obedient. Easter was taken to be [God's] proclamation of this obedience (Rom. 1:4), and the Easter gospel of the disciples was the expression of their conviction that Jesus of Nazareth was God's Israel by calling and by his faithful obedience" (van Buren, *Secular*, 53). It is not that the disciples already knew what a perfectly obedient life looked like and found that Jesus fitted that picture. On the contrary, Easter faith was and is the conviction that the life Jesus lived is the definition of perfect obedience to the God of Israel.

But Jesus is also presented as knowing fully God's will. When he commanded, it was God's command. When he forgave, God forgave. When he touched to heal, God reached out to heal. His words were the Word of God. So in him the full duality and mutuality of the covenant were proclaimed to have been present. In his presence, both the Israel of God and also the God of Israel were on the scene. Thus his concern for and involvement in the lives of those he is presented as having touched were felt to be the concern and involvement of God in the affairs of men and women. Those touched by him discovered that in the actual life of this Jew, Jesus of Nazareth, they were touched by God's Word (to use the term of the Johannine community), by God's own active self in God's concern for the totality of their lives.

iii. The commandments

The covenant, which was the context of the life, teaching, and actions of Jesus, has content: Torah, the *mitzvot* (commandments). This specificity of God's involvement with Israel for the sake of all creation was certainly not neglected by Jesus according to his witnesses. It is true that he, like other teachers of Israel, gave special weight to the fundamentals of the love of God without reserve and love for the neighbor as if the neighbor were oneself. It is also true, however, that he could pass over the fundamentals and focus on more specific commandments: "Do not kill" (or even let anger arise, Matt. 5:22ff); "do not commit adultery" (or even let the eye wander in a way that might lead to this result, Matt. 5:28ff); "do not steal; do not bear false witness; do not defraud; honor your father and mother" (Mark 10:19). As Israel's rabbis also taught, "The Sabbath was made for man," but it really was made and was really to be observed.

For the history of the Church's substitution of the first for the seventh as the day on which to abstain from work and recall that God, not we, is the creator, as well as a treatment of the question whether the Church did well in making this change, see Bacchiocchi, *Sabbath.*

The matter may be summed up in the witness of Matthew where Jesus is presented as saying, "Do not think that I am come to abolish the Torah and the Prophets; I have come not to abolish them but to fulfill them. . . .Whoever then relaxes one of the least of these commandments and teaches men so, shall be called least in the kingdom of heaven" (Matt. 5:17, 19). Only a Gentile

Church that had never appreciated Israel's testimony to God's commandments could read these words as placing an intolerable burden on Jesus' disciples. On the contrary, this burden is light because it is drawn by God's yoke—the covenant. What we are told in these words is that God has really committed himself to Israel down to the details of its daily life, and Jesus refused to present God's commitment and involvement as anything less. The commandments are there because they can be fulfilled, they can be done, so the witness to Jesus' teaching makes clear. "With God all things are possible" (Mark 10:27)—all things because God is concerned with all things; possible because God has commanded and so stands with Israel in all of them; possible, not necessary, because God has chosen to give Israel space in which to live with him; and with God, because Israel lives within the fold of God's covenant of grace. Jesus understood and bore witness to the gospel of God's freely given commandments, the path on which Israel is to walk with God.

iv. God's will for the Gentile Church

Jesus the Jew from Nazareth, according to his witnesses, lived in full faithfulness to the Torah of God's covenant and total loyalty to his people Israel. He called all who would be his disciples to follow him in the life that he led. Why, then, should there be a *Gentile* Church? Why should not all Jesus' later disciples follow him as did his first disciples, as members of Israel? Why should not every "Christian" become a Jew? This would seem to be the unavoidably primary and fundamental question posed by the apostolic witness to Jesus.

The most responsible answer to this question that I can discover is that implied by the whole thrust of Paul's calling and work: God has called us to follow Jesus the Jew, but that calling has come to us by way of the further calling of Paul (and his fellow workers) to be the Apostle to the Gentiles. The calling comes, then, specifically as a call *to* Gentiles to come follow Jesus *as* Gentiles. We are called to be the Church, not Israel. Israel and the

Church are together peoples of the God of Israel, but Israel is called to this task as a people, the Church is called to it as a community of persons called out of many peoples.

The Church is therefore in as intimate a relationship with God as Israel. It is consequently called to be Israel's co-worker in the cause of God, in its own way. Israel is to follow Torah; the Church is to follow Jesus Christ in the way in which it has been given Gentiles to follow him. That way is apart from circumcision and the *mitzvot*, and so, strictly speaking, not within the framework of the covenant of Sinai. That covenant is for Israel alone. God's purpose and love, however, are not exhausted by the covenant.

Should we say, then, that the Church has its own covenant with God, a new covenant, perhaps a second covenant? There are some notes in the Apostolic Writings in support of such language, but not enough, in my judgment, to warrant such a way of speaking without the most careful reservations.

Apart from the use of the term to refer to God's covenant or covenants with Israel, the Greek word for covenant is not widely used in the Apostolic Writings. It occurs primarily in the so-called Epistle to the Hebrews, a singular document in many ways. Outside of Hebrews, it occurs nowhere in any of the Gospels except in the word over the cup in the Last Supper scene (and so also in 1 Corinthians 11:25, in the same context). It occurs also in Galatians 4:24 and in 2 Corinthians 3:6, 14.

The author of the Epistle to the Hebrews certainly contrasts negatively the old with the new covenant, as part and parcel of his displacement theology. Since that theology, or that aspect of it, is an interpretation of Jesus that sets him in opposition not only to his own people but also to God's continuing covenant with Israel, I am unable to accept its witness on this point as overriding the contrary witness of the Gospels and Paul. I cannot do anything with that theology and its contrast of old and new covenants except to set it aside. God forbid that the Son should bring to naught the things of the Father!

The Evangelists make their various witnesses to Jesus without use of the term "covenant." They do preserve, however, as does Paul, a tradition of Jesus' use of it at his last meal with his disciples. There we find varying wordings which may depend on the scriptural expression, "the blood of the covenant." In its scriptural use, this refers to the ritual use of blood as a seal on the mutual commitment between God and Israel. The advantage of such a paraphrase is that it frees us from reading back into the first century the far more developed conceptions of the covenant that were to mark later thought, both Jewish and Christian. At the Last Supper, then, Jesus may have spoken of "*my* 'blood-of-the-covenant.' " If so, I would take this to have meant, "my seal of the mutual commitment between us." This places great weight on that seal because the mutual commitment is central in the witness to Jesus' table fellowship with his disciples. It is doubtful grounds for speaking of a second covenant. The early witness to which we owe this tradition knows no such language.

Paul speaks explicitly of "two covenants" in his complicated Sarah-Hagar "allegory" in Galatians 4, but following L. Gaston's use of H. D. Betz's recommendation, I take it that what Paul is saying is that Sarah and Hagar stand for "two world orders decreed by divine institution." One is an order of servitude, to be contrasted with the present Jerusalem which is "above" and in the order of freedom, as Isaiah had proclaimed. (On this see Gaston, "Israel's Enemies," 402–23, especially 408–11.) Gaston's interpretation casts serious doubts on the use of this text to support any idea of a second covenant.

Finally, we come to Paul's contrasting of an "old covenant" and a "new covenant" in 2 Corinthians 3:6–18, the former being written on stone, the latter on human hearts in the Spirit. Read with the traditional anti-Judaic blinders, this will support everything that Hebrews has to say on behalf of a theology of displacement. If, however, we follow the rules of interpretation that Gaston has developed, reading Paul according to his own self-designation and so within his Jewish tradition, and taking him at his word that he would address his words and work primarily to the Gentiles, the results are quite different. We may then recognize in "the dispensation of death carved in letters of stone" the same ruthless rule of Torah over the Gentile world that Paul would have known from the midrashic tradition (see Gaston, "Israel's Enemies," 405–06). Note that for Israel this same Torah came with great splendor, although something better was coming. For the Torah of the covenant between God and Israel contained a promise that had yet to be confirmed: the Gentiles too were to come to the knowledge and service of God! Paul's real complaint against his fellow Jews, then, is that they fail both to see that promise in the Torah of Moses and to acknowledge its confirmation in the Gentile mission in which Paul was engaged. A veil seemed to lie over their minds which, Paul learned from his own case, was at once removed when one saw that in Christ God has indeed confirmed his Torah-promise.

This reading of 2 Corinthians 3 is of course not traditional, but neither is any other that departs from the line running from Augustine and Luther up to Käsemann that turns Paul into a Gentile. (For another nontraditional reading, see the Bible study prepared for the Rhineland Synod of 1980 by E. Bethge, *"Erneuerung,"* 56–71.) My proposed reading is consistent with what Paul wrote in Romans 9–11, if Paul is seen (as in van Buren, *People Israel*, 146–48) as a self-consistent Pharisee called to preach the good news of God's acceptance of the Gentiles through the faithfulness of Christ. It follows that this passage does indeed lead us to say that God has done a new and wonderful thing in Christ. It gives no support for speaking of a second covenant alongside of the first; rather, it is concerned entirely with the wholly new situation for Gentiles: they have been offered in Christ the way from death to life. Now they, alongside Israel, are invited to choose life (cf. Deut. 30:19).

With so little apostolic license for talk of two covenants, it is understandable that people must turn elsewhere for support for such an idea, and so there have occurred rather frequent references to "Rosenzweig's two-covenant theory." In point of fact, however, there is no such theory in any of Rosenzweig's writings. Indeed, he has no theory about any covenant, it not being a term or category that he used in thinking through the relationship between God and the Jewish people. The German *Bund* (which can also mean covenant) occurs only five times in *The Star of Redemption,* but never in the sense of earlier Protestant covenant theologians, such as Coccejus and his many followers, or in that of more recent biblical theologians such as W. Eichrodt. Rosenzweig worked out the relationship between the Church and the Jewish people in the quite different terms of a star with its fiery core and its rays.

It seems best to say that there is the one eternal covenant between God and the Jewish people, that Jesus is portrayed by the Apostolic Writings as standing within that covenant, and that his Church is invited to hold onto him as its way into discovering the gift of the love of God and the claim upon them to love all whom God loves—a gift and claim that are certainly expressed for Israel in the covenant but which for the Church find its formulation in Jesus' summary of (itself a quotation from) the Torah.

3. THE COMMAND TO LOVE

i. *Love of God*

"You shall love the LORD your God with all your heart and with all your soul and with all your might" (Deut. 6:5). So the *Shema*, and so Jesus. If the Gospels read "mind" for "might" (Matthew and Luke) or add "mind" to the list from the *Shema* (Mark), the sense is not changed: Israel, and now also the Church, is commanded to love God above and before all else with all it is and all it has. This is what the covenant is all about.

With such penetrating and compelling meditations on this theme available as that of Kierkegaard (*Works*, especially 20–36) and that of Rosenzweig on the "Song of Songs" (*Star*, 199–204), one hesitates to write on the love of God. Yet, since this is indeed the heart of the covenant, we cannot remain silent. I shall therefore touch briefly on what seem to me to be the essential features especially needed to be noted in our time.

The first point is the utter impracticality of the supreme demand God sets before us. We are to long for one we cannot describe, bow down before one we cannot see, adore one we cannot point to. We are to love God with our whole selves, devoting all our energies and abilities to something with no conceivable consequences in, and regardless of all conceivable circumstances of, the world. No wonder we are *commanded* to do this!

The second point is that this is God's command first of all to Israel, to the Jewish people. If Jews are to pour their whole being into loving God, then they will be singled out by the nations of the world for being engaged in a foolish activity that makes no contribution to the world. And if the Church is to take up this Jewish activity, convinced that it is commanded to join the Jews in this useless foolishness, then it must learn to live with the fact that the world will not thank it for wasting so much of its energies in so pointless a task. This commandment was and is addressed quite explicitly to Israel, and any who take upon themselves to overhear it as addressed also to them and then to obey it, will find themselves singled out as Israel has been singled out for ridicule.

If it seems strange to call loving God useless, one need think a bit about how one is to go about doing it. What is it to love God? The text does not say. Other texts offer a profusion of ways in which some in Israel have shown their love for God. We are told that some danced, others sang, some went off into places of solitude to pray. Strange cults were practiced, a Temple was built. One said that it all came down to doing justice and mercy and being humble. Our modern preoccupation with consequences and results leads us to focus on the point about doing justice, but that is surely part of the other commandment, to love our neighbor. When it comes to loving God, and loving God with all we are and have, the dancing, singing, praying, and worshiping really have no earthly utility. God asks of Israel, and of those who are drawn to overhear his command to Israel, to simply love God for no other reason than that God commands this love. There are other commandments that have much to do with the course of this world. Before them all, however, comes the commandment to simply love God and to do so without reserve.

It is to be noted that the commandment lacks specificity. How shall Israel, and then the Church, know that in attempting to love God it is doing so with all that it is and has? Here it is essential to recall that this is a commandment, part of the covenant. That means that the very lack of specificity in this commandment is a sign of God's commitment to Israel. God made himself Israel's God and Israel God's people. God commands that Israel love him only because he first loves Israel. God had already shown what his love means by rescuing Israel from slavery in Egypt. Now he leaves to Israel, and also to the Church, to invent how they shall return that love. Let Israel sing and dance and pray and do whatever it will to love God, and let the Church do likewise. Let them invent liturgies, meditate, hold wild celebrations. That is the freedom that this commandment allows. If loving God is commanded, then loving God is possible, and Israel and the Church are given all the room they need to show their love. Only one other commandment has been said to be "like" it: to love the neighbor.

ii. *Love of neighbor*

"You shall love your neighbor as yourself" (Lev. 19:18). That we love ourselves is presupposed, whether we do it well or badly, to our harm or to our benefit. There is no commandment in Judaism or in the Church to love ourselves. Israel and the Church know that none is needed. What is needed is what has been provided: the commandment to love our neighbor in just the same sense in which we already love ourselves. God commands that we turn from our concern for our own well-being and make the well-being of the other, the nearest other, just as much our concern.

The witness to Jesus found in Matthew's Gospel says that this commandment is "like" the commandment to love God. It is certainly a commandment, and it is a commandment to love. Moreover, the two commandments are inseparable as the author of the First Epistle of John saw: "If any one says, 'I love God,' and hates his brother, he is a liar" (1 John 4:20). The Torah spells out in considerable detail what this commandment entails, for it seems to be basic to God's will that his creatures, made in God's image, not only should love their Creator; they should love all that God loves, and so, first of all, the human being whom they find nearest at hand.

The commandment puts its focus on the neighbor, the one next to us, whoever that may be. One need not wait until the neighbor comes along, nor need one go hunting to find the neighbor. Any and every human being will do. The parable of the Good Samaritan calls our attention to whomever lies in need by the side of the road. There is the neighbor to be loved.

From as early as Clement of Alexandria, Christians have identified Jesus with the Good Samaritan of the parable. Jesus has been for the Church the model of what it looks like to love one's neighbor. So the Apostle to the Gentiles saw Jesus' death for ungodly Gentiles as the ultimate act of love for the neighbor, a theme also known to the Johannine community (John 15:13). For the Church, Jesus is the one who proves himself to be the true neighbor, the one who loves the other. He is therefore the criterion of what it is to love the other "as oneself."

It should be pointed out, however, that while Christ is properly the model for the Church of love (being the one through whom the Church has learned of and been brought into a relationship with the God who commands love) that God and this commandment were already known to Israel. Jesus has not added something to Israel's law with this recitation of God's command to love the neighbor. He was quoting Torah, and if he gives the commandment as its embodiment a personal character for the Church, so also did the rabbis deepen the ancient commandment for Judaism by their own stress on loving for its own sake (Montefiore and Loewe, *Rabbinic*, xxv). The Jewish people and the Gentile Church stand together under this commandment against every culture, not least modern Western culture with its profound commitment to self-love that urges us to take care of "number one."

In his study, *Democracy in America*, Alexis de Tocqueville felt the need to coin a new word (which was first used in English, according to the *O.E.D.*, in the English translation of that book) to characterize what was peculiar to Americans. The new word was "individualism," and its meaning is given in that dictionary as "Self-centered feeling or conduct as a principle." In one word: selfishness, precisely the opposite of that which is commanded.

The commandment to love the neighbor is the gift of the Creator to his creatures to discover themselves in relationship to the other, to find themselves as creatures of the covenant. The commandment is therefore one more sign of God's commitment in covenant. Like God, his covenant partners are invited to go out from themselves, to give, to share—in a word, to love as God first loved them. Because it has been commanded, it can be done. "You shall—and you may—love your neighbor." That is the good news of Torah, the good news of the covenant, made available to the Church through Jesus Christ.

iii. Love of enemy

We come finally to what may be Jesus' distinctive variation on the commandment to love: "Love your enemies and pray for those who persecute you" (Matt. 5:44), to which should be added the words preceding: "Do not resist one who is evil. But if anyone strikes you on the right cheek, turn to him the other also" (Matt. 5:39). I say "may" for two reasons; we do not know for sure that these sayings, preserved only by the Matthean community, go back to Jesus, and their distinctiveness is debatable. Tertullian, for example, argued (admittedly in an anti-Marcionite polemic, *Adv. Marc.* IV, 16) that these sayings only repeat the commands of the Creator through Isaiah (reading the Greek text of Isaiah 66:5; the Hebrew text, had he been able to read it, is rather different). The point, however, is that Tertullian did not find the commandment to love our enemies foreign to the Scriptures. And although the rabbis drew the traditional line at the cruel Amalekites, they could teach that the Edomite and the Egyptian (both of which they took symbolically for Israel's enemies), whether good or bad (they added), were brothers! (On this and related themes, see Montefiore and Loewe, *Rabbinic,* 469.) With these qualifications in mind, it might be best to say that with the commandment to love our enemies, not to resist evil, and to turn the other cheek, we have at most but a slight extension of the commandment to love our neighbor (who might, after all, be a none-too-well-meaning neighbor) as ourselves. Luke has, of course, picked up this theme in his "word-from-the-cross": "Father, forgive them, for they know not what they do."

In the light of that text, and also Pinchas Lapide's realistic assessment of this commandment (*Sermon*), it should be asked whether the command to love our enemies is really so utterly idealistic and unworkable as is so often claimed. Have we tested it to reach this conclusion? Is it more unworkable and counterproductive than the unqualified—and therefore surely unproductive— love of God? And if we love our neighbor, for love's own sake as the rabbis urged, is that any more productive? One is left with the suspicion that the objection to loving the enemy and turning the other cheek could only be raised by one who has not considered carefully the commandments to love God with all that one is and has, and to love the neighbor as we in fact already love ourselves.

This is not to say that this commandment is an easy one to obey. It is, after all, a commandment. Yet it asks us to consider whether returning blow for blow, hate for hate—the normal course in this world—is itself productive. Could it be that the Creator of this world, as Jesus or his witness has interpreted him, has some clue as to how creation works? The hard case would seem to be the condition of war, but perhaps in this nuclear age the facts of war may be forcing us to recognize the wisdom in this seemingly idealistic commandment. With respect to the enemy without (the easier case) and also for the enemy within (the much more difficult case), we can only bring disaster upon all creation by not obeying the Creator's second commandment also in their case: that we love, genuinely seek the good of, our neighbor even as we might wish our own good. If we do not do so, in what possible way can we be said to have obeyed the first commandment, to love the Creator of this world with all that we are and have?

iv. Love as creativity

The two commandments, to love God without reserve and to love the neighbor as oneself, are the sum and substance of Torah for the Church. On these two commandments "depend all the Torah and the Prophets" (Matt. 22:40). That does not mean that the other commandments are to be ignored. It does mean, as Paul maintained, that the commandments concerning adultery, murder, theft, covetousness, "and any other" will in fact be obeyed by those who love their neighbors as themselves (Rom. 13:8–9). These two commandments, then, focus the whole of God's will for the Church and serve as the criteria for its response to God's love.

It has been said often that the problem with the Church's focus on love is that it offers so little by way of explicit direction in the hard decisions of real life. The problem is there, but it is compounded by the mistake of conceiving of love apart from command, thus letting it loose into a general realm of feeling or even emotion. The commandments to love God and the neighbor, however, say nothing about feelings or emotions. They point to one most unidentifiable and to one utterly identifiable focus of our attention and activity, and they order us to set about making our activity turn around those foci. We are to think about them, not ourselves, and then we are to set to work in behalf of their cause, not our own. If the commandments lack specificity about just what that activity might be, they also invite us to inquire as to the cause of God and our neighbor, as though to encourage us to make them the genuine foci of our attention and understanding before we set to work. The lack of detailed direction, then, has the merit of pointing us in the right direction.

Both commandments are as immediate and as open-ended as love itself. They are immediate because love has its life primarily in the present tense. Unlike hope which looks wholly to the future, and unlike faith which draws its present force from recalling the past, love knows only the immediate present. It is to be done now. But love is open-ended. The command to love challenges the one who hears it to be creative. It invites the exploration of every possible political and social program or proposal, to see whether and to what extent it will indeed serve the cause and need of the neighbor, whether and to what extent it might express in some new way a love of the Creator and all that is. The commandments do not define for us just how we shall love. They give us the foci of God and the neighbor and then leave to us the use of our imagination and minds as well as our will, experience, and skills to see what we can come up with that will serve God or the neighbor.

The commandments to love, then, are themselves covenantal, not only in their origin in the covenant between God and Israel, but also because they respect and call forth the creativity for those with whom God has made his covenant, Israel, and those whom he has called to work alongside of Israel in his cause of peace and justice for all his creatures. In commanding that his Church serve beside his people Israel, God has invited Jesus' followers to creative participation in God's cause of redemption.

4. THE CALL TO DISCIPLESHIP

i. Jewish discipleship

Jesus' call to discipleship was of course addressed to his fellow Jews, not to the Gentile Church. As a call to Israel to follow him in preparation for God's coming, however, it has been made inaudible by the history of the Church. God's call to Israel to be renewed came (if in a somewhat different form, yet providentially) from the rabbis of Javneh, Safed, Babylon, and from many centers of Europe and then the United States. If there had been anything distinctive in Jesus' original call to discipleship (perhaps the intensity and so the call to love even God's enemies), it was lost for Israel through Gentile pride. The Gentiles never seemed to realize that that call had not been addressed to them at all. If it were to come through to them too, it would have to come as someone else's call overheard and responded to nevertheless. If heard as a call from God (and only thus could it have a place in christological consideration), it might then have to be considered with utmost care, but in view of the change of address, it needs to be handled with far more caution than has been characteristic of the Church in its tradition.

ii. Gentile discipleship

We are led then to the only matter of legitimate Church concern: a Gentile appropriation of a call to Jewish discipleship. Gentile discipleship cannot be a matter of a direct hearing of the call of Jesus to follow him. That is because it only became possible as a consequence of two further factors: the gift to Gentiles of the Spirit and the resulting decision of the apostles to admit Gentiles into the company of Jesus' Jewish disciples.

The "gift of the Spirit" to Gentiles, of which both Paul and the author of Acts wrote, refers to the recurring event of certain Gentiles responding to the actions and preaching of the apostles in such a way that the apostles recognized in their case what they believed to be true of themselves: God was laying claim upon them and taking them into the movement that he had begun in Jesus Christ. These Gentiles and the Jewish apostles saw this recurring event as initiated by the God of Israel and they saw it as God's call to these Gentiles to serve him as Gentiles. Both of these judgments were entailed in speaking of the gift of the Spirit to Gentiles.

iii. Imitatio Christi *as creative response*

What, then, was to be the content of Gentile discipleship? It was not to be the same as Jewish discipleship, and so we need to ask about a peculiar Gentile *imitatio Christi.* The Gentiles are not to become Jews, and they are not to hold to those features of Torah that mark the Jews as Jews. It is evident that the early Christian communities had difficulty determining what that included and what it excluded, and that difficulty has continued to this day. It is not the task of the theologian to resolve this issue for the Church, but it is the theologian's duty to point out that some of the classic distinctions that have been called upon in order to answer this problem (as for example that between the moral law and the ceremonial law) have no grounding whatsoever in Torah itself, and import into the discussion of discipleship or obedience to God distinctions that impose criteria quite foreign to the matter.

The call of Gentiles to follow Christ is and will remain a call to creative response, in which the Gentile Church has to make up its own mind how it is to walk. It is called to serve the God of Israel, the God of the covenant, in a Gentile way, and that means it will have to figure out for itself how to go about serving such a God in a non-Jewish way. It has some guidance from those who first faced this problem, from Paul and the other apostles, but such guidance can only be a point of departure. Not even the apostles can take from the Church today its own responsibility before God and the world to decide how it should follow its crucified Lord in his service to the God of Israel. This it will do in part in reflection on the meaning of the cross, to which subject we now turn.

CHAPTER SEVEN

The Crucified One

The death of Jesus on a Roman cross has from the beginning been presented as an essential part of his story, defining him and his role in God's purpose. His death has been presented as having cosmic, redemptive, and revelatory consequences, all of which for the sake of credibility require reconsideration and reformulation in the aftermath of Auschwitz. God's suffering solidarity with his people Israel, and so with his whole creation, was enacted exemplarily, but not for the last time, in Jesus, showing that God's power lies in weakness.

1. INTRODUCTION TO THE PROBLEM

The cross has become unquestionably the central and most universally recognized symbol of the Christian Church. Whether the cross has at all times and everywhere been central to the Church's thinking and living is not so clear. Although the cross and the events leading to it form the climax of the story of Jesus in the Gospels of Matthew, Mark, and Luke, it is debatable whether any of these Gospels has a "theology of the cross." With the possible exception of Mark 10:45 (the son of man to "give his life as a ransom for many"), they present the cross as the destined end of Jesus' life, but they do not seem to have any theory about why it was destined or what it accomplished. The Gospel of John does have a theory of sorts, but it does not fit what one would expect from the later and especially Western tradition of a "theology of the

cross'': Jesus is lifted up to draw followers to himself. It is a moment of triumph. (The evident exception to this is the motif,
sounded by John the Baptist in the first chapter but not developed
further, of "the Lamb of God who takes away the sin of the
world.") The New Testament grounds for a theology of the cross
as central would therefore seem to be primarily in Paul's writings
and in Hebrews.

When we turn to the developing tradition, it is noteworthy that
the creed of Nicea, or rather that creed as formulated at the
Council of Constantinople in 381 C.E., simply recites the crucifixion, along with the death and burial, as being "for our sake,"
without further explanation. The formulation of the Council of
Chalcedon (451 C.E.), concerned especially to establish the humanity of Jesus, contains no reference to the cross at all (nor to
Easter!). Indeed, no ecumenical council formulated a dogma concerning the effects of the death of Jesus on the cross. The line of
tradition for which the cross is central flows from Augustine,
through the Franciscans, to Luther and on into seventeenth and
eighteenth century Pietism in both its Protestant and Catholic
forms.

The centrality of the cross in Western theology would appear
to be directly connected with the radical view of the consequences
of "the Fall" that we owe so largely to Augustine. When sin is tak-
en to be a fundamental corruption of humanity, then its remedy
will be as fundamental. Whether the seriousness with which the
problem is taken leads to stressing the importance of the solution,
or whether the magnitude ascribed to the solution leads to an
awareness of the depth of the problem, is another matter; Anselm's *Cur Deus Homo*, for example, can be read either way,
Barth's *Church Dogmatics* IV/1 allows only the second perspective.
In either case, however, the seriousness with which sin is taken
goes together with central attention being given to the cross.

Where the cross has been taken to be central, it has been seen
to be so both as the remedy for corruption, variously conceived,
and as a revelation of God, although the emphasis may fall more
on one aspect than the other. In any case, it will be well to consid-

er both aspects in our reflections on the significance of the death of Jesus.

Today, however, we are invited if not compelled to reconsider all past reflections on the Passion of Jesus at Gentile hands—consisting (according to all accounts) of a night and one morning's humiliation, and death following three hours of torture—in the light of the passion nineteen centuries later of six million more Jews at Gentile hands, consisting in innumerable cases of months or years of humiliation, starvation, beatings, and torture, before being shot to fall into mass graves, or gassed and burned to ashes in crematoriums. The invitation comes from the warning of the Roman Catholic theologian Johann B. Metz that we beware of any theological statement made after the Holocaust that is unchanged from how it was expressed before ("Oekumene"). It comes also from the Jewish theologian Irving Greenberg's recommendation that "no statement, theological or otherwise, should be made that would not be credible in the presence of the burning children"—those thrown into the ovens alive to save less than one-fiftieth of the German mark that it would have cost to provide the gas for a slightly less agonizing death (Greenberg, "Cloud," 23). It comes as well from the Protestant theologian F. W. Marquardt: "Auschwitz confronts us as a call to repentance. Not only our behavior but our faith itself should change. Auschwitz should bring forth not only ethical consequences but also consequences for faith. Auschwitz cries out for us to hear the Word of God today radically otherwise than as we heard it before Auschwitz, radically otherwise than as it was handed down to us in the preaching and theology of our elders" (Marquardt, *Schweigen*, 10).

We are thus invited anew to think through what the death of Christ was and what it effected. To ignore the invitation must appear to many to be an attempt to extol the death of one Jew—an incredible and ethically inexcusable act in the face of the death of six million Jews. And whatever the Church may say as to the unique role of that one Jew—and for the Gentile Church at the least he is surely unique—it cannot be forgotten that each and every one of the six million was one of God's elect, one of God's own people Israel. If God has authorized Jesus to represent God's self to the Gentile Church, has he not also authorized his people Israel to be God's light to lighten all the Gentiles? Surely no word about the death of Jesus will be credible, even to ourselves, if it is spoken unmindful of the deaths of six million of his people after nineteen centuries of preaching redemption, and practicing contempt, in his name.

2. THE CROSS AND AUSCHWITZ

i. *Before Auschwitz: the cross as the remedy for corruption?*

"In Christ God was reconciling the world to himself. . . . For our sake he made him to be sin who knew no sin, so that in him we might become God's righteousness" (2 Cor. 5:19, 21). "Since therefore the children share in flesh and blood, he himself likewise partook of the same nature, that through death he might destroy him who has the power of death, that is, the devil, and deliver all those who through the fear of death were subject to lifelong bondage" (Heb. 2:14–15). The witness of the early Christian communities to the cross seldom refers to its consequences apart from those of the resurrection. Taken in its own right, however, that witness provides the grounds for the theme in later Christian teaching, that Christ's death was the antidote to corruption.

The corruption that afflicts God's good creation has been variously defined. It has been given the name "sin" (in contrast to "sins"), and death has been seen as its most dramatic effect. Sin or death has been felt as a cosmic condition, in which the power of corruption has been sometimes personified as Satan, or as a human condition, with the emphasis falling on the corruption of human will resulting from the sin of Adam. More important than these differences, however, is the common conviction that God's good creation is not as God intended it, and that death is the ultimate sign of this situation.

The death of Jesus, as God's authorized agent of God's cause in behalf of creation, is then seen as God's way to defeat the power of corruption, a victory made evident on Easter. Death, with sin as its cause, was overcome in that God accepted Christ's death in place of ours, or in that Christ as God's anointed proved more powerful than death. "[God] made him to be sin" (2 Cor. 5:21), either as the one who takes the place of all sinners and so takes upon himself the punishment due them, or as a sacrifice to wipe away the condemnation against them. In God's judgment upon sin and corruption, or upon sinners, Christ dies in the place of all those over whom death reigns. The tradition has of course preserved an eschatological reserve: death in its physical or biological aspect is still at work, but it is no more to be feared as God's judgment. Only with the *eschaton,* "the end," will death itself cease. "As in Adam all die, so also in Christ *shall* all be made alive" (1 Cor. 15:22, emphasis added).

In broad strokes that has been the major line of the Church's understanding of the consequences of the cross. Millions of Christians throughout the ages have died in the conviction that physical death was but the remnant of the condition that in God's sight—and so in reality—has been overcome, that death can by no means separate them from the love of God made real for them in Christ Jesus. Death, since the cross, is no longer what it was.

And then came the Holocaust. It did not come without a long preparation and without its context. While it was taking place and shortly after it was over, Christian voices were heard to say that it came because "the Jews" rejected the Church's gospel, because "the Jews" had played a role in the death of Jesus. That longstanding teaching about "the Jews" was an important preparation for such a response, as it was for the event itself. It surely was not the sufficient cause of the horror, but without it, it is difficult to account for the passivity before the fact, not to speak of actual cooperation with it in all too many cases of so many Christians.

Auschwitz raises questions about the victory of the cross over death. In the face of that Kingdom of Death, can it now be said that death is swallowed up in victory? In the light of this unparalleled manifestation of corruption, can it now be said that the corruption of creation has been remedied? Can the Suffering Servant of Isaiah 53 be taken any longer to refer solely to the suffering Jew on the cross, when we have seen photographs of the deadened faces and stacked corpses of God's people in the death camps? Auschwitz surely makes these questions morally and theologically unavoidable for the Church, however difficult it may be to answer them.

ii. Before Auschwitz: the cross as the revelation of God?

"God shows his love for us in that while we were yet sinners Christ died for us" (Rom. 5:8). The cross of Christ has been taken to reveal the extent of God's love for his sinful creatures. Two connections are preconditions for such a conclusion to be drawn: (1) God is so closely associated with Jesus that the death on the cross was a loss to God, so that in some sense, God took this suffering and death upon himself, and (2) God willed or intended Jesus' death on the cross. Each of these preconditions has special problems requiring separate discussion.

The first connection has traditionally been made with the doctrine of the Incarnation: the second *hypostasis* of the Triune God was in Jesus. God the Father was not involved directly (personally, we might say) in the death of Jesus, but the eternal Word of God, "consubstantial" with the Father, was united inseparably with the crucified one. On the other hand, even the Word or Son did not die with Jesus, according to the orthodox tradition, because the Word or Son, being divine, cannot die. To put it sharply, Jesus the Jewish son of the God of Israel died, whereas God the Son, or God's way of being as Word, simply waited this event out. Only with the rarest of exceptions have Christians wanted to say that God died on the cross.

But if God did not suffer this death, can there not be other ways in which God shared in or suffered loss in this event? Obviously, we can think of other models, but none of them require the doctrine of the Incarnation or even the orthodox doctrine of the Trinity. God can be conceived as having forged a relationship with Jesus modeled on that of human intimacy and commitment.

Then God would suffer as a human father or mother would suffer the loss of a son or as any human being can suffer the loss of a loved one. Or one could turn to the covenant as a framework for understanding that God is hurt by any loss to the covenant partner. But the use of such models of connection are based on our experience of human relationships or of Israel's connection to God. They are neither incarnational nor trinitarian, in the usual sense of those doctrines. Moreover, those doctrines do not provide a stronger connection, only a less personal one. The issue, finally, is whether or how the love of the God whom Jesus called Father is revealed in the cross. The love in question is that of God the Father for the Jew Jesus. The inclusion of the second *hypostasis* of the Trinity is an evasion of this hard question.

Even these personal models of connection, however, leave us only with the possibility of Jesus having shown *his* love for us, if we could establish that his death was intentionally suffered for us. The passage quoted at the beginning of this subsection appears to imply that God willed the death of Jesus for us sinners, and that Jesus accepted his death as consciously undertaken in obedience to that will. The struggle of prayer portrayed in the Garden of Gethsemane scene depicts just this, although it is painted explicitly as having had no witnesses. Karl Barth's magisterial presentation of this tradition (*CD*, IV/1) works carefully through its presuppositions: God had decided to exercise his sovereign judgment on his rebellious creatures by taking upon himself the consequences of their rebellion. And so God's way of being himself as he who discloses himself (= God as Son) came to take our place as one of us, dying in our place the death we had all merited, and was raised that he might continue to stand forever in our stead before the Father, God's righteousness in our place.

At best this tradition need not say that God willed the death of Jesus, only that he had so established his creation that death was the consequence of rebellion. Sin could hardly be taken more seriously than that. Perhaps this tradition need not even lean so heavily on the story of the Garden of Gethsemane as to require that Jesus accept his death as the path he must follow because God had willed it. It would be sufficient that he maintain unswerving fidelity to God, wherever that obedience might lead. More importantly, the dynamics of what took place in the death of Jesus allow room for a more personal mode of commitment between Jesus and his Father than that provided by the doctrines of the Trinity and the Incarnation of the second *hypostasis* of the Triune God. If this was God's intention, then its dynamics are open to more than one interpretation. In any case, Paul's claim in Romans requires that a relationship exist between God—namely God the Father, the one whose love is shown—and Jesus, the one who died. A third term, the incarnate Word, seems only to get in the way.

What shall we say to this tradition after Auschwitz? Did not many of those who died go to their death in utter fidelity to God? But who would claim that God willed their death, for whatever reason? And if some good has come from their death—the reversal of the Church's traditional anti-Judaic teaching, for one— would anyone dare to say that God had willed so much misery and so many deaths for this result? And if after Auschwitz we hesitate to speak of God's intention in this horrible event, might that not suggest that we should be more circumspect in speaking of God's intention in connection with the cross?

iii. The cross in the light of Auschwitz

Perhaps the greatest question that Auschwitz raises for the tradition of Christian teaching about the cross is whether we can continue to say with Hebrews (and perhaps with Paul in Rom. 6:10), that it happened "once for all." The price of doing so is to set God's authorization of Jesus on a radically different plain from his authorization of the Jewish people. This is of course precisely what the orthodox tradition has done with its doctrine of the Incarnation. The result was the introduction of a profound discontinuity in the conception of God's dealings with Israel. That this stands opposed to Paul's insistence that all God's promises (i.e., to Israel and to the world through Israel) are affirmed and confirmed in Christ (2 Cor. 1:20) does not appear to have bothered that tradition. It must however bother a Church that has declared its conviction that God's covenant with Israel, the Jewish people, is eternal. A Church that affirms the Jewish people as the continuing Israel of God cannot coherently define the authorization of Jesus so as to undercut God's authorization of the people Israel. In a world that has known Auschwitz, consequently, the cross can only be presented as a world-redeeming event in more qualified terms than those of "once for all."

Precisely the point of hesitation in the orthodox doctrine of the Cross, the inability to go so far as to say that God was directly, personally, and immediately involved in the suffering of Jesus becomes unbearable when we reflect on the suffering of the Jewish men, women, and children in the Holocaust. If God was not there, suffering with his people, if God did not suffer a loss there at least as painful as that suffered on Golgotha, then that God is not worthy of respect by moral persons. It could be argued that the clear intention of the doctrines of the Incarnation and the Trinity were to confess the unconditioned character of God's involvement in human affairs in the life and death of Jesus. As actually formulated, however, those doctrines were blunted in order to preserve the assumption of all thinkers in the Greco-Roman world that God could not suffer, that divine omnipotence excluded such an involvement. Precisely at this point, Auschwitz may teach us what we should have learned from Golgotha: that God's omnipotence is such that God can and does enter into the pain and suffering of his children.

We shall learn to speak of Auschwitz from the perspective of the cross, then, by first learning to speak of the cross from the perspective of Auschwitz. A rule that would appear essential to govern our language in this area is that the death of one Jew, no matter whom or what he was in God's purposes, should not be spoken of so as to lessen the significance and the pain of the death of any human being, least of all that of six million other Jews. Any talk of that earlier event as eschatological in a way that reduces the importance of further events in human history is called into question by the guidelines of Metz, Greenberg, and Marquardt to which we have referred.

A second rule bears directly on the Church's understanding of God. It would seem essential that we say that the death of God's faithful son Jesus must have hurt God, and the deaths of six million of God's sons and daughters in the Holocaust must have hurt God even more. Indeed, the murder of every one of those to whom God has entrusted the keeping of his covenant and/or the ministry of reconciliation is a defeat for God and God's cause. Do the sufferings and defeats of God's authorized ones, of those to whom God has made a binding commitment, require that we deny God's omnipotence? Perhaps any answer here needs to exercise a constraint more characteristic of the Eastern Orthodox tradition than of Western theology: we should not pretend to know more about God than God has led us to see by God's operations in human history. We should therefore grant that the ascription of omnipotence to God is an act of praise, a liturgical ascription, not a definition. If the cross tells us something about God's power that is confirmed on an incredibly vaster scale in the Holocaust, it is that God evidently does not always come to the rescue of those to whom he has committed himself. It is always possible to conclude from this fact that there is no God, that God is not concerned with human life, or that God is incapable of intervening. It is always possible to conclude, that is, that if there is a God, that Being is either not good or not powerful. But it is also possible to conclude that God did not come to the rescue of his child Jesus or his many children in the Holocaust because he did not choose to do so, for reasons of which we cannot be sure. Could it be that God prefers to suffer with his chosen ones rather than solve their problems for them? Could it be that God wants his creatures to take far more responsibility for the future of God's creation than those who trust in God have generally dared to assume? Could it be that God wants such trust in him that his creatures acknowledge and understand that God has entrusted his cause to human hands and hearts, so that if the evils seen in Roman tyranny or Nazi bestiality are to be overcome, God's creatures must address themselves to that task?

If such reflections are in order, then God's omnipotence needs to be seen as God's truly unlimited freedom to *not* act even when those most dear to him are threatened and cry to him to intervene. God's failure to act in such circumstances could still be seen as evidence of his goodness, if we could see that God thereby offers us a model of covenantal love that surrenders to God's covenant partners the lead in restoring what is corrupt in God's creation. In which case, the consolation for the victims may be their trust that they do not suffer alone, and their act of trust in God in such circumstances may be to weep as much for God's pain as for that of themselves and their fellow human victims.

3. FOR US/FOR OUR SINS

i. A reasonable hypothetical reconstruction

In what sense and in what way can the death of Jesus be affirmed as having been "for us," "for sin," "for our sins"? In order to find our way toward an answer, we shall attempt a historically reasonable reconstruction of how his death came about, which of necessity, given the nature of the historical evidence, will be hypothetical. E. P. Sanders wrote that it is conceivable "that Jesus taught one thing, that he was killed for something else, and that the disciples, after the resurrection, made of his life and death something else, so that there is no causal thread between his life, his death, and the Christian movement. This is possible, but it is not satisfying historically" (Sanders, *Judaism*, 22). The question surely needs to be put after Auschwitz: what is "satisfying historically" in a world that has witnessed the Holocaust? In so carefully thought-out and written a book as Sanders's, it is painfully evident that this rationalist presupposition is never subjected to critical examination. For a historian of this actual world so minimally characterized by logical coherence, "not satisfying" is an odd criterion to use.

Sanders argues persuasively that to rely on Jesus' purported teachings for understanding his life is fraught with uncertainties. He is surely on a better track in starting with the probable actions of Jesus (and he is always careful to distinguish the possible from the probable, with several gradations of each), of which some sort of demonstration in the Temple area during the Passover time will obviously be crucial in answering the questions that the historian must ask.

On the basis of the actions that mark the story of Jesus, Sanders comes to the conclusion, with which I am inclined to agree, that Jesus understood himself as a divinely called prophet of Jewish restoration, a conclusion based on such reasonably probable facts as Jesus' baptism by John and the calling of "the twelve." In this context, a *cleansing* of the Temple makes no sense, but an act intending to symbolize the destruction of the Temple *in preparation for its divine restoration* fits nicely. The case for this probable connection between the life and work of Jesus and the Temple incident is convincing.

How Sanders moves from that incident to an arrest, summary "trial," and execution by the Roman occupation authority, however, is by no means so persuasive. The move is made by an all-too-familiar theme: Jewish opposition to Jesus. Sanders does not find this to lie in any supposed novel teaching concerning God's kingdom, the reported healing miracles, or in Jesus' attitude toward Torah. On all these counts Sanders sees Jesus well within the limits of first-century Judaism. The conflict, as he sees it, rose from Jesus' invitation to known and blatant sinners to join his restoration movement *without requiring any ritual of repentance whatsoever.* That and the Temple incident were enough to turn the Temple authorities or their leaders (just those who would have had access to Pilate) against him.

To use Sanders's careful distinctions, I think we should call that reconstruction no more than possible. Given his agreement that the trial scene is a later construction, that Jesus was executed as a rebel (confirmed by the *titulus* on the cross), and by the further fact (which Sanders mentions but does not develop) that the Temple tax from Jews all over the empire was coming into Jerusalem at just this time of Passover (turning the Temple area into something like an Internal Revenue Service center on April 15) it seems reasonable to say that Jewish complicity in Jesus' arrest, at best conjectural, is quite unnecessary. Pilate was responsible for Roman law and order, including the orderly reception of a tax on which much of the life of the city depended. We should add to this the probable status of the Temple as the national bank (see Hamilton, "Temple," 365–72, and literature cited there, to none of which Sanders refers). If, as Sanders would have it, the Temple leaders could have misinterpreted Jesus' demonstration as a rejection of God's Temple rather than as a symbol of its imminent restoration, how much more likely that Pilate would have understood it as an affront to Roman law and order? I therefore find it is more "satisfying historically" to conclude with Hamilton ("Temple," 372) that Jesus' death "was pure tragedy. An eschatological prophet acting under the obligations of his message came into collision with civil authorities who also had their obligations."

It would have been helpful if Sanders had discussed Hamilton's earlier interpretation of Jesus as a prophet of Jewish restoration (or as eschatological prophet) but perhaps he was unaware of it, Hamilton's extended treatment of the matter having been published under the totally misleading title *Jesus for a No-God World*.

To sum up, the following seems a reasonably probable historical reconstruction of the final events in Jesus' life: consistent with a divine calling to bear witness in word and deed to the coming restoration of Israel, Jesus carried out a demonstration in the Temple area, intending to show that the days of the existing Temple were over and the day of a new Temple in a new Israel, the day of God's reign over his creation, was at hand. But a demonstration in that place at that time was a conspicuous challenge to Roman law and order, and Pilate acted swiftly to have Jesus arrested, condemned, and executed. That Pilate had the cooperation of at least some of the Temple authorities is a good possibility but would hardly have been necessary. Pilate had ample reason for and ability to carry out the death of Jesus with no official Jewish help at all. Perhaps the identification provided by one of "the twelve" was all the help required.

If this reconstruction is anywhere near correct, then Jesus' intention did not include his death, although unswerving faithfulness to his calling led him into a situation of which death was a likely outcome. He died, then, because he would not let anything stand in the way of a calling he believed to be that of his Father, the God of Israel. And since the world is not yet the scene of God's reign but a world corrupted by sin, it is correct to say that he died because of sin. This last statement can of course also be made concerning every one of Hitler's victims.

ii. How the disciples came to say, "for us"

The stories of a betrayal by one of "the twelve" (Judas) and of the denial by no less a member of "the twelve" than Simon Cephas (Peter) are almost beyond doubt a part of the earliest traditions concerning the death of Jesus. They point to solid grounds for assuming that Jesus' disciples felt implicated in that death. The shepherd was taken and killed; the sheep had scattered, looking out for themselves, not for their master. They had served in God's cause together with him and under his leadership, but when the crisis arrived, in effect they turned and ran. It would be strange indeed had they not felt guilty for their behavior. It is unlikely that any of them would have thought that Jesus deserved what had happened to him; it appears a good possibility that they would have felt that they should have died for him, or at least with him. In such circumstances, if such a reconstruction has any merit, it would be understandable that they might have said among themselves, already before Easter, "He died for us," or "He died for our sins." Thus could have begun, without any theological superstructure, the early confession which Paul claimed to have received from others (1 Cor. 15:3–4).

It should be pointed out that the truth of this confession in no way depends on Jesus having had or expressed an intention to die for his followers. It is even more important to see that, if there is a profound theological conclusion to be drawn concerning the function of Jesus' death in the divine economy, that conclusion also does not depend on Jesus' intention. The intention of the Jew Jesus is no more essential here than we saw it to be in discussing the validity of the claim that Jesus was authorized by God to speak and act in God's name. In both cases, what is required is a divine decision and intention.

In the case of Jesus' death, however, we must go farther: we must say that its place in the divine economy does not depend on God's having intended *ahead of time* either that Jesus would die at the hands of the Romans or that his death should be of benefit for others. Doxologically, both were soon to be said. Was it not fitting that sorrow over his death, turned to a mysterious joy by the event of Easter, should give way to thanksgiving precisely for the most painful part of his story? How could all this have come to pass apart from the care and loving purpose of God? Any devout Jew of the time would have tried to see it that way. As Jews familiar with the Psalms, they would have been driven to see this too "in accordance with the Scriptures." It would take some time before specific passages of the Scriptures would be turned up as interpretive keys. From the first, however, it would have been a Jewish response to have felt that these events must in some way have stood in the light of and be continuous with the Scriptural story.

iii. How the Church can take up the confession of the disciples

The Church of Jesus Christ, however, is not Jewish. It does indeed see itself in the light of the Jewish story, but it is itself Gentile. How can it come to make its own the confession of Jesus' disciples that he had died for them? Further, how can it do so today with such different conceptions of time and history, cause and effect from those of the disciples, and above all separated from them by Auschwitz?

First of all, one point in that early confession must be reviewed. In our present critical reflections on the early witness to these events, there is no theological necessity to conclude that God must have worked out in advance the role that the cross was going to play in the future of God's cause. In an age in which it seemed impious to even suggest that God had not planned all this "before the foundations of the earth," God's foreknowledge, as first century Jews might have conceived it, would have to count against such thoughts. In an age in which the Church has discovered the continuing history of the covenant however, and so begun hesitantly to speak of God's own history, in a time in which we find powerful the concept of God's self-limitation and no longer see changelessness as a necessary attribute of God, above all after witnessing so massive a failure in the history of the covenant as the Holocaust, such a conclusion is less sure, having lost its logical force. Covenantal thinking, as the Church may learn from some Jews (e.g., Hartman, *Covenant*), opens for us the possibility that God did not intend that Jesus should die on the cross for us, but that he accepted what happened and the disciples' reaction to it as a fresh opportunity for a new contribution toward the renewal of his creation.

We recall in this connection the rabbinic story (*Bava Metzia* 59b in van Buren, *People Israel*, 213) of the conflict over the *halakhah* in which Rabbi Eliezer was outvoted by the majority, in spite of his having called to his aid a number of miracles and a voice from heaven. The story concludes with a report by Elijah on God's reaction: God laughed and said, "My sons have defeated me, my sons have defeated me!" If the Church could muster such rabbinic daring, it might then say that God may have discovered after the fact that the death of his faithful son Jesus would be the way to draw innumerable Gentiles to their knees before him. In which case, it could then conclude with full confidence that the cross became God's way of relating to his Church, deciding to let the one stand in the place of the many.

The step we have just taken bears reflection, both as to what it says about the Church's faith and about its implications for the church's theology, its understanding of God and the world. The Church has believed that it has died with Christ, that by his death it has been reconciled to God. Now, my hypothesis is that God in fact decided that it would be as the disciples and the developing and increasingly Gentile Church confessed: this tragic accident of his beloved and utterly loyal son Jesus having been caught up in and destroyed by human fear (in this case Pilate's) of losing control would become the event in which many could come to see their own faithlessness, the power of corruption in the world, and the offer of God's merciful love. On this supposition, the cross would still be everything that Paul claimed for it. It would be so because the resurrection would have been God's sign that God had discovered in the penitence and sorrow of the disciples that the death of Jesus need not be simply a tragic accident; it could become the culmination of Jesus' divine calling to speak and act in the name of the God of Abraham, and the means of drawing the nations into the story of his love affair with his beloved people Israel. This line of thinking is confirmed by the witness of Paul that his calling to preach Christ to the Gentiles came by God's having caused the risen Jesus to appear to him. Paul became the Apostle to the Gentiles precisely as a witness of the resurrection.

It may be asked, however, what this implies about our understanding of God, or rather what understanding of God allows such reflections. Clearly the God who could have made a new beginning of his own work on the basis of the response of the disciples is the covenantal God we have come to understand from the witness of Jewish, and especially rabbinic and Lurianic thought (see van Buren, *People Israel*, 62–64, 210–239). It is a God who entrusts to his covenant partners incalculable responsibility for the future of his cause. It is a God whose plan and purpose call upon those human partners to take responsibility for how that plan and purpose shall look. And it is a God who refuses to evade the pain and suffering that comes when his human creatures misuse their creaturely responsibility and bring such horrors to themselves and to God as we have seen in Auschwitz. It is a God, therefore, who suffers on the cross, suffering more hellishly in the gas chambers of the camps and the mass murders of the *Einsatz* teams in eastern Europe, and whose power lies in determining that God will not win our cooperation apart from our own conscious decision to side with his cause of justice and peace. It is, in a word, a God who is just the one whom Jesus called Father, just the one whom the Church has been given to see in the face of the crucified one.

iv. The cross and Auschwitz together

"O foolish Galations! Who has bewitched you, before whose eyes Jesus Christ was publicly portrayed as crucified?" (Gal. 3:1). "I decided to know nothing among you except Jesus Christ and him crucified" (1 Cor. 2:2). The Church has appeared through most if its life to want to identify with Peter in the scene of his confession of Jesus as "the Christ" (Mark 8:29) or as "the Christ, the Son of the Living God" (Matt. 16:16), ignoring that Jesus is said to have told the disciples not to say this to anyone (Mark 8:39, Matt. 16:20). It has been less inclined generally to identify itself with Peter in his repeated act of betrayal (Mark 14:66–72, Matt 26:69–75). It has chosen the cross as its primary symbol, only occasionally using the thrice-crowing cock of denial. Auschwitz made painfully clear for all to see that the Church's Petrine identification has been unbalanced. The Gentile Church of the crucified Jew seems ever again to be bewitched into forgetting that the cross is a clue to where it stands before God: not on a cross with the Jews, but standing with those who ignore, deny, or even assist in the crucifixion of God's elect and thus contributing to the agony of God.

It was precisely the Apostle to the Gentiles who made the cross so central to his gospel. As though aware of how almost totally Gentile the Church was to become, Paul seems to have felt that the intimacy between God and Israel was in danger of being missed, especially their intimacy in failure. In Paul's view of the world sin, the insidious and powerful corrupting force of decay in God's creation, was no minor blemish. The whole of creation groaned in birth pangs for a day of renewal, and the death of Jesus was a sign of that struggle. Had Paul lived to see it, he might well have included also the destruction of his beloved Jerusalem and God's Temple—and then why not also the pogroms and destruction visited on his people in later centuries, and especially the latest great agony, the Holocaust. They are all of a piece: each death was died only once, but each was a death arising from the world's resistance to God's purpose ever being worked out together with those to whom God has bound himself for the world's good. Each death was died once, but also for all, for God's purpose remains the good of all his creation.

"My power is perfected in weakness," Paul understood God to have said to him (2 Cor. 12:9). That must mean that God chooses to accomplish his purpose of good by submitting to evil, by accepting failure, by going to the cross and to the gas chamber. God's power, in this so opposite to what human beings mean by power, is made perfect in powerlessness. That has too often been interpreted to mean that God gets his work done by making use of human weakness, but such an interpretation forgets God's covenant. If we think covenantally, then we may interpret this saying to mean that God too joins in the failure of his people, that God too knew the shame and agony of Golgotha and Auschwitz, and by sharing this with his elect, God is exercising to perfection the power that is specific to God. Such a choice of "powerlessness" is in fact a choice for nonviolent, as opposed to violent or military, political power. The Scriptures present God as having used both in Israel's early history as well as in its sagas or myths. Jesus is presented as having opted exclusively for the former. If both the Scriptures and Jesus bear a reliable witness to God, then it appears that with the coming of Jesus, God changed his mind about the use of power.

By holding the cross and the gas chambers together in reflecting on the significance of the death of Jesus, we are led finally to an inclusive view of God's part in human suffering. It now seems appropriate to say that in every human being who suffers the all-too-pervasive corruption of creation—be they tortured by their fellows or killed by disease, be they murdered by chance or by intent, be they one of those whom the Jewish people and the Church believe to be of God's elect, or one of those for the sake of whom some, according to our story, have been elected—their

Creator is indissolubly incarnate. This we may say of each of them because we have learned to see it in him in whom this fundamental commitment of God has been made evident to his Church.

"In Christ God was reconciling the world to himself" (2 Cor. 5:19). God's way of slowly winning us to himself is by sharing our very life with us. This is made clear to the Church in the person of Jesus Christ, so that it may understand that God works with and in every one of his beloved creatures. Some such understanding of reality may lie behind the prayer of that student of Paul's who left us what we know as the Epistle to the Ephesians: "For this reason I bow my knees before the Father, from whom every family in heaven and earth is named, that according to the riches of his glory he may grant you to be strengthened with might through his Spirit in the inner man, and that Christ may dwell in your hearts through faith; that you, rooted and grounded in love, may have power to comprehend with all the saints what is the breadth and length and height and depth, and to know the love of Christ which surpasses knowledge, that you may be filled with all the fullness of God" (Eph. 3:14–19).

4. GOD, DEATH, AND HISTORY

i. The God of Golgotha and Auschwitz

The objection that could be raised to the line of thought here pursued is that it makes God quite superfluous, a pious relic of the tradition with no functional significance. A God whose power is exercised chiefly by a divine restraint in using power is pragmatically equivalent to a powerless God and such a God is, as far as effects in the world are concerned, indistinguishable from no God at all. The God of Golgotha and Auschwitz then turns out to be the nonentity at which Richard Rubenstein arrived (*After Auschwitz.*)

So close to the truth is this objection that it needs to be heard clearly, lest the Church fall back once more into its traditional conflation of the God of Golgotha and the Absolute. That view of God helped to "protect" God from identification with the cruci-

fied by making fine distinctions between the impassible Absolute
and the Jew dying at Roman hands. The distinction between the
Creator and the creature was indeed maintained, but the loss of
the covenantal relationship between them was the price. The Absolute ultimately cannot suffer with its "children," cannot finally
have "children," be they nailed to a cross or gassed and burned in
death camps. The Absolute cannot bind itself to a particular people and submit itself to human history, much less to Jewish history. The force of the objection lies in making clear the risk of
learning from that history a conception of God that is not compatible with the traditional Western concept of the Absolute.

The objection, however, passes too easily over a difference. Is it
really the same whether there is no God or whether there is a God
who does no more, but also no less, than to insinuate himself, so to
speak, between the Jew Jesus and that Roman cross, in order to be
co-crucified with him? Is it all the same if God is only a pious hope,
or one who steps, admittedly unseen, ahead of his children into
the gas chamber and leaps before them into the ovens? Of course
we have no proof one way or the other, yet it may be said that
there is a difference here, and the difference lies in what we take
reality to be, not just in how we feel about it. People who differ on
this live in different worlds.

Albert Einstein expressed his revulsion at the aspect of chance
in quantum mechanics by asserting that God does not play dice.
Einstein may have been guilty of confusing not only a model of
physical theory with reality (Piddard, "Scientist," 555) but also
the God of his fathers and mothers with the Absolute. The God of
Jesus on the cross and of the Jewish people in the death camps
may not play dice, but he does play the exceedingly hazardous
"game" of the covenant. A God who has decided, according to
the story of Noah, to abide by the downs as well as by the ups of
history—including the history of the covenant as well as the history of the creation for which the covenant was made, and so whose
sun rises on the evil as on the good, and whose rains falls on the
just as on the unjust—a God who has so compromised himself to
his creation, will hardly be the Absolute and so may well appear to

play dice. He may well seem, and not only in moments of crisis on the cross and in the camps, to have forsaken his beloved, but only if God is such a God is it possible to think to see his glory in the face of a crucified Jew.

God's glory then must seem more like what we generally call poverty and suffering than the splendor of an eastern potentate. Whether or not the heavens tell of this glory, God's glory as found in the crucified fills the earth in the faces and bodies of all the poor and wretched of the earth. The glory which is that of God's "only begotten," according to the community that left us the Fourth Gospel, is his as the crucified, and the hour of his glory is the hour of his death (John 17:1), and that glory is shared with his disciples in that they fill up whatever is lacking in his suffering. Some such view of God must be that of a Church that believes that God has made himself and his love known and present in the death of Christ.

ii. Death on Golgotha and at Auschwitz

"The last enemy to be destroyed is death" (1 Cor. 15:26). It was not characteristic of Paul's tradition to assign so negative a rank to death. The Scriptures, perhaps reflecting Israel's experience of the variety of human life and its closing, has no single view of death. Death is one thing when it comes to a person "full of days"; it is quite another when it takes the young. In the rabbinic tradition, death is generally seen as a normal part of created existence: Adam returns to the dust of which he was made. Sometimes death is viewed as the consequence of sin, brought into the world by Adam's sin. In the Scriptures, death is often presented as going to a place beyond human and even divine reach: the dead are cut off from Israel's communal praise of God.

For the Church from its beginning, death became redefined by the cross. It could no more be thought of as the ultimate enemy than Jesus' death could be seen as the ultimate fact about him. As the cross stood always in the light of Easter, so death could at most be the last enemy to be destroyed. Grounded as it was in Easter faith, the Church had to say that Jesus did not die in vain, but that beginning on Easter, God had used and was using him further in God's cause. Death for him, and therefore also for them, was an undeniable fact, but it was penultimate.

Was death penultimate for the many sisters and brothers of Jesus who died as Hitler's victims? It has not been revealed to the Church that they received an affirmation of the sort that the Church believed Jesus to have received on Easter. And yet the cause of the covenant, which lay behind the identity for which they died, has lived on. They are remembered, and not only by the Jewish people. In so far as the Church seeks to enter into the Jewish memory of the six million, in so far as the Church shares with Jews the determination that there shall never be another Holocaust, in so far as the Church holds most dear the Jewish State as one precious affirmation of Jewish life after so many deaths, it plays a minor part in affirming of those dead that their death is not the ultimate fact for them, that God's cause of life for his people continues.

Much of what the apostolic witness has to say about death takes it as the primary symbol of the great enemy of humanity. The symbol will no doubt continue, even among those who have learned a biology according to which death is seen to be as normal a part of the life process as is birth (which was also a good rabbinic view). The symbol, however, has always been somewhat mixed: Francis of Assisi could hail death as our "sister."

The Epistle to the Hebrews gives an interesting variation: it is not death but the fear of it that holds us in bondage (Heb. 2:15).

Death may remain for many a symbol of that which is opposed to God and God's love, but it would be contrary to Scriptural and apostolic thought as well as a serious theological mistake to make of it more than a symbol. The biblical and theological tradition implies and sometimes makes explicit the conviction that there is an enemy, one who stands opposed to God's purpose. That enemy is not given the status of a being over against or alongside of God, yet it is real and dangerous (see Karl Barth's careful treatment of what he called "Das Nichtige" in *CD*, III/3). Death and Satan may be symbols of that enemy, but they are not the enemy itself. If there is a "last enemy," it is the unnameable resistance to God's love, which as chaos resists creation and as death threatens humanity. It is that which God engaged on the cross and with which he wrestled in Auschwitz, an evil of which death is only the sign.

The cross is a place of God's engagement with evil in what certainly appears as a defeat. Easter is an ambiguous sign that evil did not finally win, that God's cause still had a future. Just this must also be said in the face of Auschwitz: the incredible and shaky birth of the Jewish State and its survival, along with every Jewish birth to this day, are ambiguous signs that the enemy has not yet won, that God's cause still has a future. The story is not over.

iii. History after Golgotha and Auschwitz

The death of Jesus was an event in history, both in the sense that it was a more or less datable occurrence in recorded time and also in that it has had consequences for human history ever since. The history and present existence of the Church is the first evidence in refutation of the absurd claim that the cross was the end of history. Indeed, the Church's most characteristic doctrine, that of the Triune God, affirms a continuity not only of Israel's story and that of Jesus but also the story of the life of the Church under the guidance of God as Spirit. The history of the Church and its doctrine of the Trinity make incoherent a claim that the cross marked the end of history.

Can it be maintained that the cross marks the middle of history? Without doubt the cross proved to be a turning point in the story that began with Abraham. The coming and going of Jesus, to use the terms of the Fourth Gospel, was a major turning point leading as it did to the inclusion of Gentiles in that story in an unprecedented manner and in unprecedented numbers. But there have been other turning points since. The parting of the ways of the Church and the Jewish people in growing hostility was one. The divisions of the Church between East and West and again in the sixteenth century should also be mentioned. And the Church's awakening to the continuing validity of the covenant between God and the Jewish people surely must count as a major turning point.

The last turning point mentioned reminds us that the history that matters most to the Church is the history into which it believes itself to have been grafted: Israel's history. That history certainly has continued with turning points more radical than, but not unrelated to, those produced by the coming and going of Jesus. Israel's history includes centuries of oppression and destruction at the hand of the Church, and its horrendous culmination in the slaughter of European Jewry at the hands of ex-Christians. More recently, Israel's history has included the amazing return to the Land and the founding and endurance of the Jewish State. When the Church considers not simply world history and not simply its own ecclesial history, but the history on which its own is built and in the context of which the coming and going of Jesus had to occur in order to have been of so great importance for it, it does not seem fitting to call the death of Jesus even the middle of history. In its proper context, the cross appears rather to be for the Church the beginning of its own existence and participation in a much older history, the end of which is clearly not yet in sight.

We may also ask about the place of the cross in God's view of history, although of course any answer can be only a human judgment. Our tentative answer is that the cross manifests God's involvement in the history of Israel in such a way as to confirm his involvement in that history from Israel's beginning, making more clear that he had entered into Israel's history for the sake of all the nations of the world. More specifically, the cross shows that that history runs without guarantees. It can include defeats and death. Even the event of Easter, showing that God's can turn defeats into new opportunities, holds no guarantees, as the Gentile Church's growing hostility and enmity to the people Israel was soon to disclose. Auschwitz too was one of the bitter fruits of the particular turning point marked by the cross.

Since the Holocaust and the birth of the Jewish State (and not unrelated to them) has come most recently the beginning of the Church's *metanoia* (turning around, repentance) and so the beginning of a reconciliation between God's Gentile Church and God's people Israel. God's Apostle to the Gentiles thought that this should have been one of the major consequences of the cross. His student who wrote the Epistle to the Ephesians thought it was the primary consequence, although his attention was only on the reconciliation taking place within the Church and did not cover the hostility developing between the Church of Jews and Gentiles, and the bulk of the Jewish people. What has begun only in the last third of the twentieth century may therefore be one of the major factors to be taken into consideration in a divine judgment as to the place of the cross in the history that began with Abraham and is not yet over.

To understand the death of Christ as a significant moment within the continuing history of God's covenantal relationship with creation excludes any understanding of the atonement as a divine transaction carried out "over our heads" without our participation. God's involvement in the death of Jesus was rather his engagement against sin and for us, calling on us to engage for God and against sin. The "transaction," in short, is still going on, and God's history with his creatures and their history with him is not over. In history, in our history now, is where God's unfinished, continuing transaction of reconciling the world to himself is happening.

CHAPTER EIGHT

The Novelty of Jesus Christ

The coming and going of Jesus Christ produced the utter novelty, within the continuing history of God's covenant, of effecting the hidden goal of God's Torah to bring the nations into the plan that began to develop with the calling of Abraham. It is hardly surprising that Israel on the whole did not see this and has not been able to see it over the centuries. Both Israel and the Church are therefore faced with the challenge of living cooperatively their unshared visions of their shared convictions.

1. THE HIDDEN GOAL OF TORAH

i. Novelty and continuity

The things concerning Jesus of Nazareth, his coming and going, have been seen by the Church from its beginning as both an utter novelty and, at the same time, also integrally continuous with their context—the history of God's covenantal purpose. "If anyone is in Christ, that one is a new creature; the old has passed away, behold, the new has come" (2 Cor. 5:17), and yet all this is "that which was from the beginning" (1 John 1:1), even from "before the foundation of the world" (Eph. 1:4). New wine had come that could not be contained in old wine skins, yet the new commandment is "no new commandment but an old commandment which you had from the beginning" (1 John 2:7). The followers of Christ are to walk "in newness of life" (Rom. 6:4), yet they are directed to the Torah with the command and promise, "Do this and you will live" (Luke 10:26–28). Novelty and continuity are both stressed.

This dual stress was not confined to the early witness; it continues in the classical creeds. The "only begotten Son of God," so the Nicene Creed runs, "came down from heaven . . . and was made man," but this Son was "begotten of his Father before all worlds" and by him "all things were made." The Church's Christology in its many forms has always had to do justice to both the discontinuity of radical novelty and also the fundamental continuity apart from which Christology would lose its bearings. Christ in context: neither side may be neglected.

The duality of novelty and continuity is presented in Colossians 1:12 in a manner well suited to open up just what was new and what continuous; here thanks is offered to the Father "who has qualified us [i.e., Gentile believers] to share in the inheritance of the saints [i.e., Israel]." The specificity of the new and the continuous is developed at length in Ephesians 1–3, especially in 2:1–5 and vv. 11–13: the novelty is the unveiling of a mystery hidden from all eyes until now, namely, that in Christ "the Gentiles are fellow heirs" of the promises to Israel (Eph. 3:6). The mystery was hidden before, but it was always there: Christ is the *telos*, the goal, of the Torah. What is continuous is Torah, God's covenant and covenantal purpose. What is new is the implementation of what God had always intended: that the Gentiles now receive a place in that purpose. The goal of Torah is the restoration of all creation.

ii. The goal of Torah

The rabbis also thought that the Torah had a goal, but their concern was its immediate goal of shaping the life of the Jewish people. Rather different was the concern of Paul and of the author of Ephesians, whose eyes were on the Church and its conformation to Christ. The goal of Torah that they had in mind might be called its ultimate or final goal. So the author of Ephesians can speak instead of God's plan or economy, of his will, and of his purpose (Eph. 1:9–10). There is a divine plan or intention behind the covenant, Torah, and the coming of Christ. The question about the covenant that preoccupied the rabbis, on the whole, was how it should be applied and obeyed. Paul and the author of Ephesians are largely responsible for having made another question central on the Church's agenda: where is the covenant going, and what is its final goal? The two questions are not mutually exclusive, but they are different.

The concept of a divine economy is susceptible to at least two different interpretations, depending on two different understandings of God. In one view, "God's plan or purpose" implies that God has foreseen all that is to take place for all time, and that he reveals his plan bit by bit, slowly educating his elect and drawing them on to discover over time what was always present to the mind of God. God, so to speak, has dealt all the cards and we find out how the game will go as we pick them up one by one. God, in this view, is understood to be unambiguously omnipotent and omniscient, having perfect foreknowledge.

There is however at least another possible interpretation, one modeled more on the concept of covenant. In this view God's intention, so to speak, is to engage us in a game in which his moves depend on ours. The course of the game is mutually determined by both partners. Our moves are made in response to God's, but then God has to decide how to move next in the light of our response. God's intention, in this view, is for the future to develop covenantally. Here, but not in the first model, it would be appropriate to speak of God being surprised or displeased by what his creatures do, and one could also say that God can grasp with pleasure new opportunities presented by human initiatives. In this view the attribution of omnipotence and omniscience to God will be quite ambiguous, since God's power is exercised so as always to leave room for human initiative, and God does not appear to know in advance the choices of his creatures.

Although the overwhelming weight of the theological tradition lies on the side of the first model, I find the second to be more in tune with the covenantal context and language of the Scriptures. It is certainly possible to interpret the language of the Scriptures to fit the requirements of the first model, but the second model can do as well or better.

My choice is partly influenced by the feminist hermeneutic of Elisabeth Schüssler Fiorenza (*Memory*). In the first view, God is more dominant and, in the modern sense, "goal-oriented"; in the second, God is more committed to process and to give-and-take persuasion.

The merit of the covenantal model for thinking of the divine economy or purpose is that it makes it possible to see the response of so many Gentiles to the preaching of the Jewish apostles and Paul's own creative interpretation of his calling as providing opportunities, not all planned in advance, for God to bless and encourage with his Spirit a movement that could serve the cause of the restoration of God's creation, understood as God's underlying but unspecified intention all along. Certainly Paul was convinced that the promise to Abraham already included within it the opening to the Gentiles to which he was devoted, but who is to say to what extent that was already in the text he read and to what extent it was Paul's creative reading of that text? The mystery hidden from the beginning and now revealed could also be called the discovery of a new reading of Israel's Scriptures. To call it a newly revealed and hitherto hidden mystery is to assert one's conviction that it is truly pleasing to God. The possibility that it was a pleasant surprise for God was hardly in the mind of the author of Ephesians, but in a covenantal model of God's relationship to those whom he has called as his co-workers for the sake of his creation, this too may be allowed. The goal of Torah may be one that calls for human contributions before it can be specified. In which case, Paul's assertion that "Christ is the goal of the Torah" should be read to mean that in Christ fresh new steps were made toward the ultimate purpose of bringing the world into God's service.

iii. A living covenant

"If anyone is in Christ, that one is a new creature" (2 Cor. 5:17). This radically new creation, the Church, is the novelty that came from the things concerning Jesus of Nazareth. One has only to look at the Church's Bible to see what was new: there, bound together with Israel's Scriptures, is "The New Testament," a new additional step in the strange history of God's covenant with Israel. In the coming and going of Jesus, there began, first within Israel then increasingly alongside of and outside Israel, a community drawn from the nations of the world that served the God of the covenant. From the perspective of the covenant, this was a new occurrence that was seen by some (the majority of Jews) as an aberration, and by others (the Jewish apostles and disciples of Jesus, together with other Jews who joined them) as a promised development. From the perspective of the Gentiles who joined the new community and increasingly made up its membership, it was a transformation from darkness into light, from death to life. They had been as though born again. They became alive to the God of the covenant and the covenant had now become living for them. For them it was indeed a new covenant.

This covenant, however, was seen to be none other than the one covenant of the One God, the old covenant renewed as it had been again and again, but this time renewed in such a way as to make it possible for Gentiles to serve the God of Israel as Gentiles. This renewal of the covenant proved once more that God's ancient covenant—from Creation, through Abraham and Moses—was a living covenant, ever alive and changing, ever open to new possibilities. The tragedy in this renewal was that neither the Church nor Israel was able to see that the range of those possibilities could cover both the development of the oral Torah and rabbinic Judaism, and the apostolic and patristic Church. And neither side even entertained the thought of other possibilities outside of both communities.

Both Church and synagogue knew the reality of a living covenant, but they knew it only in part. What was lacking on both sides was sufficient attention to the grammar of that which they knew. Consider first the noun: covenant. That means that God has committed God's own future into human hands, that the course of history is determined in part by human action. So it must be if "the word is very near you", if "it is in your mouth and in your heart, so that you can do it" (Deut. 30:14), as Israel believes. And so it must be, if "the word became flesh and dwelt among us" (John 1:14), as the Church believes. Covenant means that all creation is caught up in one interconnected and interactive dynamic between God and God's creatures.

Next, the adjective: living. This covenant is alive. To live is to change. To live is to grow. A living covenant cannot possibly be today exactly what it was yesterday. A living covenant means new possibilities, new responses to new challenges, and new surprises for both parties. It is a love affair that grows and changes, or else it dies. So the Church and Israel have been constantly changing, all the while pretending and insisting that they were always just what they had been before.

On this see Montifiore's introductory essay in Montifiore and Loewe, *A Rabbinic Anthology* and Wilkin's excellent study, *The Myth of Christian Beginnings.* The myth of an unchanging orthodoxy appears to be a common feature of both traditions. Indeed, it may be endemic to any community that claims to have a tradition. The fact of a community's survival and therefore of having a tradition, however, points to its vitality and so to the fact of its constant change and adaptation to new challenges and opportunities.

Finally, the article. "A covenant" refers to something specific, particular, and perhaps quite distinct, but not to all that is. There may be other covenants, or there may be other ways in which covenantal existence can be realized. A living covenant depends for its life only on the vitality of the relationship between the partners, and this is in no way affected by other relationships that the one Creator may have with other parts of creation. The Church especially has been slow to come to this realization, and for most of their history, neither the Church nor the Jewish people was able to see the other as living evidence of the fact that covenantal relationships other than the one each knew firsthand were possible and actual. The Church believed itself to have displaced Israel as the sole covenantal partner of the God of Israel, and Israel could not conceive of any form of the covenant other than the one it knew and lived.

2. WHY ISRAEL DID NOT SEE IT

i. *Those who did see it*

Before we consider the larger part of Israel that did not see, we should remember the smaller part of Israel that did see, for apart from them there would have been no Gentile Church. As we have pointed out (van Buren, *Discerning*, 84; *People Israel*, 81), "he came to his own" and enough of his own received him in order to make possible the Church of Jesus Christ. But we must first reflect on what it was that some saw and others did not see. Was it the messiahship of Jesus, or the incarnate Word? One could put it this way, yet that is to focus on titles which themselves only function within another context. The matter that was at stake, as events proved, was a strange renewal of the covenant. It began with the mission of John the Baptist calling Israel to repentance. It centered in the mission of Jesus as the prophet of Israel's restoration. It took its definitive course from the response of Gentile God-fearers and Paul's calling to preach Christ to the Gentiles. Taken in its totality, what there was to see or not see was a turn in the course of the living covenant such that Gentiles were now to have a place in it as Gentiles, alongside of, not within, Israel.

Because a turn in the history of Israel's covenant was the issue, it is evident that only Israel could have seen it. Only from within that history could one notice a turn in a new direction. Gentiles would not have had even the vocabulary with which to describe such a turn; even Luke's Ethiopian eunuch (Acts 8:26–39) and his Roman centurian Cornelius (Acts 10), who had learned already from Israel to speak of the covenant, can only ask questions. So indeed it was Jews who first described the new turn. Of these Paul has left us the fullest expression, but he was not the first. Peter, according to Acts, was the first to see it and then only with great hesitation.

In the ninth chapter of his letter to the Romans, Paul wrote of his "great sorrow and unceasing anguish" over the fact that most of his fellow Jews did not seem able to accept the new stage of the covenant which he had been called to further, namely, that in his day that which God had spoken through Hosea was happening: "Those who were not my people I will call 'my people' " (Rom. 9:25, citing Hosea 2:23), and he points to himself as an example of the remnant (Rom. 11:1) who carry out on its behalf the calling of Israel to recognize that the time had come when the Gentiles too were to be drawn into God's covenantal purpose. Thus the covenant was renewed to include Gentiles in the form we have come to know as the Church, because some of Israel saw and acknowledged the novelty of what God began in Jesus Christ. This having been seen, we can then turn to consider the other side, the vast majority of Israel that could not, or at least did not, see this novelty in the history of God's covenant.

ii. Israel's nonanticipatory zeal

Paul granted to his fellow Jews that they were zealous in their service of the Torah of the covenant (Rom. 10:2, 9:31), but in their very zeal they did not anticipate (*ephthase*, Rom. 9:31) what Paul was sure was already there in the Torah: God's promise to gather the Gentiles, the nations of the world, into his covenantal purpose. In his faithfulness, Christ had become God's righteousness for all who trusted in him and so the goal of the Torah. This is what some Jews saw and what most Jews did not see.

It should be said that, after all, it really was not all that obvious. It was certainly possible to read Israel's Scriptures as pointing to this new turn of events, and so from the beginning the Church has read them. But Israel's Scriptures were written from within and focus surely on the covenant between God and Israel, with little attention paid to how God relates to the other nations of the world. The nations are there—usually in the background, usually the enemy, and, if subject to the one God of Israel, not generally seen as having any positive relationship to God. Israel's Scriptures can certainly be read as saying very little positive about the Gentiles, and so on the whole has Israel read them.

From the perspective of Judaism of the first century of the Common Era, and especially of the Pharisees who were giving the lead to what was to become the course for the Jewish people for centuries afterward, Israel's overriding responsibility under the difficulties of Roman dominion was to become more exactly obedient to the covenant made with God. Israel was to become a more thoroughly holy people, a people set apart. Precisely those regulations of the Torah that marked the distinctiveness of the Jewish people—Sabbath observance, circumcision, and the rules governing foods and eating—were the ones to be developed in greater detail, as defenses against the temptations to assimilation in the sea of Hellenism. From this perspective, a movement leading Jews to find their identity in the closest fellowship with Gentiles must have seemed an invitation to betrayal of the covenant itself, if not national suicide. It should be remembered that they were reading their Scriptures in the light of their experience since the Babylonian Exile, not as Gentiles who had discovered Deutero-Isaiah for the first time. For them, the Prophets were commentary on Torah, not the reverse. The new reading of the Scriptures that put the Prophets in first place must have seemed arbitrary and contrary to tradition. Surely Moses was the greatest of all the prophets. The zeal of the Pharisees and their followers was for what had been Israel's all along: the Torah of God given at Sinai by the hand of Moses, both in its written form and in the oral traditions, said to have been passed on from generation to generation and also going back to Sinai.

That most Jews found the Christian movement bizarre if not downright apostasy, therefore, is hardly surprising. Much more in need of explanation was the faith of those Jews who saw the hand of the God of Israel in this new movement. They were indeed "anticipating," "going before," Moses: they were finding in Torah things that opposed the very traditions handed down from Moses. Maybe the Christians called it anticipation; for most Jews, it must have looked more like a radical departure from Israel's covenant.

iii. The "hardening"

In his speculative interpretation of what was happening in his own day, Paul suggested that "a hardening has come upon part of Israel, until the full number of the Gentiles come in [to the renewed covenant], and so [thus] all Israel will be saved" just as it was promised through Isaiah and Jeremiah (Rom. 11:25–27). In line with his argument in chapter 10, Paul saw the events of which he was a part as all having God as the prime agent. Thus the resistance of the majority of Israel to Paul's gospel of Gentile inclusion is presented as God's hardening of their hearts or wills. Their decision was of course their own, yet behind it lay the decision of God in furtherance of the covenant. First let the Gentiles be drawn in, and then God would come to redeem his whole creation, Israel in its totality first of all.

Whether God had so planned things in advance, or whether God's will was to make the most of human decisions, it is worth reflecting on the divine options concerning which Paul had his own ideas. How, after all, was the experiment to be carried out? For it was a radically new experiment to open the covenant to those not schooled in Israel's history and to invite them in as Gentiles. Their path was also new, to be walked in conformity to Christ, without the controls of the written and oral Torah. If all Israel had accepted them, it could have done so either by incorporating them into Israel on Israel's terms of the covenant, in full conformity with the Torah, or else by joining them under their new terms and so abandoning the commandments especially given to Israel. The first option would have retained the *status quo* prior to Christ: Gentiles could always become Israelites by conversion and circumcision. The first option would allow the Gentiles to come in, but not as Gentiles. They would have to have become Jews, thus defeating the experiment.

The second option would have opened Israel to all the trials and temptations of Gentile Hellenistic ways. Had all Israel accepted this new stage of the covenant, could Israel have survived as Israel? Would it not have lost its anchor in God's holy Torah and so ceased to be God's holy people, distinguished from all the nations of the earth? The very covenant that was to be renewed to include the Gentiles would have been in serious jeopardy.

There was, however, a third option: let Israel remain Israel, faithful to God's original covenant and loyal to Torah, but let a remnant of Israel, a small part acting on behalf of all, take the risky step of apostasy to welcome the Gentiles as Gentiles into a new life of this new stage of the covenant. In this new gathering, the distinction between Jew and Gentiles would have no place, so it was important that most of Israel hold on in the path of Torah already being worked out before this new experiment was started, so that the young Church might never be without the faithfulness of Israel as a reminder of the rock from which it had been hewn, the root onto which it had been grafted. In this way, the Gentiles might indeed be taken into the covenant as Gentiles, and Israel continue in the covenant as before, both in the united service and praise of the Creator of the heavens and the earth.

Something like the third option (although in a radically eschatological framework that I have not used) seems to have appealed to Paul. It may even have been God's choice, for if it seems less than ideal and had its dangers, it should be recalled that all options were covenantally conditioned. The God of the covenant had to allow room for the choices of the covenantal partners. As we heard from the later witness of the Talmud (p. 172 above), God lets his Torah be what the majority decide, and this confirms the saying attributed to Jesus, that it will be in heaven as his disciples decide on earth (Matt. 16:19, 18:18, John 20:23). So the young Church continued in this covenantal pattern of thought in reaching decisions cooperatively with the Holy Spirit (Acts 15:28). On this point, the witness to God, to Christ, and to the Holy Spirit is all one.

iv. God's novelty and God's continuity

Israel on the whole did not see what a remnant of Israel saw. Therein stands a witness, absolutely fundamental for the Church, to a sort of duality in God and what God accomplished in Christ and continues in the Spirit: God's act in Christ is novel precisely in the context of God's continuity. We might think of novelty and continuity in God dialectically, so long as (with Franz Rosenzweig and against Hegel) we insist that the two are never resolved into a third, that novelty and continuity are features of God's action in continuing tension, since both together, but neither alone, are the essential features of God's covenantal reality.

God's covenantal self-determination guarantees continuity in God and all his works: God has committed himself eternally to be what he is in his covenant with Israel for the sake of all creation. But because this self-determination is covenantal, room is also guaranteed for the original contribution of God's covenantal partner and so of God's openness to novelty in response. Since, covenantally conceived, God cannot know ahead of time what his partners are going to do, he also cannot know how he will respond in order to make the most of the opportunities presented by their new actions. When in the light of human action God does a new thing however, one who trusts in God's fidelity will always try to see it as a new step toward the goal of the good for all creation to which God has committed himself.

The Church has formulated this duality of continuity and novelty in God primarily in its doctrine of the Trinity, in which it confesses the one God (continuity) in all the diversity of God's work as Father, Son, and Spirit (novelty). Tri-theism, thinking of Christianity as a new religion, and talk of a second covenant would all be examples of a denial of God's continuity, whereas Unitarianism and speaking of Christianity as "Judaism for the Gentiles" would deny God's capacity for novelty. The doctrine of the Triune God is thus fundamental for the Church's understanding of God's covenantal self-determination.

The consequence of these reflections is that the question of the novelty of Christ takes us to the very center of the Church's understanding of God. When God's continuity and openness to novelty is reviewed in the light of the doctrine of the Trinity, God's covenantal self-determination, as this works its way out in the things concerning Jesus of Nazareth and the opening of the covenant to the Gentiles, implies that God has become pluralistically the God of Israel and also the God of the Church. And if the God of Israel and the Church, then why not also the God of all his creatures? God's continuity may be able to contain far more novelty than either Israel or the Church have dared to imagine.

3. WHY ISRAEL CANNOT SEE IT

i. The blindness of Israel and the Church

Israel on the whole not only did not, but to this day still does not, see that something new has taken place precisely in the history of the covenant between God and Israel. That is largely because the Church did and does not see it either. Israel did not see and does not see that the coming and going of Jesus, that Jesus himself, and then the community arising in his name, were events within its own history with God and God's history with Israel. The Church did not see, and only in our time is perhaps beginning to see, that the novelty of Christ and then of his Church was and is a part of the continuity of Israel's life and covenant with God, and that its own life is to be lived cooperatively alongside Israel.

At rare moments and by rare individuals, at least some of this was understood. Calvin was one who saw the continuity of the covenant as well as the novelty of its renewal with the coming of Christ (*Institutes*, I, XII, xxx), but he ignored almost totally the continuity of Israel alongside the Church. Karl Barth went a huge step further in seeing continuing Israel and the Church as two parts of a single but divided people of God (*CD*, II/2, 195–305), but he clearly considered the division a sin to be overcome only by Israel joining the Church in its confession of the novelty of Christ. The exceptions only highlight the general pattern: the Church has been as blind as Israel to the real novelty of Christ, which is a novelty precisely in the continuity of God and his covenant with Israel.

One might almost say that the Church has been more blind than Israel, for the exceptions on the Jewish side are more evident. Maimonides was sure that the church had made a terrible mistake, but he did allow that its function in the divine purpose was in the ultimate service of the covenant. Judah Halevi and especially Rabbi Jacob Emden (see Falk, *Pharisee,* for Emden's irenic letter on Christianity to the Jewish Council in Poland in the 1750s) could also be mentioned. From a Jewish perspective, the continuity of the covenant would of course be the starting place for making sense of anything, and the novelty of the Christian movement had always been maintained. The exceptional position was to see any positive connection between the two. Outstanding in this regard was Franz Rosenzweig who, almost half a century before any Christian thinker followed his move, found his own way to see the Church and the Jewish people called to mutually supportive if distinctively different patterns of life in a cooperative service of the one God. When one compares the exceptions on the two sides, one must wonder that the Church has talked so much of Israel's blindness and so little of its own.

The accusation of blindness, it should be admitted, is made here from the perspective of the Jewish-Christian reality, from the awareness and appreciation of the continuing place of the two different realities within the one reality of God's covenantal self-determination. It is a disputed point as to whether the Jewish Apostle to the Gentiles held such a perspective, for we are today caught in what may be a "paradigm shift" in the interpretation of Paul (Gager, *Origins,* 198). What cannot be disputed is the blindness of the Church to the continuity of God's covenant with Israel in the context of which alone the novelty of Jesus Christ is anything other than an arbitrary event. Jesus Christ made for something radically new within the continuing covenant between God and the Jewish people. That is what the Jewish people and also the Church of Christ failed for so long to see.

ii. The Church as Israel's blinders
Israel has remained blind to the covenantal novelty of what began with Jesus Christ primarily because of the Church. Jesus was not the only Jew to have taught that a tree may be judged by its fruit or a teacher by his disciples. If the fruits brought forth, or what the disciples claimed to be true teaching, be looked at from

Israel's point of view, it is hardly surprising that the Jewish people have felt that whatever novelty there might have been in Jesus of Nazareth, it was bad news for Israel and a danger to the survival of the covenant. The Church in its teaching and behavior guaranteed that Jews would not see a radical new move in God's covenantal history in the things concerning Jesus of Nazareth.

The Church appears to have begun its obscuring course from at least as early as the time of the destruction of the Temple in 70 C.E. The rabbis interpreted that disaster as a punishment of Israel for their many failures of not living according to God's commandments, as a chastisement of the Jewish people—that is, within the framework of the covenant. The loss of the Temple therefore pointed to the renewal of the covenant. The Church, on the other hand, taught that it marked the end of the covenant between God and Israel, a sign that Israel's life in the covenant had come to a close, to be replaced by the life of the Church (Matt. 22:1–10). It appropriated Israel's Scriptures as its own and claimed as its own Israel's calling to be a royal priesthood and a holy nation (1 Pet. 2:9), and soon began to say that it was the true Israel (Justin Martyr, *Dialogue*, 123, and especially 135). It built anti-Judaism into the foundation of its theology (Tertullian) and set an anti-Judaic course that lasted into the twentieth century, all in the name of God's novelty in Jesus Christ. No wonder the Jewish people have not been able to see it!

The Church has hidden the novelty of Christ from Jewish eyes behind the novelty of its own self, presented as "a new religion," ignoring completely the judgment of Israel's Scriptures on all "religions," new or old. It even presented itself in terms utterly foreign to covenantal eyes and ears, as neither Jew nor Gentile, but a "third race." In a word, it lost sight of the continuity in which alone the radical novelty of Christ could be seen, ignoring or denying the continuity of the covenant between God and Israel that was and remains his context. Christ out of context is a meaningless Christ, and certainly one to whom the ascription of novelty makes no sense. But that is the Christ that the Church presented. The wonder is not that Jews have remained blind to this monstrosity; the wonder is that the Church has survived with it.

iii. And now?

Nostra Aetate, the fourth paragraph of which is rightly seen as the first step since the first century toward a positive Church teaching about Jews and Judaism, is nevertheless a most limited document. In the light of the Jewish-Christian reality, it is notable for what it failed to say. The failure of the Church for nineteen centuries to acknowledge the eternal covenant between God and the Jewish people is not so much as hinted at. The failure of the Church to acknowledge that the Scriptures are and continue to be Israel's first of all is not acknowledged. Antisemitism is denounced as though it had not been the Church itself that taught the Western world contempt for the Jewish people. Seen against the historical record of the Church, *Nostra Aetate* is all-too-typically ecclesiastically self-serving and self-justifying. It surely represents a new step for the Church, but it also reflects faithfully the pride that has characterized the Church's relations with the Jewish people. Repentance toward those from whom they learned it comes hard to Gentiles.

Since *Nostra Aetate*, however, there is no question that a fair number of Christians have come to acknowledge the Jewish as well as the Christian reality, and so to recognize what I have argued is the context of Jesus Christ. At the same time, a few Jews have begun to rethink the calling of the Church in a more positive light. Whether Israel in larger numbers comes to see the novelty in continuity for which we are arguing will depend largely on whether the Church comes to see it, whether the Church ceases to obstruct the vision of the Jewish people.

But in the last analysis, it may not matter whether Israel on the whole comes to see it. The cooperation and mutual support of the Church and the Jewish people in the service of God still may sound to Jews, in any way in which the Church could present it, too much like uniformity. It should be recalled that the Church has not found a way to speak of union without uniformity even among the divided churches. It appears that God is far better able to deal with diversity and plurality than is the Church. So it may not matter that much to God that the Church and the Jewish people are and behave so differently. Paul may have been wise to leave to God (Rom. 11:33–35 as an answer to vv. 28–32?) any final vision of the harmony of novelty and continuity, as they are represented in the Church and the Jewish people.

4. LIVING UNSHARED VISIONS

i. *In the meantime* . . . .

Since we live and are responsible to God in the here and now, not in the *eschaton*, the Church, as it is continually reminded by the life of the Jewish people, has no choice but to respond to the novelty of Christ in the context of his continuity. That is, after all, the way in which he is before God and for the Church. In its rejection of the Church and its faith in Christ, the Jewish people offer for eyes to see a witness on just this point, of much value to the Church, that is both negative and positive. Its negative witness is to Christ's novelty: the Jewish rejection says that Jesus Christ is something new and different. What has happened with his coming and going is not simply part of Israel's story. He has caused a break in the history of the covenant. Its positive witness, on the other hand, is to the continuity of the covenantal context of Christ. It reminds the Church that Jesus was a Jew, one of Israel, faithful to the covenant and understandable only in that context. Thus, regardless of Jewish interpretations of Jesus and his Church, the Jewish people by their continuing existence are of inestimable value in keeping the Church clear about the things concerning Jesus of Nazareth. They help the Church precisely in its Christology.

The Church and the Jewish people may share important aspects of a common goal in an eventual reign of God's peace and justice on earth, but they do not share a common vision either of that goal or of the way to it. Israel's vision centers in Israel's restoration; the Church's eye is on the figure of Christ. Israel's vision of the way to that goal turns around its own faithfulness to the commandments; the Church sees trust in Christ as the way. These are major differences with which both the Church and the Jewish people have to live in the here and now.

Because the novelty of Christ is inseparable from his identity in the continuity of the covenant, the Church has no choice but to live with the Jewish people in the here and now, not simply in the sense that both are given entities having no choice but to inhabit the same earth, but in the sense of living with eyes open to the other, conscious of the other, having to take the other into account precisely in order to make sense to itself of that which God has done for the Church in Jesus Christ. It has to live with the Jewish people for the sake of its own Christology. And that means that the Church has to live with the Jewish people while accepting all the differences that exist between them. It has to learn to live with those differences.

What makes this task difficult as well as important is the fact that the major differences between them show up in their radically different interpretations of just those matters that unite them, and none is more crucial than in their understandings of Jesus of Nazareth. Both see him as a novelty in continuity, but for Jews, the novelty consists precisely in the Church's claims about him that seem to them to constitute a violation of the continuity. Jews hear the confession of Jesus as Son of God as a violation of the covenantal reality of one God in relation to human partners. The Church sees in him a novelty within continuity, but traditional Christology absorbs the continuity of the covenant into the figure of Christ so that the role of Israel no longer has any continuing significance.

It is essential to see that the task of the Church's Christology is not to make it appealing to Jews. A Christology for the Jewish-Christian reality is not a Christology so formulated by the Church that Jews might come to accept it or at least find it permissible for the Church. On the contrary, a Christology for the Jewish-Christian reality will be a Christology for a Church that acknowledges that the reality in which it lives is rightly definable only when Israel's continuing covenant with God is recognized and confessed as essential to it. It will be a Christology that the Church believes to be the truth concerning Jesus of Nazareth. Nevertheless, the Church has to come to terms with the fact that the Jewish people also claim to speak the truth when they speak so differently of the things concerning Jesus of Nazareth. The issue appears to be one of conflicting truth-claims.

ii. Whether truth is one

The Church and the Jewish people both claim to speak the truth, but what they say about the things concerning Jesus of Nazareth do not agree. Can two who do not agree both be speaking the truth? The answer is not simple and depends on the context and so the manner of putting the question. The addition of two plus two, for sure, does not allow of different answers both being true. There, at least, truth is one. But what may appear as conflicting claims about God and his involvement in the things concerning Jesus of Nazareth is more complex. Appearing as claims, what believers say are also confessions and so partly expressions of convictions and commitments. Wittgenstein once remarked that religious people never seem to think that they are affirming exactly what the unbeliever denies (*Lectures*, 55). To say that they disagree on any subject, then, is in large part only to say that they are what they are, believers and unbelievers, or in our case Jews and Christians. Speaking the truth for each of them is part of their fidelity to the path on which they understand themselves to be traveling. It would not be the truth for them to be in full agreement on matters that mark the difference between the two.

At a trial by jury, each witness is asked to tell the truth, even "the whole truth." But of course, no witness can tell the whole truth; that is the jury's special responsibility to determine. What each witness can and should do is to tell as faithfully and accurately as possible what one saw or heard. That same fidelity is of concern to Jews and Christians, for steadfastness and loyalty are part of the meaning of "truth" in the Scriptures, and, often coupled with mercy (Ps. 25:10, 86:15, 89:14, etc.), it is one of the attributes ascribed to God. Before God, that is to say in confessional fidelity to the path which God is believed to have shown them, Christians and Jews speak the truth in disagreement. Truth may be one, as God is one, but the Church and the Jewish people stand in—have been called to—different relationships to the one God. "Conflicting truth-claims" is an expression that does not do justice to the different callings by which they understand themselves to have their identities. In their differing witnesses to the continuity and the novelty in God's character and work, they present together what may be the whole truth for a Church that acknowledges the Jewish-Christian reality.

iii. Radical continuity in the present

In a variety of ways, the Apostolic Writings bear witness to the radical continuity of God's actions, from Creation through the coming and going of Jesus Christ. One of the earliest, apparently, if not one of the most successful ways of doing this was the use of the title Messiah. Jesus was said to be the Messiah of Israel, the long foretold and promised rescuer of his people. By this title, Jesus was placed in the direct line of Israel's history, and all of Israel's history was seen as leading up to him. That certainly stresses the continuity, but it does so at the price of having then to redefine not only the role of the Messiah but also Israel's hope and God's promises to his people. As it turned out, Jesus did not "restore the kingdom to Israel" (Acts 1:6), possibly the decisive messianic task. In proclaiming Jesus as the fulfillment of God's promises to Israel, the Church had to fill those promises full of new meanings, which meant emptying them of the meanings they had and continue to this day to have for Israel. The early Church's use of the title Messiah was thus a less than successful means of expressing the continuity between Jesus and Israel, since it also contradicted it.

An extension of this self-contradictory attempt to secure the continuity of Jesus with God's history with Israel may be seen in the doctrine of the *muneri Christi,* the three "offices of Christ," developed especially in the Reformed tradition of the Church. Christ fulfills by taking up perfectly the three offices of prophet, priest, and king (which, in reverse order, became the organizing themes of Barth's christology in *CD*, IV/1, 2, and 3). Forgotten or overshadowed was the fact that the so-called offices were institutions within and for Israel. The roles or offices were those of *Israel's* prophets, who addressed themselves to *Israel*, calling it back to covenantal fidelity, priests of *Israel's* worship in the Temple of the God of *Israel*, and *Israel's* kings who ruled this particular people in its covenantal life with God. However Jesus' continuity with his people is to be defined, these roles were clearly not the ones which he exercised in historical fact. They could be taken over by the Church only when emptied of their specific content in their original setting in Israel's life and history.

Paul found a better way of defining the continuity between Jesus and Israel. His claim was that Christ (already for Paul primarily a proper name, not a title) "became a servant of the Jewish people [perhaps, the covenant—literally: 'circumcision'], to show [or in the cause of] God's truth [or fidelity], in order to confirm [not fulfill!] the promises given to the patriarchs, and so that the Gentiles might glorify God for his mercy" (Rom. 15:8–9). That is not only a less problematic but a far stronger way than the earlier use of the messianic title, preserved for us in the Gospels, of stressing the radical continuity of God's history with Israel, Christ, and the Church. It is stronger because it secures the continuity triply: Christ himself was in the service of his own people as a faithful Jew; God's fidelity or steadfastness is thereby served and shown to be served; and this happened in order to confirm God's promises of old. On top of this, even the Gentiles are drawn into this continuity, glorifying God because there is now made available to them precisely the mercy which God continues to show to Israel.

Whether Paul's definition receives a better confirmation from history than the messianic claim is a question that confronts the Church in the late twentieth century. New scholarship seems increasingly to support the probability of the thesis that Jesus did indeed mean to serve his people, and the Church today is coming increasingly to recognize God's continuing fidelity to the Jewish

people. The Church may even come to see that Paul's theme of
Jesus as the confirmation of God's promises to Israel is to be preferred to the Evangelists' theme of fulfillment (see van Buren,
People Israel, 28–30 for a discussion of this issue). In so far as the
Church moves in this direction, it underscores the radical continuity even to our own day in the context of which alone the radical novelty of Christ may be appreciated fully.

iv. Radical novelty in the present

The question about the novelty of Christ is usually put in the
past tense: what was different about him, what change took place
with his coming and going? Asking the question in that way corresponds to speaking of the resurrection as an event in the past and
asking what "really happened." Questions about the past certainly have their rightful place, but they will not be in first place for a
living Church. In first place will always be Christ present. What
was new about Christ in the past is what is new about him today or
the Church's faith is vain. That is not a so-called "existentialist"
retreat from history. History matters and may not be ignored or
reduced to present concerns, but history, as far as the Church's
life and faith is concerned, needs to start from today as a part of
that history. Living faith will begin in the present, as we have argued, look to the future, and then retell the past. So it will be with
the novelty of Christ.

The novelty of Christ, first of all then, is the novelty to be seen
in our own time, and that is the novelty discernible from time to
time in the Church, a novelty truly to be seen with eyes of faith.

Karl Barth once remarked (in a seminar on the Nicene Creed) that the
hardest words of the creeds to recite with conviction were the confession,
made with eyes open on oneself and the other members of the congregation about one, "I believe one holy catholic and apostolic church." Dare
I believe this of myself and of my fellow members of this congregation?
Are we all there is to be seen of the coming and presence of Christ?

The novelty of the Church is hard to see because the Church
too readily takes itself for granted. But is it really so self-evident

that Gentiles around the world in vast numbers should worship the God of the tiny Jewish people? Is it really to be passed off without wonder that so-called "Jewish values," the great themes of peace, justice, mercy, and forgiveness, which the Church learned from Israel, are at least honored by hundreds of millions of Gentiles in all lands? Whose novelty is this if not Christ's? "All things [including all of Israel's things] are yours and [= because] you are Christ's and [= because] Christ is God's" (1 Cor. 3:21–22).

The radical novelty of Christ in the present that is most evident for the Church, however, is found from time to time in the attractive power of individual persons whose lives have been conformed to Christ. Christians call them saints, but one hesitates to name examples lest it be forgotten that all in the Church have been called to sainthood or holiness, and what we see especially striking in individual cases are only what to a lesser degree is at work in the whole Church. Nevertheless, it is a fact of Christian experience that we see love, or mercy, or justice, or forgiveness in particular lives, and when we see it, we know it and are deeply attracted by it. When this happens, and it is not all that rare, we have run into the radical novelty of Christ in the present, transforming selfish and self-centered lives into something a bit nearer God's purposes for his creatures.

Perhaps even more striking are the cases when we run into the fruits of the novelty of Christ not in individuals so much as in situations, in social patterns or in economic or political institutions. When God's justice and mercy begin in however limited a measure to appear in social and economic structures, when political or judicial powers exercise any degree of forgiveness, there can be seen a novelty in this world that is radically beyond what we usually find to be the case. There is to be seen the novelty that is Christ's. Not unfailingly, but in enough cases to support the Church's faith, the marks of Christ may be detected as the source of such situations.

The novelty to which I am referring may be traced to Christ. It may also be traced to other sources: to Judaism, for example, or even to pagan humanism. Yet I would contend that there is a novelty that comes from Christ that is not that of Judaism and not that of humanism. There is a novelty in human life, in human behavior and human institutions, that bears the marks of the cross and of Easter, of the parables of the penitent tax collector or the Good Samaritan, that bears the stamp of Jesus Christ peculiarly. Such novelty recalls the figure of Christ to the Church: specifically him, and not the good life and witness of his people nor the many respectable features of pagan humanism. His coming into the world brought something new that the church has usually been able to recognize and sometimes to embody. That novelty occurs precisely in the context of continuity. It was and is a new way in which the eternal God was and is with and for his creatures. The Church's characteristic confession of this fact takes the form of confessing Jesus Christ as the eternal Son of the Father.

CHAPTER NINE

The Eternal Son

The apostolic witness to the life, death, and resurrection of Jesus Christ presents God as behind these events, as well as acting in them, to confirm his covenant purpose. This tension between God's entering into and standing above and behind human history was reflected in the Arian controversy over the Church's confession of Jesus Christ as the eternal Son of God: Was the Creator's engagement in creation's troubled course really God's involvement (the pro-Nicene concern)? Was God really involved (the Arian concern)? A Christology for the Jewish-Christian reality needs to make clear that at stake is a claim about God's covenantal self-determination, which is at the same time a claim about the seriousness with which God takes the course of the covenant in human history.

1. THE TENSION IN THE WITNESS

i. God in the events

The witness of the various Apostolic Writings shares with the witness of Israel's Scriptures a tension in the way in which God is believed to live his history with his creation. On the one hand, God is spoken of as the direct agent of events, as in the creation stories of Genesis 1 and 2; on the other, he is the indirect agent who causes a wind to part the sea (Exod. 14:21). Already the stories of God's indirect agency, however, tend toward another narrative pattern in which God's will stands behind events as their ultimate cause, but the events unfold as if entirely the result of the intentions of human agents, as is evident in the narratives of the arrest, trial, and crucifixion of Jesus. Yet the two patterns are so interlaced and overlapping that it is seldom that one appears in isolation from the other. Nevertheless the two patterns, apparently mutually exclusive, have been noted (Frei, *Identity;* Root, "Dying" in *Christology and Exegesis,* 155-69) and we take them as clues to understanding the witness to Jesus as the eternal Son of God.

The Apostolic Writings nowhere clearly call Jesus God, yet it can be said that the story of Jesus is told as the story of God. His coming is God's visitation to and redemption of his people (Luke 1:67). His cures are effected by "the finger of God" as evidence that God's reign is breaking in (Luke 11:20). He does what only God has the power and right to do (Mark 2:5–12; Matt. 9:2–8; Luke 5:18–26). His deeds are the deeds of God, his words are the words of God. Only John 1:14 makes explicit the claim that this man is himself the creative and saving Word of God, but John's "the word became flesh" is not so far removed from other writings that together provide a basis for seeing a broad pattern in which God is presented as at work in Jesus. We could say that one aspect of the witness to Jesus reflects a conviction that God was present in his deeds, words, and life. His story is told with the conviction that when confronted by him, the disciples were confronted by God.

The one step beyond this comes in the confession of Thomas upon being challenged by the risen Christ: "My Lord and my God" (John 20:28), yet immediately following this story comes the summary statement (v. 30) that these things were written in order that the reader might believe that Jesus is the Son of God, echoing the conclusion of the Prologue that Jesus is "the only Son" who has made God known (John 1:18). For the author and the community that produced the Fourth Gospel, as for the individuals and communities that preserved other witnesses to Jesus, he is the Son of God. But if the Son is not the Father, he who has seen the Son has seen the Father (John 14:9), for the Son is "in" the Father and the Father is "in" the Son (John 14:10–11). In short, God himself is present in this man; the Son of God is God's way of being present in the event of Jesus Christ.

With a reserve perhaps reflecting a fear of calling any creature God, the apostolic witness and the Church following it confesses Jesus as the Son of God as a way of acknowledging that God, always the Creator of his creatures, was and is present in this man, acting for the furtherance of his covenantal purpose for his creation. In Jesus Christ the covenantal God has come all the way into the creaturely situation of his covenant partners. There is something of continuity in this, but it is certainly also a novelty. After this, the covenant will no longer be quite the same, for God or for Israel.

ii. God behind the events

The apostolic witness to Jesus Christ as the Son of God has another side to it. It also tells his story as the story of Jesus—not as God's act, but as a story that unfolded according to the will of God as its hidden author. God is not so much present in the event as noticeably absent and behind the scene. Jesus becomes a relatively passive figure and events proceed according to human decisions: Judas' betrayal, Peter's denial, Pilate's "trial" and execution of Jesus as an insurrectionist. At the moment that came to be seen as God's decisive engagement, Jesus cries out that God has forsaken him. Yet all this is said to be according to the will of God (Acts 1:23, 3:18; Rom. 8:32, etc.). God is presented not so much in as behind the events.

In the pattern of God directing events from behind the scene, the Son of God comes closer to mediating God's presence as Israel does. Like Moses and the other prophets, the Son of God is authorized to speak God's word and act in God's name. Like Israel, the Son of God is a litmus test of how people stand with God: the enemies and friends of the Son of God, like those of Israel, show by their behavior whether they are enemies or friends of God. So the Son of God may suffer as Israel may suffer, and God suffers because of this as a parent suffers when a child is hurt. But in this pattern, the heavenly Father suffers behind the scene, involved, however deeply, only indirectly in the life of the Son.

It should not be concluded that this second pattern results in God's being any less involved in creaturely affairs than the first. Both "acting in" and "behind the scenes" are metaphors. Creaturely talk of the Creator can not expect to reach further than metaphor. Jesus used the metaphor of Father for God, and the disciples used the metaphor of Son for Jesus. Whether "Son of God" expresses the presence of God in Jesus or the intimacy of the relationship between Jesus and the God of Israel, it is only a way of speaking, a metaphor that expresses the conviction of the Church that, in one way or another, we are to trust that what Jesus did and what happened to him are of God, that we may trust that he brings us as near as we need ever come to the heart of God.

This trust has been the basis of the Gentile Church. The Church of Christ has come to know the God of the covenant and thus to know itself invited into the covenantal relationship with that God who formerly had been known only by Israel. The Church therefore knows itself as "fellow citizens" along with Israel and "members of God's household" (Eph. 2:19)—not as a part of Israel, not in the covenant on Israel's terms, but as Gentiles and on terms given freely to it by God in the person of the Jew Jesus. Jesus' authorization by God to perform this function for the Church is what the Church acknowledges when it confesses him Son of God.

God the Father; Son of God. The familial terms express the intimacy of the relationship, such that the Church can speak of God's will being done in Jesus as well as saying that in Christ God was and is present and at work. The second metaphor says no less than the first, and the first implies as great a unity of the two as the second. In either case, the intimacy of the covenantal relationship is pushed as far as language makes possible. It is the Church's confession that it finds itself drawn into the life of God that first began to make itself known with the calling of Abraham and is embodied for it in the life, death, and resurrection of Jesus Christ.

iii. Events, faith, and God

To confess Jesus Christ as the Son of God is the Church's fundamental way of speaking of a historical event as the focus of its faith that God is and acts for the good of God's creatures. The Church, like Israel from whom it learned to speak in this way, trusts that particular historical events are occasions that make clear the Creator's commitment to and engagement in his creation. The unseen, hiding God makes himself visible in this way: God chooses a historical event as an occasion to open creaturely imagination to God's love, judgment, and mercy. Formally speaking, the Church's confession stands together with Jacob's confession at Bethel: "Surely the LORD is in this place; and I did not know it. . . .How awesome is this place! This is none other than the house of God, and this is the gate of heaven" (Gen. 28:16–17).

This place, this moment, this person—here is God! It may be perfectly natural to ask how one comes to say such a thing, but neither Israel nor the Church has ever been able to give an answer to this so-called natural question. The Church, like Israel, is defined by the fact that it does so speak. Its answer to why it so speaks can only take the unavoidably circular form of replying that that is who it is. In so far as revelation is an "offensive idea" (Rosenzweig), it is so because it cannot and will not ground itself in anything else. The conviction—that in this place, this moment, this person, one has been met by God—is unqualifiedly foundational.

For Israel, that foundational moment is Sinai. Sinai is indispensably important for the Church because, apart from Israel, Jesus and the Church are inconceivable. Yet Sinai is not foundational for the Church as it is for Israel. Sinai does not make the Church to be itself, even if the Church would never have come into existence without Sinai. For the Church, Jesus himself is foundational. He and he alone (of course in context) is that place, that moment, that person which made and makes the Church aware of the presence, claim, and gift of the God of Israel.

Strictly speaking, as Sinai continues to be foundational for Israel as the story of Sinai, so for the Church Jesus continues to be foundational as the story about him. The Church lives and knows God and itself in rehearsing the things concerning Jesus of Nazareth. In its Eucharist, which it does "in remembrance of him" it "proclaims the Lord's death until he comes" (1 Cor. 11:24–26). In its prayers and preaching, it recalls, appeals to, and "publicly portrays as crucified" (Gal. 3:1) the person of Christ. He is the event, ever recurring in the story about him, that the Church finds to be the continuing occasion of its faith, its becoming aware of God and of itself before God. In "seeing" him, it "sees the Father." That is what the Church means when it confesses him as the eternal Son of God.

"That is what the Church means," I just said, yet that is not so evident. The Church has been divided and at war over this confession. As I have presented it, the confession refers to the continuing common life of the Church, its recurring rediscovery in the story of Jesus Christ that God is its God and that it is God's Church. As the Church tells this story to itself, it finds its collective identity, and therefore it judges that all attempts to sum it up (doctrine) should be faithful to that originating event. Dogmas are thus rules for the linguistic conformity of later efforts to restate the story and its role in the life of the community.

This seems to be close to what George Lindbeck calls the regulative role of doctrine (*Doctrine*), a role worked out in more detail in Dietrich Ritschl's *Zur Logik der Theologie*.

The Church's confession of Jesus as Son of God came early to be called the doctrine (or teaching) that Jesus was the Son of God. That transition from confession to doctrine, though slight, may have been part of the reason why the Church came to blows and worse over the meaning of calling Jesus the Son of God. This happened most dramatically in the Arian controversy that developed in the fourth century.

2. THE ARIAN CONTROVERSY

i. The rule that mattered to the Arians

As the papers of the Ninth International Conference on Patristic Studies brought to our attention (Gregg, *Arianism*), the traditional view of the Arian controversy has undergone considerable revision by scholars in recent years. It is now being seen that Arius and his followers had a point, a profound insight into the witness of the Apostolic Writings that the orthodox appear to have missed. The Arians felt the rule of faith demanded that Church teaching conform to the apostolic witness that the one who had actually suffered and truly died for our salvation was the Son of God himself. Christ's suffering and death could only be effective if it was granted that he was a divine being: the Word of God had really become incarnate in Jesus and had died for our redemption. "The mainspring and primary motivation of the movement [was] its determination to safeguard the presentation of Christ's passion and crucifixion as unequivocally the passion and crucifixion of God" (Miles, "Asterius," in Gregg, *Arianism*, 136). That was the rule that mattered to the Arians.

The Arians felt that the orthodox, the pro-Nicean party, were endangering this crucial element of the apostolic witness by their talk of "very God" and "of one substance with the Father." "By speaking of Christ's Godhead in such exalted terms," the orthodox had "ruled out the availability of Christ to be the saving God who in his person became man and died for us on the cross" (Gregg, *Arianism*, 137). In short, in Arian eyes the orthodox appeared to be ashamed of the scandal of the cross (cf. also Hanson, in Gregg, *Arianism*, 203).

There was of course a price to pay for insisting so boldly on this single rule of faith: the God who suffered and died had to be a lesser being than the God who is the origin of all things, Creator of heaven and earth, beyond all change and so incapable of entering into creaturely experience. What God did and underwent in Christ, therefore, "necessitated a reduction or a lowering of God, so that it had to be undertaken by a being who, though divine, was less than fully divine" (Hanson, in Gregg, *Arianism,* 182). This was because the Arians (no less than the orthodox, it must be pointed out) were firmly committed to the rule that the One God, the high God, God the Father, was incapable of incarnation, suffering, or death. Patripassionism, the claim that God the Father had suffered or even could suffer, was regarded by the Arians as well as by the orthodox as a monstrous blasphemy.

If you have in your sacred writings the assertion that "*God* shows his love for us in that . . . Christ died for us" (Rom. 5:5, emphasis added) and are also committed to the rule that God cannot suffer, you have a problem, whether you are Arian or orthodox. The Arians tried to meet the problem by saying that God created a divine being capable of that which had to be done, thus in effect teaching "two unequal gods, a high God incapable of human experiences and a lesser god who, so to speak, did his dirty work for him" (Hanson, in Gregg, *Arianism,* 203–4). The orthodox chose the hardly more satisfactory "solution" of saying that the second God is one in *ousia* with the high God, "true God of true God," but then necessarily (by the rule that both sides accepted) inactive, passive, merely standing by, so to speak, while the passible Jesus suffered and died. The controversy between them never got around to a critical reconsideration of the assumption they shared and that was the heart of their problem and the weakness in both "solutions": that God cannot suffer.

ii. The rule that mattered to the orthodox

If the Arians were primarily concerned to stress God's deep involvement in the life and death of Jesus, the orthodox wanted to stress that it really was God who was so involved. What happened in the life, death, and resurrection of Jesus really can be trusted as God's doing, as the orthodox saw it, because the eternal, creative Word of God, who took to himself a human body capable of death, was and is one with God, of the same being as the Father. It may be that the orthodox focused less than the Arians on the suffering and death of the body that the Word had taken to itself, and more on the theme of the Word having taken on that body and entered into the human situation of corruption and death, but that divine movement of incarnation was itself for them the heart of the matter. "As Athanasius put it in an analogy, it was as if a king had come to a city and had taken up residence in one of its houses. Forever after, not just that one house but the whole city could claim the honor and the protection of the royal presence" (van Buren, *Secular,* 37, referring to *De incarn.* 9). God had moved to make the human situation his own, and he had done this in his eternal way of being as God the Son. That was the rule that mattered to the orthodox.

From the perspective of the orthodox, the Arians were violating this rule by their doctrine of a divine but created Son, a being less than and so other than God. How could this creature, even if the first of all God's creatures, rescue creation from corruption? How could it do the work of God and so fully reveal God, being itself only a creature? Only "God of God, light of light, true God of true God, begotten, not made, of one being with the Father," only such a one could rescue creation from corruption and death. And such a one there was: the eternal Son, God's way of being as Son, in distinction from but not less than God's way of being as Father, had assumed corruptible flesh and had offered up that body to death in our place and raised it up as our way to life in God.

The orthodox "solution" was not without its problems, as the debates of succeeding centuries show. Clearly the scandal of the cross was a difficulty for the Church. Somehow, a line had to be drawn between the crucifixion and the being of God, and this was a problem for the orthodox no less than for the Arians. Whereas the Arians drew their line between the Son and the Father by making the former a creature, the orthodox drew a line between the Son and his assumed body. The price of this move was that either the reality of Jesus as a human being such as we are was endangered, or else the unity of Jesus of Nazareth and the incarnate Son became questionable.

From the perspective of the Jewish-Christian reality and for a Church that wishes to acknowledge the continuing covenant between God and Israel, it must be said that the orthodox creedal decision of Nicea appears to have ignored almost completely the context of Christ. The first clause reflects the opening chapter of Genesis but skips the whole story of the covenant. With the second and central clause, we are led through a series of anti-Arian affirmations of the eternal Son who came down from heaven "and was made man." The summary affirmations of birth, suffering, crucifixion, ascension, and a future coming in glory of Christ then bring us to the third clause, in which we are reminded that Holy Spirit "spoke through the prophets," and that is all. The context has become the Son of God's movement "for our salvation" and the grounding of that movement in the being of God. That is well and good, but that we are to understand this movement apart from the context of God's call of Abraham and his heirs, the covenant of Sinai, and the history of Israel, up to and including its occupation and oppression by Rome, as a victim of which Jesus was put to death, invites serious distortion if not utter incomprehensibility. Is the God defined only from the opening of Genesis and the Prologue of John really the God and Father of the Church's Lord Jesus Christ? Is the eternal Son of that God really the Son of the one whom Jesus called Father? Nicea is not so much wrong as inadequate for a Church that wishes to live within the Jewish-Christian reality.

iii. The problem common to both sides

Arians and orthodox alike felt the need to draw a line between God and the death of Jesus. The rule that determined this agreement was their shared conviction that God cannot experience the suffering of a creature, for suffering involves a change and God cannot change. God may appear to change, God may present himself as changing as a way of adapting himself to our limited perception, but in reality, God is beyond all change. Change is a category applicable to all that is creaturely; it is strictly inapplicable to God.

Logically, this assertion is metaphysical. It is a finding neither of analytical reasoning nor of empirical observation. It is a rule governing how one is to speak of what is ultimately the case. As such it is difficult to assess. Why, we might begin, should one want to say that change is a category inapplicable to God? A reason might be that change is a sign of imperfection. Change is either for the worse or for the better, and neither is proper to a being who is perfect. Since perfection seems an eminently proper quality to assign to God, change must be excluded.

If the assertion that change is a category inapplicable to God is metaphysical, so, logically is its denial. Arguments over this issue are not going to be settled by appeal to evidence, yet an appeal to evidence will mark every attempt to argue either side. The issue is over a root understanding of that which is thought to underlie all reality, so appeals to any and all parts of reality will always be relevant. The case for the applicability of the category of change to God, then, will probably best be served by beginning with that aspect or those aspects of reality most closely associated with the concept of God. That is to say, my concern here is to present not just "a case" but more specifically the case that a Gentile worshiper of the God of Israel can make to a fellow Gentile worshiper of the God of Israel. I am concerned to ask whether change is applicable to this God, to God as the Church has been invited (so it must believe) to know him. I am concerned with the God of Israel as he has shown himself to the Church in the face of the crucified and risen Jew Jesus Christ. Is the God whom Jesus called Father, is the God of Jesus' people, the people Israel, is the God of the Scriptures that were sacred to Jesus and his disciples, is that God capable of change?

In the light of our earlier discussion, it seems reasonable to say that God is capable of novelty as well as continuity, and that God's covenantal self-determination would be better confessed by saying that God is able to and does change, even if we add some qualifier such as "of course in his own way." To ascribe change to God need not necessarily involve saying less of God. Indeed, it may be, as Schubert Ogden has argued (*Reality*, 57–70), a form of praise. Ogden's (and others') "neoclassical" theism may be a religiously appealing alternative to "classical" theism, and a God who can and does respond to his creation, rather than simply act upon it, is a metaphysical alternative that appears more congenial to the covenantal context of Christ than the one with which the Arians and orthodox of the fourth century were working.

John Macquarrie (*Diety*) argues that what he calls "Dialectical Theism" has been in fact an important strand in the Western tradition, of which "neoclassical" theism is but one example.

When we reflect on this alternative, it becomes clear that the Arian controversy was to a large extent over how to solve a problem that might not have arisen had either side or both had their eye upon the covenantal context of Christ.

iv. The common failure

The decision that confronts the Church in its Christology today is clearly not that of choosing between Nicea and the Arians. A choice for either position involves accepting what they held in common, and it is just this that makes both their Christologies inadequate for a Church that is beginning to acknowledge the continuing force of the covenant between God and the Jewish people. The relationship that will be at the center of a Christology for such a Church will have to be that which was and is between the God of the covenant (the one Jesus called Father) and this Jew whose life, death, and resurrection, and the gospel preached to the Gentiles in his name, has led to the gathering of the Gentile Church into the service of this God and his covenantal purpose. The doctrine of Incarnation that can serve such a Church will have to help the Church confess that it is in just this Jew that God has caused his light to shine upon the Gentile Church, that in the presence of just this man they have found themselves in the presence of God. In short, the Church today is called to confess a more radical notion of Incarnation than either side was able to hold in the Arian controversy. The challenge now is to understand how we can confess of this Jew, Jesus of Nazareth, that he is the eternal Son of God.

Just this is what the orthodox failed to do. They made their claim of eternal Sonship and full divinity of the second hypostasis of the Triune God. This eternal Son of God took to himself flesh, a human body. One wonders what and where the Jew Jesus of Nazareth was in all this. Is he the result, so far as the eye can see, of the Son of God having assumed a human body? It appears to have been of little interest to the Fathers of Nicea that the assumed flesh was Jewish flesh or that the title Son of God was there in Israel's Scriptures referring to Israel. What, one must ask, was the connection between the story they confessed in their creed and the story of Scripture on which they claimed to stand? If they saw a connection, they certainly did not go out of their way to make it clear. The Jew Jesus of Nazareth is lifted right out of that context and set in another with the result that he is already Jesus Christ our Lord, totally the end product of the action of the eternal Son of God. He is, one might almost say, no longer a Jew; he is the body of the incarnate Son of God.

The Arian controversy is worthy of reflection, not because the Arian Christology is more adequate than that of the orthodox, nor because it offers us a better understanding of God, but because the conflict exposes the failure of the orthodox as well as of the Arians to face up to the covenantal context of Jesus Christ. The God in which both sides believed was one defined by metaphysical commitments drawn from another context. To understand Christ in context requires that we understand God in the light of the same context. The resulting Christology will have to spell out its understanding of the claim that Jesus is the eternal Son of God on the basis of a concept of God drawn from Israel's story of its life with God. It will have to begin with a God who is covenantally self-determined.

3. GOD'S COVENANTAL SELF-DETERMINATION

i. The compromised God

God, the only God Israel knows and so the God whom Jesus called Father, is one who has committed and so determined himself to be the God of his creation. Israel knows this by the covenant that God has made with it.

We pick up here from where we left off in *People Israel* (62–69), "God's Involvement." There, with special attention to Isaac Luria's teaching of the divine contraction (the *tzim-tzum*) that God suffered in order to make room for creation, we explored the self-determination of God that Israel's doctrine of Creation entails. Here we turn our attention primarily to the covenant as the revelation of God's self-determination, for I understand Israel's doctrine of Creation to be historically a product of its covenantal experience and life.

Whatever God may have been "in the beginning," Israel knows God only and always as the One committed to Israel for the good of all creation. However universal God's purposes may be, Israel knows him only as one who chooses to achieve his ends by tying himself to the particular history of this particular people. Jesus knew no other God, and so neither does the Church. The God of Israel, of Jesus Christ, and of the Church is a compromised God.

This is not to make any claims for the exclusivity of God's concern for Israel or for the Church. The compromised God is still compromised first of all by becoming Creator of the heavens and the earth. Israel really does not know much about how the compromised God has gone about achieving his ends in cultures and lands beyond its own ken. Since the Church is becoming increasingly aware in the modern era of other cultures and histories, it is beginning to think about God's relationship to other peoples and traditions, but that is a new situation for which the Church has few guidelines. However the Church is to respond to this new situation, its point of departure will be from what it knows, and that is what it has learned from Israel: the God of this whole earth, in so far as God's ways have been shown to Israel and the Church, is the God who carries out his universal purposes by means of utterly particular historical peoples to whom he commits himself. God is, in himself and forever, a compromised God. That is the unavoidable conclusion to which the Church is forced by its confession that its God is the God and Father of the Jew Jesus Christ.

Therefore when the Church tries to think out the relationship between God and Jesus, it is forbidden by Israel's witness, which Jesus himself lived in, from working with such general terms as God and man, or the divine and the human, unless those terms are anchored in and colored to their depths by the particular context in which the compromised God has made himself known to Israel and the Church. Whatever further is to be said about the relationship between God and Jesus, the Church's starting point can only be that it is speaking of the relationship between the God who has compromised himself in his covenant with Israel, and a Jew, one of that people Israel.

It is obvious that the Church throughout almost its entire history has not started at this point. Even today with all the new talk about "the Jewishness of Jesus," what might be called "the Jewishness of God," the compromised reality of God, goes unnoticed, so that when we start to hear of "incarnation" what we get under the name of Christology turns out to be anthropology, since Christ is really only "the theological symbol" of the fact that "each human person is somehow divine," and a "revelation to the whole human family that its humanity can be made whole because of the ability of people to be touched in the deepest realms of their consciousness by the humanity of God" (Pawlikowski, *Light*, 115, 119). The Church had better leave to others such attempts at broad generalizations about universal human abilities. On this it has no special wisdom to offer the world. What it has been given to see, if it would open its eyes to it, is that the God of whom it speaks is a thoroughly compromised God. Whatever else may be true of God, including a hypothetical "humanity of God" (and what Karl Barth had to say under that heading was something far more particular than the words just quoted), the Church should begin its thinking with the little it knows: that the God and Father of Jesus Christ is the God who is covenantally self-determined and to that extent thoroughly compromised.

ii. The involved God

God is compromised by his involvement with Israel. He is compromised by the covenant. Consequently, Israel too is compromised. Neither God nor Israel can be fully themselves without the other, for to attempt to be without the other involves them both in a self-determined self-contradiction. The relationship between God and Jesus was and is a relationship within and shaped by this dual reality. The God who was involved with Jesus was the God already involved with the people of whom Jesus was one, and Jesus as a Jew was already born into Israel's involvement with God. The novelty of Christ was and is embedded in that continuity.

Whether it would be better to say that God became more involved with Israel, or became involved in a new way when he became involved with Jesus, the fundamental point to make is that in Jesus, God was doing something already predetermined by his covenant with Israel. This new involvement was grounded in and shaped by that already ongoing involvement. What the Church has referred to as the incarnation is fully coherent with the covenant between God and Israel. If the incarnation be reduced to a "theological symbol," then let it at least be a symbol of that covenant, not of some general anthropological claim. That would at least treat the "symbol" within the framework of the "symbol system" in which alone it could function as a symbol. I much prefer, however, to speak of an event, of something happening between the already-involved God and one member of the particular people already involved with God. As John 1:14 would read, when set in the context of the Scriptures, "The covenantal Word of the God of the covenant *became* flesh and dwelt among, being one of, the covenanted people."

We may clarify further what we mean by God's involvement by addressing briefly four questions: (1) How far does that involvement go? (2) Is anything of God held in reserve? (3) Is God wholly involved? (4) Is God really there?

1. God's involvement in the covenant and so in Jesus knows no limits. Israel's Scriptures explore this question in many ways, and the final answer is that God will be Israel's God no matter what happens. It is not often said so clearly, for evidently Israel thought that God cared a great deal about what happens. Nevertheless, no matter how far Israel strays from the path, God will not forget it. No matter how he heaps pains and grief on Israel for

its infidelities, he will call Israel to himself again, be it even as a valley of dry bones (Ezek. 37).

2. God's involvement is as God. He is Israel's God as the Holy One of Israel. He is never delivered into Israel's hands. Rather, his involvement delivers Israel into his hands. God is God and not a human being, and his thoughts and ways are not those of creatures. What there may be of God that is not immediately involved in the covenant is clouded in darkness. God speaks, even to Israel, out of the whirlwind. Yes, Israel spoke always in awe and with reserve of God, even in the great intimacy of the covenant. There is good covenantal reason, therefore, for saying that the Son, not the Father, happened as this Jew Jesus.

3. But that is not to say that only a part of God committed himself to Israel, or that God determined anything less than God's own self in making covenant with Israel. Whatever God may be that is not revealed, that stands, as it were, above or beyond the covenant, it cannot be uninvolved in God's covenantal partnership.

4. Therefore it is proper to say that where God is involved, there he is, though we know it not. This is precisely how God is present with and to his creatures: in covenantal partnership. But that leads to our final point about God's covenantal self-determination, for the covenant means, among other things, suffering on the part of Israel and so suffering on the part of God.

iii. The suffering God

God's commitment to his creatures, already established in Creation but made explicit and particular in the case of Israel by God's covenant with it, ties God to the human condition as Israel lived and lives it. That is not Israel's decision; it is God's own choice. God has determined himself for ever to be with Israel for better or worse, and that includes Israel's suffering whether this comes from Israel's failures or, as is more usually the case, from the actions of Israel's enemies. If the covenant has any substance, God weeps with those who weep and hurts with those who hurt. God "knows"—takes part in—the sorrows of his people

(Exod. 3:7). "In all their afflictions he was afflicted" (Isa. 63:9). Such is the compassion—the suffering with—of Israel's God, the God and Father of Jesus Christ.

It has been given to the Church to see God's suffering primarily in the compassion and suffering of the one Jew singled out by God to be his means of making himself known as he is to countless Gentiles. What should not be done at this point is to start redrawing the lines that orthodox as well as Arians drew between God and the cross. The insight of the Fourth Gospel is that no such line exists: he who has looked into the face of this suffering Jew, the Jew from the Galilean village of Nazareth who was nailed by the Romans to a cross, has seen the Father (John 14:9), not a being of one substance with the Father, not a divine creature, but God the Father of Israel and of Jesus Christ. That is how God makes himself present to and known by his Church—he addresses them in just this way: they are addressed by that Jew. Consequently their fully appropriate confession, made while looking directly into the face of this crucified Jew, is, "My Lord and my God!" (John 20:28).

How can this be? How can the Church look at this man and say, "My God"? Certainly they say this to this man's face. The Church does not thereby think for one moment that Jesus has become other than a man. It is quite misleading to talk about the divinity of Jesus. The Fourth Gospel demands an infinitely more daring move than to call Jesus a divine man. On the contrary, he is a thoroughly human, a thoroughly Jewish man. And so he was and is a crucified man, the victim of a cruel Roman occupation. He is every bit as much a human being and a Jew as were all his fellow Jews who died in the death camps.

The move that the Fourth Gospel dares the Church to make is that of risking and trusting the judgment that this man is precisely the way in which the suffering Father of Israel and all creation has chosen to open a radically new chapter in the continuing history of his involvement in human affairs which he began with Abraham. To risk that judgment and trust that it is right is to let oneself be defined by it. But even more important, it is to let God define himself by it. God may not be seen as incapable of what he has already done, especially not when what he has done in this one Jew, for all its novelty, is so consistent with his compassionate involvement with Israel from its beginning and up to our own day.

4. THE SERIOUSNESS OF THE COVENANT

i. *The creatureliness of the covenant*

"It is not in the heavens" (Deut. 30:12). This absolutely crucial word of Torah about the Torah meant for the rabbis that Torah was not only given into Israel's hands, but that the interpretation too was up to Israel. God has given to his covenant partner the freedom and responsibility to say what his holy word shall be, and as it is decided on earth, so shall it be in heaven. God's word shall now be settled in human words. God's holy covenant is to be worked out entirely by creatures in the creaturely realm.

So seriously does God take his covenant with Israel that he waits upon Israel to see how the covenant shall progress. Certainly the Word of God, God's call, address, or election, comes first, but Israel's response is what makes the life of the covenant. Israel's response makes the difference between life and death, between whether God's purpose goes forward or is thwarted. This is reflected in the fact that Israel's life is the major subject of Israel's Scriptures.

The major subject of the Apostolic Writings is Jesus' life and that of the apostolic communities. Here too the call of God has priority, yet the subject is primarily the response, first of Jesus, and then also of the early Christian communities, for whom Jesus' response functions as the call to which they in turn respond. The covenantal pattern of call and response, or commandment and willing obedience, seems therefore appropriate for understanding the early Church's confession that Jesus is the eternal Son of God.

Readers may recall that I came to this same conclusion some twenty-five years ago and worked out a "Christology of Call and Response" (*Sec-*

ular, 47–55). The difference in what follows comes from my having since worked through *A Christian Theology of the People Israel.*

We should begin by recalling the use of the expression "son of God" that would have been familiar to Jesus' disciples. The expression is covenantal in context, and it refers to God's faithful covenant partner. It refers to Israel first of all, and then to the principal figures who represented Israel before God: Israel's king, Israel's high priest, perhaps the messianic king of Israel's restoration. The son of God carries on and carries forward the history of the covenant which embodies God's purpose for his creation. The response of the son of God is what shapes the future, God's as well as that of God's partner.

The Church confesses Jesus to be not just another son of God, but God's special Son, whose response to his and Israel's calling led to a quantum leap in the history of the covenant. His Jewish disciples evidently saw him as embodying all that Israel's response was ever to have been. He was evidently for them such a personification of that response that they found themselves defining Israel on the basis of his person and life, rather than the reverse. From him they learned in a new way what it was to be God's son.

They confessed Jesus to be not only God's Son, but God's eternal Son. It does not seem that they meant to say that the Jew Jesus was eternal, but rather that God's involvement in the things concerning Jesus of Nazareth was of such depth that God was to be conceived as always having been the God who would do this thing. "Eternal" means that the factor of time is ruled out. God's Word as the call of Jesus comes from God without respect to time (to express it negatively). God is in himself (to express it positively) this call to which Jesus' life was the response. When the Church beholds this response, therefore, it sees into the heart of God ("He who has seen me has seen the Father"). God's call cannot be seen when it occurs: all that there is to be seen is the response to it. The response is what God's call looks like. And because God has determined himself covenantally, he abides by the response to his call. That means that the response is to be trusted as the call-made-visible ("The Word happened as flesh and dwelled among us"). Such is the seriousness with which God has taken the creatureliness of his covenant.

ii. *The covenant as God's*

The covenant, we have been arguing, is a fundamental self-determination on the part of God. It is not, according to the witness of the Scriptures and the Apostolic Writings, and according to the witness of Israel and of the Church, a secondary or minor aspect of God. On the contrary, it is God's own expression of God's self. It is God's way of being God for his creation and so of showing his creatures what it is to be God. God is not a being in and for himself. God is love, grace, self-giving, self-binding to others, and God is this in his very being. God is covenantal in his essence, so it would make no sense to say "there was a time when he was not" covenantal. God's covenantal self-determination, then, is to be thought of as God's own eternal reality revealed in time but itself the innermost fact of God's own life, or so Israel and the Church claim, each in its own way.

Does either Israel or the Church know enough about God's inner life to make such a claim? Clearly they do not, but Israel and the Church trust God not to be a deceiver. What God has shown in his action, what he has revealed by entering into the covenant by which both Israel and the Church live in their different ways, leads both to think that God is not other than what he has shown himself to be to them. On this basis, the Church confesses that God is and must be in his own heart what he has shown by addressing it in the response of Jesus to his calling as God's utterly faithful son. And if God has made Jesus to be the Son of God for them, then they can and must trust that God is eternally God in just this way, covenantal in a way that draws also the Gentiles into his covenantal purpose.

None of this makes the covenant less creaturely. None of this makes God's Word in its fleshly reality any less human. On the contrary, it is precisely in its fleshly, creaturely reality that God has uttered his Word of personal address to the Church, truly

God of God, light of light, true God of true God, begotten not made, of one being, substance, reality with the Father. God's covenant, precisely in its being given into the hands of his covenant partner, is totally God's.

iii. *God's only begotten Son*

The relation of the Son to the Father is radically unlike that of any creature: so the Church taught and teaches. The calling of Jesus was of course fully in the line of and coherent with the calling of Abraham and the calling of Israel. But it was unlike any other calling in that its response opened the new chapter in the history of the covenant that came to be called the Church.

It is perfectly understandable that Israel and the Church make such different responses to that new chapter. For Israel, it would be at most only an appendix to the story, moving off somewhat tangentially from what Israel knows as its central thread. It had to do with Israel only indirectly. It was surely about Israel, in one sense, since it was the work of the God of Israel, and it led to the carrying out of an important part of the reason for Israel's original calling to be a blessing for the nations of the world, but it was not, as it turned out, addressed to Israel directly. For the Church, on the other hand, the new chapter was the beginning of its life. For the Church, God's relation to this Son was literally creative as was no other. God's calling of Jesus was therefore spoken of by the Church as being unique, and Jesus was, as God's only child, the sole one to bear in his calling, and in his response to it, the foundation of the Church's existence. The Church confessed Jesus to be God's only child, because he proved to be the sole origin and foundation of its life. He alone became the ground of the Church's existence in the realm of God's covenantal purpose. For Israel he might be perhaps an outstanding son among many sons of God. For the Church, Jesus is God's only begotten Son.

The Church believes, with Israel, that it is possible that in the mercy of God every human being might be a daughter or son of God, but the Church has discovered in its own life that this possibility is realized by its becoming sisters and brothers of Jesus. Je-

sus as God's Son is never for the Church either a symbol or an
example of what is possible for every Christian, not to speak of
every human being. He is rather the doorway by which Gentile
men and women can enter into God's covenantal purpose. God
has used him to effect this possibility and make it actual. That is
why the Church confesses him, not as a son of God, not as a symbol of the potential sonship of all human beings, but as God's only
begotten Son.

This confession is made about the one Jesus Christ. Its reference is at once God's utterly unique calling of Jesus and Jesus' totally human—and Jewish—response to that calling. The two may
be distinguished for purposes of analysis as, following the Christological tradition, I have done, but they are in reality inseparable.
This is because we are dealing here with the way in which God's
covenantal self-determination has met, called, and created the
Church. We are dealing with a new chapter in the covenant and
so with a new facet of God's covenantal self-determination. If the
Church's Christology dealt only with what happened in Jesus of
Nazareth without respect to the consequences, if it were only an
expression of the Church's convictions concerning the inner relationship between Jesus and God, then the Church's Christology
would have to speak of God's call as it is to be seen in Jesus' response, and that response was addressed solely to Israel and its
lost sheep. But the Church's Christology is always and fundamentally a confession of the God before whom the Church finds itself
in the presence of Christ, and of itself uncovered as standing before God as it stands before Christ. Its confession, therefore, refers to God's calling of Jesus and to Jesus' response always as they
have issued in the calling of dead Gentiles into the life of God's
covenantal love alongside Israel.

Israel, we have said, can at most confess Jesus as one outstanding son of God among others, and this is in recent years increasingly happening. More than that he cannot be for Israel, for his
calling, as seen in his response, was to call Israel back to its ancient
covenant in ever deeper fidelity (recognized by the Dutch Reformed Church in its statement of 1970, referred to in van Buren,

Discerning, 175). For the Church, however, his calling, as seen in his response, had the effect of bringing those far from the God of Israel into the realm of God's loving and purposeful presence. That is why the Church, unlike Israel, confesses him to be God's only begotten Son.

iv. The eternal Son

The seriousness with which God takes his covenant and so his covenant partner, and therefore the seriousness of God's covenantal self-determination, which the Church acknowledges in confessing Jesus to be God's Son, calls for a response. The appropriate response is trust—trust that God is fully and faithfully true to God's own reality in God's calling of Jesus, itself revealed in Jesus' response as this has been used by God to bring the Church into existence in God's presence. When the Church says, as it has from its beginning, that it believes in the Lord Jesus Christ (Acts 11:17), it means that it trusts that Jesus' life was an obedient response to God's calling, and that that Jew, determined as he is for the Church by that call and response, has been God's way of bringing it before the humble throne of God, itself supported by the prayers of Israel (Ps. 22:3 = v. 4 in the Hebrew). To believe in that Jesus is to trust God's faithfulness to God's own self.

The apostolic witness to Jesus does not admit of the possibility that God was doing anything contrary to his own inner reality both in his calling and in his confirmation on Easter of the response of Jesus. As the Apostle to the Gentiles put it (Rom. 15:8, emphasis added), "Christ became a servant to the Jewish people *in order* to show God's truthfulness." The truthfulness and faithfulness of God to God's own self is the sole matter at stake in the Church's confession of the eternity of what God has done in Christ. To speak of the eternal Son or the eternal Word may sound as if it were being said that God's calling of Jesus happened a very, very long time ago (e.g. before Abraham, or before Creation), but that would be a misunderstanding of the logic of the confession. The issue is not one of time and it is not of change; God may, for all we know, be constantly changing. The issue is solely whether God can be trusted to have been and to be faithful to himself and to his own covenantal self-determination in calling Jesus and responding as he did to Jesus' response. The Church lives by the conviction that God was being true to himself on Easter, so that Easter becomes God's and its own joint affirmation of Jesus' calling and response, united in his life and death. Thus united, they express God's own covenantally determined self. God's face and God's fullness, and therefore God's faithfulness, have been shown to the Church in the face of the Jew Jesus, crucified and raised, so the Church confesses. It makes this confession solely because it believes that the God who has shown and made effective his covenantal self-determination also for his Gentile Church is no other than the God of Israel, and it is led to this belief by the fact that this manifestation and efficacy confronts it in the Jew Jesus Christ. That is what the Church acknowledges when it confesses that Jesus Christ is the eternal Son of God.

We have come at this point to the very center of the Church's Christology. That means, we have come to the center of the Church's faith and identity. The confession of the eternal Sonship of Jesus Christ is spoken out of the reality of the Church's life into which it finds itself awakened by the gospel concerning Jesus of Nazareth. Baptized into and rehearsing his life and death in its Eucharist and in its retelling of the things concerning Jesus of Nazareth, the Church finds itself in his presence. In that presence it finds itself on its knees before the God of Israel, the God of the covenant now opened up also to it. In becoming aware of him, it becomes aware of the Father, the God who called Jesus of Nazareth to be his only begotten Son for the Gentile Church. The Church makes this confession of trust as the primary way of confessing that its own existence is grounded in the fact that the God of Israel has effectively made use of Jesus of Nazareth's response to his calling to confront the Gentiles with himself and to open them to see themselves as claimed, judged, and loved by the God of Sinai and of Abraham, Isaac, and Jacob, the Creator and re-deemer of his people Israel and now also of his Church. The Church knows no other God, and it knows this God as just this and in just this way. It is therefore always to the glory of God the Father that the Church confesses Jesus Christ as the eternal Son of God.

CHAPTER TEN

The Incarnate Word

A Church that acknowledges the continuing covenant between God and the Jewish people will wish to reassess its patristic legacy of the doctrine of the Incarnation of the Word of God. Such a reassessment will strengthen its weaknesses and affirm its contributions to recognizing that God's involvement in Christ took place within the context of and as a further step in God's covenantal involvement in creation for its good. The aim of this reassessment would be to affirm more adequately the covenantal unity between the God of Israel and Jesus of Nazareth in including the Gentiles in God's covenantal purpose of redeeming the world.

1. THE PATRISTIC LEGACY

i. What the Church has from the Fathers

From its early history, and especially from the councils of the fourth and fifth centuries, the Church has inherited many things, not the least of which are conciliar formulae that have shaped its christological tradition. At the center of this legacy is the doctrine of the Incarnation. This received its major formulation in the so-called Nicene Creed, in which the conciliar fathers confessed their faith in "one Lord Jesus Christ." Of this one, they confessed, among other things, that he was "God of God . . . of one substance with the Father," who "for us and for our salvation came down from heaven and was incarnate . . . and was made man." Of this same one they also confessed that he "was crucified ... suffered and was buried." In short, they bequeathed the Church a Christology of one subject with a dual predication.

The one subject of Nicea was the "one Lord Jesus Christ." Of this one it was confessed the he is the eternal Son of God, "of one substance with the Father," and of this one it was also confessed that he lived, suffered, and died as the man Jesus of Nazareth. The foundation on which this dual predication was based is obviously the Prologue to the Fourth Gospel: "In the beginning was the Word, and the Word was with God, and Godly was the Word .... and the Word happened as [became, was made] flesh and dwelled among us." A duality of predication that is peculiar to the Fourth Gospel was thereby made a primary guideline for Christology (and not only that of the orthodox party), although it took over a century to develop conceptual tools for saying how this could be done without detriment to one form of predication or the other, or to the unity of subject. The first question that we must face is whether we wish to abide by this primary patristic guideline.

One argument for at least qualifying it is that it condenses the cloud of apostolic witness to what God has done in Christ into one drop: that of the Fourth Gospel. The doctrine of the Incarnation is really the legacy of the Johannine community only. On the other hand, it could be answered that the Johannine witness is only the articulation of that towards which the other witnesses were tending in their own ways (see Dunn, *Christology*). And even if we do not wish to give such exclusive dominance to one out of many witnesses, we are left with the fact that it was one important witness with which we would have to come to terms in any case. I think we should listen to this objection primarily to remind ourselves that the Fourth Gospel itself has a context and should not be read in isolation. The fact remains that the Johannine image or figure of incarnation has worked its way into the language and worship of the Church so deeply that it would be difficult indeed to dismiss it.

Another objection is that the conceptual tools developed to

make possible the dual predication of the one subject—two "natures" in one *hypostasis*—are terms of a physics and metaphysics which no one has found workable for many centuries. The terms can be used only if translated radically into a metaphysics quite other than that of the late patristic era. I think the objection is in order, but with sufficient translation or even transmutation of the terms (and their metaphysical underpinnings), a good part, if not all of the intent of the ancient formulas, can be preserved. Undoubtedly, that will remain a matter of dispute, and sides will be taken perhaps as much due to different understandings of the workings of our language as to the degree of concern to remain loyal to the council of the past. I am inclined to think that the question of whether one can say the same thing in other words does not admit of a simple yes or no, but that to say that one can keep the substance of a doctrine when one changes the words may be based on a misleading picture of how our language works.

A further objection is more substantive. The classical christological doctrine presents the incarnation as itself the saving event. The reason for the insistence on the full humanity of Jesus (one of the fruits of the Council of Chalcedon) was the thesis that what is not assumed (by the eternal Word) is not redeemed. If the Word assumed only human flesh and not a human soul or mind, then only the body is redeemed but not the soul or mind that is the root of our unredeemed condition. In order for the whole of corrupted human nature to be rescued, a complete human nature had to be assumed. This is why at Chalcedon it was confessed that in the incarnate one there was a full human nature consubstantial with ours as well as the full divine nature of the eternal Word, consubstantial with God the Father. To hold to the single subject of this dual predication, it was argued that the two "natures" were united in a single *hypostasis* with a single *prosopon*. Leaving aside for the moment both the reason for and the terms of this conclusion, it may still be asked whether this focus on the incarnation as itself redemptive does not spring from just that which the Arians feared in the orthodox position: evasion of the scandal, indeed even of the fact, of the cross. Redemption is accomplished precisely in the event of incarnation itself, regardless of the rest of the life and the death of Jesus; one might say that the Virgin's womb has replaced the cross as the locale of the world's redemption, and one may fairly wonder if that is being fair even to the Fourth Gospel, not to speak of the many other voices of the Apostolic Writings.

ii. The weaknesses of the legacy

If we reconsider the classical christological tradition, the patristic legacy as it has worked itself out in the life of the Church, and do so first of all in the light of the whole witness of the Apostolic Writings against their background and in their context of Israel's Scriptures, we find six interrelated and partially overlapping difficulties which should be recognized before turning in the next subsection to the patristic legacy's great strengths.

1. Jesus of Nazareth is slipping from our consciousness. The Jew from Nazareth, the one called rabbi who spoke Aramaic and thought as a first century Galilean, has been largely displaced by "man," "human nature," or even "flesh." In the classical doctrine he represents the human condition, standing in for all humanity, but in the process he seems to lose his individual identity as a Jew of his time and as one of his people living under Roman occupation. I do not think that the conciliar fathers intended to slight the Jew Jesus, only that they were so focused on the incarnate Word that this Jew in his Jewish human particularity was in fact neglected. He has been recovered again and again through the centuries, but it has always been a recovery of something constantly slipping from the Church's consciousness. The Church's Christology ought to do better than that. It ought to help the Church to be fully aware that it says "My Lord and my God" precisely while looking fully into the face of the Jew Jesus of Nazareth. The Church's confession is not made in the face of "man" or of "human nature" but of that particular Jew.

2. A redemption of humankind conceived as being accomplished by God's Word having taken into himself one human being, that is, by the divine act of incarnation, constitutes so radical

a break with the Scriptural witness to God's previous redemptions and promised future redemption of Israel and, through Israel the world, as to leave in doubt whether it can be conceived as the work of the same God. Not only is the call and election of Abraham and his descendants, the call of Moses, the redemption from Egyptian slavery and then the gracious gift of his Torah, not only is the whole story of the eternal covenant between God and Israel undervalued in this view; it is simply ignored. Now a new and quite different story begins. But because the Church carried with it Israel's Scriptures, these now had to be radically retold as a collection of types and shadows of the real event of redemption. In short, in place of the scriptural witness to God's covenant with Israel, we have the Church's Old Testament, and this is just what we find in the formula of Chalcedon's reference to "the prophets from of old" as having spoken of Christ in perfect agreement with the council's conclusion. A Church that is coming to acknowledge the reality of the eternal covenant between God and the Jewish people is going to have to make a choice: either abandon this dawning recognition of the Jewish-Christian reality, or revise its legacy of redemption accomplished (or set in motion) by means of the incarnation. With all due respect and even reverence for Miriam, the mother of Jesus of Nazareth, a virgin's womb is no substitute for this created world as the locus of God's promised redemption. And when redemption no longer refers to Israel and the nations of this world, but to a generalized fallen creation, Christ loses his specific context. Precisely for the sake of the novelty of God's act in Christ, a Christology for the Jewish-Christian reality must do better justice to its continuity than that.

3. Classical Christology, as a means of preserving the unity of subject, produced the idea that the divine and human natures of the incarnate one were united in a single *hypostasis*, that of the divine Word. The Council of Chalcedon provided no definition of *hypostasis*, but Leontius of Byzantium and John of Damascus later worked out a possible meaning: that which every existing entity has which makes it to be itself—its peculiar ground, we might say. With some such sense of the term, the tradition leaves us with the

following conception of the incarnation: God the Word, having in himself, so to speak, his own ground (*hypostasis*) and (divine) nature, took to himself also a human nature, that which we know as Jesus of Nazareth, which had no independent ground, but was grounded in that of God's Word. Thus it was said that the full, complete, and personal human nature (i.e., Jesus), although without an independent grounding (*anhypostatic*), was in reality *enhypostatic*, having its ground in that of the Word.

We shall consider in the next subsection the strengths of this idea, but its weakness needs to be noted. This does *not* lie in what is so often said, that the humanity of Jesus is thus defined as being "impersonal." *Anhypostatic* does not mean anything like our English term "impersonal" because our English word "person" is a most misleading translation of the patristic term *hypostasis*. What the classical tradition meant was that Jesus of Nazareth came to be as a human, historical being only because God the Word was there as the ground of his very existence. What existed was a fully personal human being, but his existence itself depended absolutely on the presence of the divine Word in which he was grounded. Precisely that was his fundamental difference from all other human beings.

For all that may be said in behalf of this conception, it is clear that it moves us into a radically different line of thought from that of the tradition in which Jesus and his disciples lived. Whatever else is to be said of this conception of unity, it is not that of the covenant between God and Israel as this is reflected in the witness of the synoptic Gospels to the relationship between Jesus and the one whom he called Father. *Enhypostatic* might just conceivably be a term that would cover part of the witness of the Fourth Gospel to Jesus of Nazareth, the part which presents Jesus as so totally grounded in God as to seem hardly to be an independent human being, and so who prays not out of human need and a human, personal relationship to God, but only "on account of" his disciples in order that they may believe (John 11:42). It hardly does justice to Israel's witness to the existence of God's covenantal partner who is grounded independently of God by God's gracious gift of Creation. The witness of the Apostolic Writings to the obedience of Jesus to God and God's calling, an obedience "unto death," has as its context Israel's own witness to its call to obey God, and the novelty is striking precisely because it is set within the context of that continuity of the covenant. The covenant, precisely as a gift of God's grace, is between partners and depends, by God's own decision, on both of them, not on just one. The hypostatic union of the classical tradition fails to preserve this fundamental feature of the context of and so of the witness to Jesus Christ.

4. In classical Christology, the Son of God is the eternal Word, "God of God, light of light, true God of true God." In Israel's Scriptures and in the Apostolic Writings, on the contrary, the Son of God is God's covenant partner: Israel and its principal representatives, and Jesus of Nazareth as God's utterly faithful servant.

To refine the contrast, we should note that according to the classical tradition, the term "Son of God" is applicable directly to the eternal Word, the second *persona* of the Trinity, but then also indirectly to the man Jesus. The indirect application was held to be legitimate because of the union of the Word with the man assumed, so that the attributes and characteristics of the one may also be ascribed to the other. Thus it may be said that the divine Son of God suffered and died, because the human nature that he had assumed suffered and died, and it may be said that Jesus was before Abraham, because the Word that had taken this man to itself was before Abraham. For a penetrating discussion of this doctrine of the *communicatio idiomatum* (the sharing of attributes between the divine and the human in Christ) as it was debated in the patristic period and then greatly refined in the debates between Lutheran and Reformed theologians of the sixteenth and seventeenth centuries, see Karl Barth (*CD*, IV/2, 36–116), who has left us a superbly penetrating and original review of the whole issue.

This change of reference of the term is another sign of the fact that the classical christological tradition was developed without sufficient attention to the covenantal context.

5. The classical Christology of the creeds and the tradition certainly constitute and can serve as a confession of Jesus Christ as Lord. It is less clear that it helps the Church to make this confes-

sion "to the glory of God the Father" (Phil. 2:11), because so much attention is given to the glory of God the Son. This is not to say that the tradition makes it impossible to confess Christ as Lord to the glory of the Father, only that it makes it difficult. A Christology for a Church seeking to affirm God's covenant with the Jewish people should make it evident that the Church wishes not only to honor the Father but that its confession of Christ is unambiguously part of its worship of the God and Father of Jesus Christ.

6. The orthodox Christology of the councils is as burdened as was that of the Arians by the concept of the impassibility of God. Consequently, its doctrine of the Incarnation is crippled at a crucial point: since God the Word or Son can no more suffer than God the Father, the incarnate Word as well as God the Father must forsake the crucified one. At what the Church has often held to be the decisive moment of God's battle with the forces of evil, Jesus is left alone to suffer and die. God has no place in that last bitter and final struggle. Thus the tradition leaves the Church with its primary symbol working against its own faith: the cross marks a breach of God's faithfulness, and at the decisive moment, the christological unity of subject breaks down.

iii. The strengths of the legacy

The weaknesses just discussed are serious, serious enough to invite hard thinking about finding a better way than that of the orthodox tradition for speaking of the things concerning Jesus of Nazareth. Before we do this, however, we should review the strengths of the christological heritage, for these can be helpful guides to a better understanding of Christ in context. As we pointed out six problems in the tradition, so we single out six features of it that should guide any reformulation.

1. For all of the weaknesses appearing in its development, there can be no doubt but that "incarnation" is a powerful metaphor or figure for God's intimate, active involvement in the affairs of his creation. The concept of incarnation present God as entering directly and personally into the struggle of human affairs and doing

so on a fully creaturely level. It speaks, therefore, of God's deeply personal engagement in the world. It dares to say that now, here, in this place, in this person, God is present to and for his people Israel and, in this particular way, present to and for his whole creation. In its own (Gentile?) way, it could be seen to proclaim a covenantally committed and self-determined God. It could be a proclamation of the God of Israel, of Creation, of Sinai. In its novel way, then, it can also bear witness to the continuity of the ways of the God of Israel. In order for it to do so, however, each of its original Johannine terms would need to be anchored in Israel's witness to God's covenant.

2. Behind the doctrine that the Incarnation is itself God's act of redemption lies the insight that the world into which God has come in this new or more intensive way is a threatened creation, profoundly corrupted by sin. Incarnation says in a powerful way that God is not indifferent to the threat to creation, that he comes to help, restore, and above all suffer with all those who suffer in this world. Incarnation can remind us of the word attributed to Jesus, that to visit the jailed, feed the hungry, and care for the poor is to visit, feed, and care for Jesus himself. As he is incarnate in them, so the poor do not just have God on their side; they are before us as a way in which God is present to us.

3. The doctrine of the Incarnation expresses the conviction that the initiative in the relations between the Creator and creatures is God's alone. "Conceived by the Holy Spirit, born of the Virgin Mary" underscores Israel's witness that God initiated the covenant. It also reminds us, however, that God does call his covenant partner into action when he makes that first move. Mary's "Let it be to me according to your word" expresses active cooperation, not passive resignation. She wills to be what God calls her to be, "the handmaid of the Lord." Divine initiative and full human cooperation both could find their place in the doctrine of the Incarnation, which therein could reflect faithfully Israel's witness to the covenantal relationship between God and Israel. In doing so, it would call the Church to humble thanksgiving to God the Father and to active engagement in the world that God so loves.

4. With its conception of the hypostatic union, the doctrine of the Incarnation is the Church's confession that the relationship between God and Jesus is unique, fundamentally other than that which God has with the Church or any member of it. Repeated attempts to find parallels or even analogies to this union have always finally been rejected, beginning with such early ones as that of the soul and the body, and of fire and metal in a blacksmith's glowing iron. More recent attempts deserve the same judgment. The ideas that there is also in us a spark of divinity, and that we are all also sons and daughters of God are not comparable to that of the hypostatic union. Donald Baillie's "analogy of grace" (*God*), which he thought to derive from Paul's words of 1 Cor. 15:10: "I worked . . . . though it was not I, but the grace of God which is with me" is also not analogous. All of these attempted analogies may point to profound truths, that the body and soul are one, that all persons are created in the image of God to be God's children, and that God's covenant partners are glad to give the glory to God alone, but none of these truths compares with the single truth that God's call of Jesus and Jesus' response has been used by God as the way in which he has called his Church into existence in the continuing history of the covenant. The hypostatic union, so the fathers thought, was incomparable.

There was one comparison or possible analogy that does not seem to have been considered in the tradition, that of the covenant between God and Israel. The connection between the incarnation and the covenant, however, is so basic that comparison and analogy seem misguided. Since we have been trying to understand the incarnation in the context of and with the help of the terms of the covenant, as we see this already in the *Magnificat* and *Nunc Dimittis* of Luke's Gospel, it would be a reduced estimate of the connection to compare them or see one as analogous to the other. Rather, my concern is to understand the doctrine of the Incarnation as an expression of the Church's awareness of the covenant between God and Israel and that new stage of its history in which the Gentiles began to be drawn into its course. To that new movement out of which the Church received its life, the Church can hardly want to make any comparison.

5. The classical christological tradition maintained that the man Jesus of Nazareth was enhypostatic. By this it meant that Jesus appeared in this world and on the stage of history solely and totally because God had come to this world and chosen to do so in just this way. This idea underscores and expands on the point we have noted under the heading of God's initiative. In spite of the dangers of depriving Jesus of his historical, biological, and cultural identity as one of his own people Israel, this teaching does express the Church's discovery that in its confrontation with Jesus, it has been met by God. This discovery, in turn, corresponds to and reflects the witness to Jesus as himself having given all the glory to God. For the Church, Jesus is precisely the one whose Jewish, human identity was determined first of all by his calling. With the teaching of the enhypostatic Jesus, the tradition has signaled the inadequacy of every sort of "Christology from below" that would begin with Jesus' response. How can the Church wish to begin other than from where God has begun with it, namely with God's enacted decision to be for the Church in just this way of presenting it with a Jew in whose presence God is present to it? This doctrine calls for a Christology that begins and ends with the God and Father of our Lord Jesus Christ, confessing the Jew Jesus as Lord to the glory of God the Father.

6. In its classical doctrine of the Incarnation, the Church has insisted on the full humanity of Jesus, then, now, and forever. It did so out of its conviction that the things concerning Jesus of Nazareth concern also the Church. All the debate on this matter has arisen because so much hangs on the substance to which this teaching refers: it has to do with us, with the Church first, and then with the whole human family. It has to do with human life, social life, political and economic life, and it has to do with our life in the midst of our environment. It has to do, that is, with our redemption and the redemption of all creation. A Christology for the Jewish-Christian reality will want to endorse that concern.

The classical doctrine expressed this concern by insisting on the unqualified involvement of both God and humanity in the incarnation, by saying that the divine and human "natures" of the one subject were *homoousios* respectively with the Father and with the rest of us human beings. At Nicea, only the consubstantiality of the divine Son with the Father was confessed; at Chalcedon, a century and a quarter later, it was felt necessary to add the consubstantiality between Jesus and the rest of humanity. That is just as much a claim about ourselves as it is about Jesus. The claim is that we and every human being are involved in the incarnation. It was all "for us and for our salvation."

The terms "salvation" and "redemption" will need to be handled with care. Israel bears continuing witness to the Church of the all-too-evident fact that this world is not yet redeemed, that it is a world full of poverty, sickness, suffering, and death. God is the Redeemer, but God's redemption is still in the future. When the Church speaks of the incarnation for our salvation, therefore, it needs to take Israel's witness into account and recall that God's Jewish Apostle to the Gentiles spoke of redemption consistently in the future tense, even if it was a future which he thought to be imminent. The Church and the whole world may be involved in what God has done in Christ, but the fruit of that involvement that is referred to as salvation or redemption is not yet here. As the rabbis could say, "All Israel has a place in the coming world [of redemption]," so the Church can say that the whole world has a place in the redemption promised. What has already been accomplished is not that reign of God to which Jesus bore witness, but the inclusion of the Church in Israel's hope. Indeed, the Church can hope that all humanity and humanity's environment will be included in God's rescue of his whole creation. Its confession that Christ was and is *homoousios* with all humanity supports no less a hope than this.

2. THE ETERNAL WORD OF THE FATHER

i. *The present form of the problem*

The Church today as in the past confesses its trust that Jesus of Nazareth is the incarnate Word of God the Father. It has decided, however, to confess also that the covenant between the same God and the Jewish people, as the continuation of Israel, is unbroken and enduring. The evidence is also clear, however, that the Church for centuries has confessed Jesus as the incarnate Word without affirming the covenant, even claiming that it had been superseded by a new covenant between God and the Church. The issue before the Church today, then, is not simply if it can confess Jesus as the incarnate Word and also affirm the covenant. That would be possible by forgetting or ignoring the past. The issue before a Church that is willing to own its own past is rather how to confess Jesus as the incarnate Word of God so as to make it clear, by its very manner of making that confession, that it *thereby* affirms God's covenant with his people Israel.

This issue is at once prudential, moral, and theological. It is prudential because the Church is confronted with a question of its credibility before a world already skeptical enough. Does the Church mean what it says? Can the Church be believed in any matter if it makes such solemn pronouncements about Christ and also about its newly discovered awareness of the Jewish people as the Israel of God? Given the Church's record of preaching and practicing contempt for the Jewish people, can it change itself in that respect without that having any effect whatsoever in its most central affirmation? Maybe its central affirmation should not be taken so seriously after all.

The question is also moral, in that it bears directly on whether the Church is concerned to speak the truth. To continue to make its central confession of faith in the same terms as it used while persecuting the Jewish people calls in question its new affirmation of the Jewish covenant. An outside observer, not to speak of a Jewish observer, might wonder about the moral integrity of the Church.

Above all, the issue is theological, for with its new affirmation of the covenant, the Church has confessed to a new understanding of God, namely that God remains the God of Israel, still the God of the Jewish people and committed to them, while also being the God of the Church as the God and Father of Jesus Christ. That recognition of the continuity in the history of God's relationship to a crucial part of God's creation must surely have its impact on how the Church understands and confesses the piece of that history centering on the things concerning Jesus of Nazareth out of which the Church was born.

The challenge to the Church, then, is how it can confess Jesus to be the incarnate Word of the God of Israel in such a way as to make it unavoidably clear, as it certainly has not been to this point, that in that very confession it is affirming the continuing covenant between God and Israel.

ii. The Word in covenantal terms

In order to meet this challenge, the starting point for the Church would seem to be a reconsideration of the terms with which it makes its central confession. The task before us, then, is to set the language of incarnation unmistakably within that of Israel's covenant. And the first word with which to begin is that which stands out so prominently in the principal text, the Prologue to the Fourth Gospel, on which the doctrine of the Incarnation rests: the Word of God. The first step is to understand "the Word of God" in covenantal terms.

This raises an interesting problem of biblical interpretation, for if the Church wishes to take Israel's covenant as the primary context to be affirmed, it would seem necessary for it to listen to Israel's own understanding of that covenant. Israel, at least from the time of Ezra and on throughout its history up to our time, has given clear priority to that part of its Scriptures that it calls Torah in the narrower sense, as distinct from the Prophets and Writings. That is to say, it has seen the Five Books of Moses, the Pentateuch, as the written form of God's Torah that is the heart of the Sinai covenant between God and Israel, with the prophetic books and the Wisdom literature taken as commentary on that Torah. When the Church, by contrast, has spoken of the Word of God, it has tended to think first of the Word that came to the prophets and so has given a certain priority to the prophetic books over the Torah. Further, a consensus has developed among Christian biblical students that the background to the Prologue's use of "the Word" lies in the figure of Wisdom developed in, among other places, the eighth chapter of the Book of Proverbs. The Church, then, has been inclined to place a part of Israel's Scriptures that Israel knows as the Writings, and especially the part known as the Prophets, ahead of the part known as the Torah.

The Church has traditionally placed a higher value on the Prophets and the Writings because it has thought that the Apostolic Writings generally draw more on those parts of Israel's Scriptures than they do on the Torah. The Church traditionally has placed a relatively lower value on Torah because it has assumed that Torah has been left behind with the coming of Christ. In short, the traditional valuation of the parts of Israel's Scripture is of a piece with the Church's supersessionist theology. Since Vatican II, however, the Church has claimed that it now rejects supersessionism, that it repudiates the anti-Judaism of its past, and that it wishes to affirm that the covenant, and so Torah, is eternal. There is no way in which it can carry out this new program, however, unless it changes its relative valuation of the parts of Israel's Scriptures. A Church that means to affirm the eternal covenant between God and the Jewish people will have to put the Torah first and come to see, along with Israel, that the Prophets and the Writings are to be read as commentary on and elaboration of Torah and the history of the Sinai covenant.

The consequence for the Church's Christology is that the term "the Word of God" will need to be thought through primarily from the perspective of Sinai. God's Word will then be seen first of all as God's covenantal Word, the word that "is very near you, in your mouth and in your heart that you may do it" (Deut. 30:14). From that starting point, the Church will then be able to follow the rabbinic lead that saw Torah as prior even to Creation and therefore be able to take the witness of Proverbs 8:22–31 as commentary on Sinai: the Wisdom that was with God and helped to guide the work of Creation was the Torah given to Moses. If the Church wishes to so preach the incarnation of the Word of God as to make it clear that it *thereby* means to affirm the covenant, it will preach *this* wisdom and Word: the Torah given to Moses, the Word of God's covenant.

iii. *God's covenantal outgoingness: John 1:1–5*

The Word of God, then, is God's creative word "through whom all things were made," the word with which God said, "Let there be light," and there was light (and as we argued in *People Israel*, chapter 2, this is Israel's peculiar witness and the Church owes it wholly to Israel). It is also the word that called Abraham and made a covenant with him and his descendants forever. And it is the word that came to Moses from the bush and above all and most fully, the word from Sinai that is "very near you . . . in your mouth and in your heart, so that you can do it" (Deut. 30:14). It is God's commandment as a gift, God's covenantal presence, incarnate in the heart and lives of his people Israel, and, as incarnate, a word to be done. The Word of God, then, is God's outgoingness that let the world be and bound Israel to himself, and himself to Israel, for the world's good. It is God's covenantal outgoingness. Whether the author of the Prologue to the Fourth Gospel meant all of this by the term he used is not the point. It may be disputed whether he meant to affirm the covenant of Israel with his witness to Christ. What seems indisputable is that a Church that wants to affirm Israel's covenant and acknowledge the Jewish-Christian reality will be obliged to read that Prologue as saying that "in the beginning" God went out from himself in covenantal love to create the world in which that love would be manifest.

Perhaps creation involved a movement of divine contraction (Isaac Luria's hypothesis of the *tzim-tzum*, discussed in *People Israel*, 63–64). That must remain only a hypothesis. What we do know is that this One who went forth from himself is the One that Israel and the Church knows as the covenanted One. Robert Alter (*Art*) has shown that a person's character is presented in Israel's Scriptures not by description but in that person's words. The same is clearly true also of Israel's God. Who and what God is, is shown in what God says. God's word is God's outgoing relationship to Israel, God in his relationship to Israel that became manifest at Sinai. The Word of God, then, from "the beginning," is God in his covenantal presence calling Israel, in covenantal freedom, to take up and do the word that it hears—and is to be—for all the nations of God's world.

A Church that means to make clear that its witness to the incarnation of the Word of God is an affirmation of the covenant between God and Israel will therefore read the opening of the Prologue of John as follows: In the beginning, so the Church has learned from Israel, and as Israel had learned from its own covenantal relationship to God, God was what he has shown himself to Israel to be: a God who goes out from himself toward the other. This is God's self-determination. God's outgoingness is God's own being, and so everything that has happened and come to be is the fruit of this outgoingness. So Israel learned primarily from its own creation out of Egypt at Sinai. That is Israel's life, given to it through the covenant. And since Israel was given this life for the sake of all the nations, so the light of God's outgoingness is the life of the whole world. That light, which Israel holds aloft to this day, shines in a dark world, the measure of its darkness revealed again and again in its hostility to Israel. As Israel's continuing life shows, however, that light has not been extinguished.

Along lines such as these the first five verses of the Prologue to John will be read by a Church that wants to make clear, as it begins its christological confession, that it is affirming the covenant between God and Israel.

3. INCARNATION AND COVENANT

i. *Covenantal incarnation: John 1: 6–14*

There follows a passage which may or may not have been part of the original Prologue. It tells of a Jew, John the Baptizer, as he was known, who came to herald another Jew, Jesus of Nazareth, as the light that was to be Israel's light for so many Gentiles who as yet had no idea of what God, whom they did not know, was about to do for them: they were about to become fellow citizens of the household of God (John 1:12–13). Then comes the decisive witness: the Word was spoken anew, and, behold: the Jew Jesus of Nazareth.

"And the Word happened as [or became, was made] flesh" (John 1:14). It was of course Jewish flesh, for the only God whom the Church knows is just this God who has chosen to work by means of this particular people for the good of the whole. "Incarnation" cannot say less than this. The Church cannot properly say "incarnation" without saying "Jew" at the same moment. It has no Lord but the Jew Jesus, and Jesus had no calling from and made no response to any but the God of the Jewish people. If the incarnation comes from the heart of this God, then it points to the heart of the covenant and so, in pointing to Israel's God, it points also to God's Israel.

In so carefully crafted a construction as the Prologue to John, it can hardly be an accident that the verb *egeneto* (happened, came to be, became, was made) of John 1:14 is exactly the one used twice before in verse 3, which directs us back to Israel's story of Creation. "In the beginning" (John 1:1 and Gen. 1:1), "everything *egeneto*" through the Word, and nothing *egeneto* apart from the Word (cf. "and God said . . . ," in Gen. 1:3, 6, 9, 11, etc.). So if the Word now *egeneto* a Jew, one of the people of the covenant, is this not all of a piece? Everything happened through the Word, and especially Israel happened through the Word, for the Word is God in his covenantal nearness, in Israel's mouth and heart. If the creative Word is so incarnate in Israel, is it so different to say that the Word now also happened as this Jew for the sake of Israel's service to the world that happened through him? Along such lines may verse 14 of the Prologue of John be read by a Church concerned to acknowledge and then find its own identity in the context of the eternal covenant between God and the Jewish people.

I think we should notice that the text we are interpreting says something more subtle than that Jesus *is* the Word. It says that the Word went forth into the world and the result was this Jew. Confronted with this Jew, then, the Johannine community was sure they were confronted by the God whose Word now confronted them in just this way. This is how God chooses to meet his Church and give it life and direction.

ii. Incarnational covenant: John 1:17

The conclusion of the Prologue directs us explicitly to the covenant by juxtaposing "the Torah given through Moses" and the "grace and truth [that] have come through Jesus Christ" (v. 17). It should be noted that they are juxtaposed, set side by side, not compared or contrasted. The text simply adds the second to the first, paratactically, as if to say that first there is the one, and now there is the other. Something more has happened. The unseen God who is the Father is now being made known. The something more, then, is a further step in the story of God's covenantal relationship with his creation, reaching out beyond those who already know the Father; it has to do with those who do not know the God whom Jesus called "Father." These are those Gentiles who, being "alienated from Israel" were "without God in this world" (Eph. 2:12). Grace and truth now come to claim them as well and place them alongside of and as "fellow citizens" with Israel. That is the grace and truth that has come through Jesus Christ.

We can say, therefore, that Jesus Christ is in important respects for the Church what Torah is for Israel, not only direction and instruction—although certainly that too—but life, the way in which God is present and that to which it is to be conformed and so transformed into the children of God. God's outgoingness, his self-determination as a covenantal God, took shape for Israel as Torah "through Moses": in a fully creaturely form, that is. As the rabbis said, "Torah speaks in the language of human beings." But Torah was given to be done, to be lived, to take flesh in the life of Israel, the Jewish people. It is to be in Israel's mouth and heart, that Israel may live, holy as God is holy. Torah was given that Israel might be God's own light to the world. And that is to say, Israel is itself to be the incarnation of God's covenantal presence in the world.

To this incarnational covenant has now been added the incarnate outgoingness of God directed to God's Church, drawn from all the nations. For their sake the Word has become the one Jew who is to draw them into the life that God is for Israel. He is to be for them what Torah is for Israel: when they hear him, they will hear God's Word; when they serve him, they will serve the Father. When they speak their highest words of praise to him, therefore, they will do so always in order to give the glory to God the Father, who has come to them and claimed them in this Jew. The incarnation of the Word of God that has appeared for the Church in Jesus Christ, full of grace and truth, is grounded in and added to the incarnate Word of God spoken anew every day to Israel in the Torah.

The Christian concept of incarnation means God, truly the God of Israel, Creator of heaven and earth, present and at work for the world's good in fully earthly, utterly particular, creaturely existence. It means God's own reality fully present in definite, identifiable members of the human species. That is what Israel's whole history has been about, by virtue of the covenant between God and Israel. Both God and also Israel are fully engaged in this way in which God means to lead the world to its redemption. In the context of Israel's life in God's incarnational covenant, the incarnation of the Word of God in the Jew Jesus will be seen to be a further, novel step in God's continuing covenantal relationship with the world. The incarnation, then, is God's radical new expression of his eternal faithfulness to his creation, whereby he has added to his beloved Israel also his beloved Church in the service of his redemptive purpose. To what he has given through Moses, he has now added what he has given through Jesus Christ. In both cases, what he has given is ultimately himself as the life of his whole creation.

4. THE COVENANTAL CRITIQUE OF THE UNITY OF SUBJECT

i. The identity of the covenant partners

For all of the intimacy of the covenant, God is God and Israel is Israel. Israel clarified the distinction with its teaching that God alone is the Creator, and everything that is not God is a creature (cf. *People Israel*, 67–68). The christological formula of Chalcedon had its own way of setting limits on what could be said of the unity of God and Jesus in the incarnation. The Council settled on four negative adverbs: the divine and human were without mixture or change, but also inseparable and indivisible. The question to be addressed is how this linguistic rule works when the incarnation is set in its covenantal context.

Before beginning, however, it should be noted that the Chalcedonian rule was an attempt not so much to define as to set limits on what should be said about the "one Lord Jesus Christ" of the Nicean confession. Nicea left the Church with a single subject yet with dual predication. Of the one it was said both "God" and "man." Did the one turn into the other? Were the two really only the one? How could the one become the other and still be the one, and was the other then still another? Nicea did not say, and the following century saw many different answers to these questions. Chalcedon was an attempt to limit the range of possibilities.

It should also be noted that the fathers at Chalcedon did not seem to be concerned with the covenantal context of Christ. They addressed the question of the involvement of the Creator and creation in the particular case of the incarnation without reference to the covenant. We are asking a question that was not theirs, because we do so for a Church that is concerned, as theirs was not, to affirm the covenant between God and the Jewish people, and to do so clearly in its central confession of faith. This difference may be expected to show up in any answer to which we are led.

We begin, then, with the rule that God—the Creator of heaven and earth, the God of Sinai, and the God and Father of Jesus Christ, but then also God in his outgoingness to become Creator of his creation, and then to bind Israel to himself and himself to Israel for creation's good, and again to call Jesus of Nazareth and to seize on his obedience to his calling and to bless it as a way to call Gentiles into his covenantal purpose, and so also the God whose Presence (*Shekhinah*) accompanies the Jewish people and whose Spirit enlivens the Church to this day—is and remains the initiator and renewer of Creation, the covenant, Jesus of Nazareth, and the vitality of the Jewish people and the Church. He is deeply involved in his creation, as that whole story bears witness, and he has determined himself for all eternity to be God in just this involved way. In precisely this self-determined way, however, he remains God. He is not a creature, not Israel, not Jesus of Nazareth, not the Jewish people, and not the Church. He is the one before whom all these draw near in praise and worship. He is the one they all seek to serve and when they do so, they are not serving themselves or even a part or an aspect of themselves. They serve another: God. God, in his covenantal self-determination from "the beginning," and so precisely in his outgoingness that the Church has called the Word, remains eternally God's Self. In God's most intimate involvement in the world for its good, God is in no sense mixed with or changed into anything of this world. Even in the incarnation, said the fathers of Chalcedon, God is God without mixture or change.

The same is true, *mutatis mutandis*, of Jesus of Nazareth, said those same fathers. Like creation, like Israel, Jesus, crucified and raised by God, is forever the Jew born of his mother Mary. He is forever that Galilean who lived with and served his people under Roman occupation and was crucified by Pontius Pilate. One with us in his humanity, he is distinct in his calling and his response to that calling. He remains that particular human being for all eternity in the service of the God he called "Father." The Jew Jesus, as well as God in his outgoingness, remains forever distinct in his own identity. How could it be otherwise with a son of the covenant?

ii. *The closeness of partnership*

A Church that has preached and taught the world contempt for the Jews for over eighteen long centuries, and which now regrets that past and wishes to make it clear that it affirms the covenant between God and the Jewish people as the rock from which it was hewn and the root onto which it has been grafted, could make this affirmation no clearer than by understanding, teaching, and preaching the closeness between God and Jesus as a special case of the closeness of the partnership in the covenant of Sinai. In order to do so, given its past, it will have to learn from Jews about that closeness. It will learn from Jews the Jewish teaching of God's love for Israel and Israel's love for God; of God's presence going with the Jewish people into exile and suffering with all their suffering; of Torah as God's gracious gift to his people as loving instruction in how to walk a path that leads toward God's redemption of his people and, with them, the whole of creation; and of Shabbat—not a teaching but an experience lived anew each week—as a tiny but glorious taste of that coming redemption.

If the Church does not learn from Jews of the closeness, the intimacy, and also the fear of this partnership, of the freedom it gives and the claim it makes, it is not clear where it will find words to speak of the closeness of God and Jesus, for these teachings (or their foundations in the Scriptures he held sacred) were precisely those that the Jew Jesus would have known and within which, as the apostolic witness presents him, he expressed the closeness between himself and the God he called "*abba.*" A Church aware of the Jewish-Christian reality will be grateful to Israel for having given it the lived reality and so the vocabulary with which to speak of the closeness of a divine-human relationship.

Separation or division? Between the God of Israel and the Israel of God? Never! Israel is only Israel and fails God ever again, but God is God and he will never retreat from his own self-determined identity: Israel's Creator will be Israel's redeemer! So said the prophet-author of Deutero-Isaiah, and so has Israel said ever since. He who touches the Jewish people touches the apple of God's eye (Zech. 2:8), and God's salvation is of the Jews (John 4:22). When the world has to do with the Jewish people, it has to do with God, and when the world would know of the God of Israel, it will have to listen to the Israel of God. Neither is understandable without the other. Noetically and ontologically, they are inseparable and indivisible.

Does the Church want to say more than this about the partnership between God and Jesus that has given it life out of death? Of course it wants to say that Jesus was not only an example or illustration, but also a quite special case, of the closeness between God and Israel. He was indeed a special case, for with his particular case God began a new chapter in the history of his covenantal dealings with the world. With his case, the life of the Gentile Church began. But the novelty stands within the context of the continuity of God's covenantal self-determination. The closeness of the partnership between God and Jesus is grounded in and also expresses, because it is a part of, the closeness between God and the people of Jesus. *That* is why and how Jesus "binds the peoples of the world to the people of God" (*cf.* the Rhineland Synod, 1980). In the Church's realization of its closeness to the Jewish people, it confesses that the Jew Jesus and the God of Israel in his outgoingness are inseparable and indivisible.

iii. A covenantal unity of subject?

Nicea bequeathed to the Church a hypostatic unity of subject in its Christology. Israel's witness to the Church is that this at least approaches, and may actually be, blasphemy. A Church that paid no heed to Israel's witness, from the last third of the first to the last third of the twentieth century, could develop its Christology on the basis of Nicea. It could and did argue about whether that unity controlled the duality of predication (the tendency of Alexandrian theologians in the fifth century and Lutheran theologians in the sixteenth and seventeenth centuries), or whether the dual predication controlled the unity (the tendency of Antiochene and later, Reformed theologians). The issue was whether the Church was speaking the strict truth in saying that Jesus existed before Creation and was omniscient, and that the Word of God was born, suffered, and died, or whether it was more correct to say that the Word of God remained omnipotent and impassible, while the man Jesus was born, suffered, and died.

A Church that wishes to affirm the covenant between God and the Jewish people, however, and is therefore open to hearing Israel's witness to the duality of subject in the covenant, as well as the duality of predication, will be able to reconsider Nicea's unity of subject and decide how it will interpret it. Neither side of the issue, as just formulated in the last paragraph, is satisfactory. Clearly, if Jesus was omniscient by virtue of the incarnation, he was not "of one substance" with the rest of humanity. And if God's outgoingness cannot reach as far as the cross and death, then God's commitment to his creation is put in doubt.

If we listen to the witness of Israel to the covenant, we hear also of a unity, but it is not a unity of subject. On the contrary, there are always two subjects, God and Israel, but it is precisely of their unity that Israel speaks. It speaks first of all, of course, of the unity of God: "Hear O Israel, the LORD our God is one," but this central confession is of the one LORD who is "our God." The confession of God's unity is therefore also a confession of the covenantal bond between God and Israel.

The unity of the covenant, however, is personal. God and Israel are one as husband and wife are one (cf. Gen. 2:24; Hos. 2:16–20). They are united by covenantal commitment, and the goal of this union is that Israel be holy as God is holy, righteous as God is righteous, merciful as God is merciful. There is, then, a certain *communicatio idiomatum*, a sharing of characteristics, but this sharing comes about by intention and action in history, by Israel's *imitatio Dei* on the one side and by God's sharing Israel's joys and sufferings on the other. That is a real unity but, being personal, it is always of two distinct subjects, of two partners in the one covenant.

It might be objected that this concept of unity, in contrast to that of the hypostatic union of classical Christology, is not ontological. That is true only in so far as the metaphysical question is begged. What metaphysics is to govern the discussion of union? If it is predetermined that reality is to be analyzed in terms of *hypostasis* (substance or subsistence) and *physis* (nature), then the hypostatic union will be judged ontological and the unity of the covenant only volitional. If, on the other hand, reality is analyzed in personal terms with the relationship of love between human beings taken as the highest visible form, if reality consists primarily of relationships of love and trust and forgiveness, and then, only secondarily, of material relationships, then it could be said that the covenantal model of unity is indeed ontological by its own metaphysical presuppositions. It is clear that Israel's witness to the covenant implies a metaphysics different from that implied by Nicea, but it is by no means self-evident that that of Nicea is better adapted to support the claim of the Church that, in the Jew Jesus of Nazareth, it is confronted by the God of Israel, Creator of heaven and earth.

It is useful to recall that what we have been calling the unity of subject (with dual predication) is shorthand for the Church's confession (given first of all in the present tense) that confronted by the Jew of Nazareth as he is present to the Church in preaching, Eucharist, prayer, and in acts of love, justice, and forgiveness done in his name, it finds itself confronted by the God of Abraham, Isaac, and Jacob. The unity to which the Church's Christology bears witness is the unity realized in the Church's trust that in its meeting with Jesus Christ, it finds itself before the God and Father of Jesus Christ. With "doubting" Thomas it finds itself saying as it looks at this Jew, "My Lord and my God!" Not that Jesus becomes God—what Jew could ever want such a thing said of him?—but that God has effectively used this Jew to make himself present to the Church. The unity of subject of Nicea is one way in which this can be expressed, but a Church that wishes to make it clear that with its central confession it is affirming the covenant between God and the Jewish people will want to qualify Nicea by setting it within the terms of Israel's witness to the covenant. The result will be a doctrine of the Incarnation expressed in covenantal rather than material terms.

CHAPTER ELEVEN

Christ the Lord

In confessing Jesus Christ as Lord, the Church accepts him as God's invitation into the freedom of life in the Spirit, which is its witness to the conviction shared with Israel, that the story of the covenantally self-determined God of all creation is not over.

1. ONE GOD, ONE LORD

i. The LORD and the Lord

One of the earliest recorded confessions of the young Church is that God has bestowed on Jesus "the name which is above every name," that is, God's own name, so that "every tongue" should confess "that Jesus Christ is Lord, to the glory of God the Father" (Phil. 2:9, 11). Israel's standard way of avoiding vocalizing God's ineffable name, written in the scriptures as YHWH, was and is to say *Adonai*, "the Lord," (and we follow the practice of the Revised Standard Version in putting the word in capital letters when so used: LORD). What is being confessed when Jesus Christ is given this same name, and how can this be confessed to the glory of God the Father?

The same question, together with the suggestion of an answer, is raised by a passage in Paul's letter to the Corinthians (1 Cor. 8:6). In connection with a question about eating meat that had been offered in pagan rituals, Paul made light of the many gods and lords of paganism adding, "yet for us there is one God, the Father, from whom is everything and for whom we are, and one Lord, Jesus Christ, through whom is everything and through whom we are." Everything is *from* God and *through* Jesus Christ, and we are or exist *for* God and *through* Jesus Christ. The variation in prepositions suggests the following: the world, and with it Israel and now also the Church, has the God of Israel whom Jesus called Father as its origin and its destiny. Israel has known this since its infancy. The Church has come to know this and to be a part of this because of the things concerning Jesus of Nazareth. It is through him that it can join Israel in giving the glory to God the Father. He is the Church's Lord, sharing in God's own name, because God has used him, in his calling and his response, and now in the response of his disciples to him, to bring Gentiles, as Gentiles, into the story of God's covenantal love.

Israel to this day confesses God in the words of the *Shema*, which reflects what Jews count as the first of God's Ten Commandments: "Hear, O Israel: the LORD is our God, the LORD alone." The Church joins with Israel when it says, "for us there is one God, the Father, from whom is everything and for whom we live." Israel continues its confession by reciting the great commandment, to love God, and then by speaking of God's other commandments. It continues, that is, by referring to the covenant of Sinai, which is its founding moment in which it lives to this day. The Church's confession continues in another way. It refers instead to its own great founding moment through which it lives: it speaks of Jesus Christ, not of Sinai. So fully does it believe this novelty to be in continuity with Israel's story of God that it confesses that God has conferred on Jesus Christ his own name.

The question can and has been put, however, whether this confession preserves the continuity and whether, therefore, the Church is still speaking of the God of Israel's story.

The question has been put by Jon Levenson, *Sinai and Zion*, and even more pointedly by Michael Goldberg in an unpublished paper, "God, Action, and Narrative: *Which* Narrative? *Which* Action? *Which* God?" It is a fair question for a Jew to put, but it is even more important for a Christian to ask and to be able to give an affirmative answer, not to satisfy a Jewish question, but rather for the sake of the coherence of Christian faith.

An affirmative answer is possible, but only if the Church so confesses Jesus Christ as Lord and so tells his story as to show that God's deed in Jesus Christ is sufficiently "in character" for it to be recognizably the deed of the One who made a covenant with Israel "at Sinai." Classical Christology, we have argued, fails to meet this text. A Christology for a Church that wishes to affirm the covenant between God and the Jewish people can meet the test only if it makes clear at every point that it gives the glory to God the Father, and only if it shows at every point, especially when it speaks of Easter, that God was and is acting covenantally. That is why, in chapter 5 above, we had to stress how much the event of Easter was and continues to be the work of the Church as well as the work of God, and why in chapter 10 we had to present a covenantal interpretation of the Church's doctrine of the Incarnation. It remains to carry through with an interpretation of the lordship of Christ that is equally covenantal.

ii. Covenantal lordship

We begin by asking how God's lordship is covenantal. How does the LORD rule? The answer that Israel discovered was that the LORD rules by making a covenant. He rescued Israel from slavery and made it his vassal to be a royal priesthood and a holy nation. He rules, that is to say, by calling an otherwise undistinguished people to conform its life to God's commandments. He rescued it, not from sin but from the domination and attacks of its enemies, and led it to a place where it was to serve the LORD and the LORD alone. His rule is covenantal in that it is really up to Israel whether God's rule will be effective on earth. He rules by invitation, by pleading, by threatening, by enticing, but he gives to his covenant partner the responsibility of making his rule effective.

When I say that Israel discovered that the LORD rules by making covenant, I am referring first of all to the discovery of rabbinic Judaism, not to one obvious in the Scriptures of ancient Israel. The covenant of Sinai is indeed central in the canonical Scriptures of Israel, but that canon contains a wealth of other views of God's rule. God rules through mighty acts and wonders, through moving the nations of the world as his instruments, and through wisdom. The rabbis of postbiblical Judaism, having pondered this diverse witness and also the course of the history of their people, came to the discovery that shaped almost all of Judaism up until the modern period, and shapes much of it to this day: the LORD rules by making covenant.

The Church has been drawn into this history of God's covenantal way of ruling "through" the Lord Jesus Christ. It would appear to follow that the lordship of Christ must also be covenantal, but it is not clear that is how the Church has understood it. That is because the Church has not attended to Israel's reading of its own Scriptures. When it has thought of the covenant at all, it has thought first of the Abrahamic covenant and then of the covenant with David. That is how it read its "Old Testament" in the light of its "New Testament." The result for the anti-Judaic Church was that it took the scriptural witness to be fundamentally a covenant of total grace. God does it all. He creates, he elects, he redeems, without any place for humanity other than to trust in God and wait for it all to be revealed in God's good time. Thus God and also Christ were thought to rule as absolute monarchs, even if that rule could only be seen by the eye of faith. That eye could hardly have been expected to take note of the Jewish reality, since all was subsumed in the single reality of the Church and its one Lord, Jesus Christ.

What "the eye of faith" saw is vividly represented in the figure of the Pantocrator still to be seen in some surviving Byzantine churches. And the unaided eye could also have seen in the Byzantine emperor how the Church thought that God's rule was to be reflected on earth.

Douglas Hall has argued ("Rethinking Christ" in Davies, *Anti-Semitism*) that, although this monarchal, triumphal melody has dominated the Christian tradition, there has also been an antiphonal minor melody of a more humble sort. It is certain that a Church that wishes to affirm the covenant between God and the Jewish people will have to rethink Christ along some such lines as those that Hall has called for and as we have attempted in these pages, but it will also have to rethink the meaning and implications of the actual covenant between God and Israel, the one which has been and continues to be central for the Jewish people. That covenant, the Sinai covenant, calls for a different conception of God's rule than the Church has generally held. Yet just this view of the covenant, in which God confers genuine responsibility on his covenant partners, coheres with the witness to Christ of the Apostolic Writings concerning living by God's commandments (Luke 10:28), about daring to forgive each other (Mark 2:10), and of God in heaven abiding by what human beings decide on earth (Matt. 16:19, 18:18; John 20:23). It coheres with a Christ who rejected the temptation to rule as a monarch (Matt. 4:8–10; John 6:15) and refused to call heaven to his rescue (Matt. 26:53). In short, when it is seen that God's rule is presented in Israel's witness as being covenantally determined, the apostolic witness to the rule of Christ can also be seen to be covenantal. Indeed, the rule of Christ is no other than the covenantal rule of God now extended over the Church.

From the perspective of the Church, however, the matter can be put in the reverse order: it is from Christ's covenantal rule that the Church first became aware of God's covenantally determined rule. The Church's one Lord refused and refuses to "lord it over" the Church. He is present to it in humility, as one who serves and who calls the Church to join him in his service to God, to Israel, and to the least of his brothers and sisters. But if it is indeed the case, as the Church believes, that in his presence it is in the presence of God, then God's rule must be of just this humble sort. God's covenantal rule of Israel and in the world, then, is not of another sort than the covenantal one he has given Christ to exercise over the Church. It is his rule as the Holy Spirit.

Before continuing, we would note that there is a passage in the Apostolic Writings that appears to present a rather different view of the relationship between the one God and the one Lord Christ. In 1 Timothy 2:5, a later author wrote that "there is one God and there is one mediator between God and human beings, the man Christ Jesus." The term "mediator" occurs elsewhere in the Apostolic Writings in three places in the so-called Epistle to the Hebrews, but there it is always in the sense of Jesus being the mediator of a new covenant, as Moses was the mediator of the original Sinai covenant. Mediator in that sense means the bringer, messenger, or agent of a new stage in God's plan. Is this what the author of 1 Timothy had in mind? That is possible, for the verse quoted comes in the context of God's wish to be the savior of all and to bring all to know him. If we read the verse from 1 Timothy in the light of 1 Cor. 8:6 and with an eye also on Hebrews, we may be able to resist the idea of Jesus as an intermediary, standing as it were between human beings and God and being the only way from one to the other (as if God could not reach his creatures other than through the one who turned out for him to be his way to call his Gentile Church into existence, or as if his creatures could not pray directly to him, but had, as it were, to pray to Jesus, who in turn would then relay the message to God). That view of Christ as mediator may well be based on some forms of Christian piety, but it is a distortion of the apostolic witness. Its existence, however, suggests that the very term "mediator" is a poor one to use in speaking of the relationship of the one Lord Jesus Christ and the one God, the Father. Far better at this point that we follow the line more widely attested in the Apostolic Writings and speak of the Spirit.

2. THE LORD IS THE SPIRIT

i. *The Holy Spirit of the one God*
From the Church's beginning, apparently, Christians have spoken of the Spirit in a broad variety of ways.

In the following I am indebted to G. W. H. Lampe's provocative and suggestive *God as Spirit*, not so much for its conclusions as for its extensive exegetical discussion and its stimulating openness to some fresh thinking about traditional doctrine in that light. His thesis is that the experience of the post-Easter presence of Jesus and the experience of God as Spirit were one and the same thing, both referring to the experience of God as he works upon and within the human spirit. God as Spirit could also be called the Christ-Spirit, he wrote, "the indwelling presence of God as Spirit in the freely responding spirit of man as this is concretely exhibited in Christ and reproduced in some measure in Christ's followers" (Lampe, *Spirit,* 144). This attention to the cooperative working of the divine and the human suggests that Lampe might have found useful the model of the covenant, but he made no use of it. This is possibly because for Lampe it was the modern world, not the Church's new acknowledgment of the Jewish people today, that led him to this rethinking.

We may sum up this rich witness as saying that the Holy Spirit is the God of Israel present and acting, reaching into the lives of human beings and turning them to serve God's cause and so through them continuing his story. The Spirit is God giving understanding or wisdom or prophetic insight into his continuing purpose. The Spirit is the way in which God rules, by guiding, leading, and enlightening those through whom the story is to be carried forward. To speak of the Spirit, therefore, always involves saying something about the one or ones to whom the Spirit comes. This should hardly be surprising, however, if by Holy Spirit the Church means the Spirit of the Holy One of Israel, for to speak of the Spirit is neither more nor less than to speak of the effects of God's outgoingness, of God's covenantal self-determination not to be without God's covenant partners nor to do his work without their cooperation.

According to traditional Church teaching, the Holy Spirit is a distinct *hypostasis* or *persona* of the one God, one of God's distinct ways of being himself. The distinctness is perhaps best left unstressed. That the Church is touched by the one God when it is touched by the Holy Spirit, that God is the sender and giver of the Spirit, that the Spirit is "of God"; these are the themes that must matter to the Church, and it can be argued that the inclusion of the Holy Spirit in the creed of Nicea occurred for the sake of just these themes. Under the heading usually called the unity of God, the Church has in fact borne witness in its trinitarian language of prayer and doxology to the continuity of the story of the one God, the Holy One of Israel, who created this world, spoke through the prophets (of which Moses was the greatest), called and fully authorized Jesus Christ to claim the Church for himself, and is yet working among them to realize his will on earth. When the Church speaks of the Holy Spirit, it is claiming that its own life is also part of the story of the one God.

The claim to have a place in the story of the one God, however, has consequences which the anti-Judaic Church could not see, but which a Church wishing to acknowledge the covenant between that God and Israel will have to develop. When God by his Holy Spirit draws the Church into his story, he draws it into an intimate relationship to Israel's story and so to the living Israel whose life is where that story continues today. In so far as the Church's prayer "Come, Holy Spirit!" is answered, therefore, it is moved into the proximity of Israel. The Spirit of the One God ties the Church to the people of God, and a Church that would not accept that tie would to that extent be rejecting the rule of the Spirit of God.

ii. The Spirit of Jesus Christ

Historians tell us that before the Church came to something of an agreement to work out its Christology in the terms of an incarnation of the Word of God, it also had ample room for a Spirit-Christology. The grounds for this alternative were abundant in the Apostolic Writings. Jesus is presented as a man endowed with the Spirit and who worked by the power of the Spirit to cast out demons. When Jesus returned to the Father, according to the Johannine Gospel, the Spirit came to take his place, as it were, or to continue his work. And there was Paul's word, "The Lord is the Spirit" (2 Cor. 3:17).

Even more abundant, however, is the witness to the Holy Spirit as the Spirit of Jesus Christ. What does it mean to say that the Holy Spirit is the Spirit of Jesus Christ? It means first of all that to be touched or moved by the Spirit has the effect of being touched or moved by Jesus. His story, and so the larger story of Israel's covenantal life with God which was and remains his context, acquires a hearing and is therefore acted upon. A person touched by the Spirit becomes an actor in the covenantal story of God, and does so through the story of Christ. The person moved by the Spirit is moved by the words and actions and the person of Jesus. Christ's words "come alive," his compassion stirs a corresponding compassion, his cause is taken up.

The context of Christ, however, was and is Israel. The cause of Christ was and is no other than the covenantal cause of the God of Israel. To be touched by Christ's Spirit is to be touched by the Spirit of God. It is God's own Spirit that God sends through Christ when he reaches out to include new partners in his covenantal cause. For this reason it would be better to remain with the original wording of the creed and drop the later Western addition of the *filioque* clause (the words, "and the Son"), and this appears to be the tendency in ecumenical discussions of the matter. The Holy Spirit "proceeds from the Father." Or we might say, as some have suggested, the Holy Spirit "proceeds *from* the Father *through* the Son." For the Church worships and glorifies the Holy Spirit, as it worships and glorifies the Son, always and only to the glory of the Father who has moved to be present to his Church and has caused his Church to be present to him, in this way that draws the Church along the path of God's covenantal purpose.

The *filioque* clause has the unfortunate effect of masking the temporal development or historical sequence of the movement of God's cause in the world. It tempts the Church to contemplate the invisible inner life of the Triune God, rather than to reflect on and give thanks for the visible economy of God's way with his creatures. The movement of the Spirit that matters fundamentally to the Church is the continuing covenantal initiative of God: having led Israel to Sinai and there given it responsibility for his cause, he later reached out to lead Gentiles to acknowledge Jesus Christ, who in turn leads them to accept enlistment in the cause of the Father. This triune movement, in which the Church comes to life and takes responsibility along with Israel for the future of God's creation, is what the Church confesses when it calls the Spirit of God also the Spirit of Christ. In making this confession, the Church accepts its place alongside of Israel in God's cause. Its place and its very existence are from the Father and move toward the Father, and this comes about through Jesus Christ in the Spirit.

This interpretation of the Spirit may be clarified by setting it alongside that of Calvin. When one has come to the end of Book II of the *Institutes*, one might well conclude that Calvin has considered all that is necessary for the salvation of the world, and that what had to be done to remedy the sinful condition into which the world had lapsed had all been carried through to completion on the cross. Christ had taken without reserve the place of sinful humanity and suffered the death that was its due. Nothing more needed to be or could be done. But then, at the beginning of Book III, Calvin stopped and asked how all this of which he had written could have anything to do with himself and his reader. There, at a great distance (Calvin preferred a spatial image where we might today use a temporal one), was all that God had done in Christ. How does it get from there to here? His answer was the Holy Spirit; it is the Spirit who brings to bear on us in the present that which God has done in Christ in the past.

The present interpretation differs in not presenting the things concerning Jesus of Nazareth as complete in themselves, needing only a means of applying their effects in a later time. Rather, we have presented those things as the beginnings of a new development in the continuing history of God's purpose. The role of the Spirit, then, is God's continuing role of leading his Church to Christ who leads it to the God of Israel and the Israel of God, so that it will join Israel in God's praise and in taking up responsibility for how it walks today and into the future.

iii. The Spirit in the Church

The lordship of Christ is demonstrated by the power of the Spirit to build the community that is the Church. Whom the Spirit touches reaches out to make contact with others who are similarly touched. Therefore where the Spirit of Christ is, there is the Church. Being the Spirit of Christ, it invites and encourages Christ-likeness. This is why one of the fruits of the Spirit can be the gift of distinguishing between spirits (1 Cor. 12:10): only in the Spirit may it be seen that the Spirit which leads to an *imitatio*

Christi is the Holy Spirit. In the exercise of that discipleship, the rule of Christ is realized. And where Christ rules, there is the Church.

Whether we say that Christ rules by the Spirit, or Christ rules as the Spirit, is not so important as to be clear that the lordship or rule in question is understood to be that of one who is witnessed to as having said that he was among his disciples as one who served (Mark 10:45) and as having refused to take from them their own responsibility and power to make decisions (Luke 12:14). The imitation of Christ therefore includes acceptance of the precept that among his disciples there shall be no ruling of the sort exercised by the rulers among the Gentiles (Mark 10:42–44). It is noteworthy that this last saying contrasts the rule of Christ, and so also rule among Christ's followers, with rule among the Gentiles. The rule of Christ and within his Church has its model elsewhere. Its model is God's rule in Israel—the rule as it is to be conducted among the people of the covenant.

The interpretation of lordship as service and of the Lord as the servant is becoming a fairly common theme in contemporary theology. My interpretation is not at all unique in that regard. The distinctive feature that I am giving to the motif of service is provided by the model of the covenant: God's servant-lordship is an empowering one that sets his covenant partners free to cooperate with him in service.

The Spirit makes for community. It binds the Church together into one body. This has been said in the Church from its beginning. But the Spirit, precisely as the Spirit of the Father and of Christ, makes for another sort of binding: it ties the Church to Israel, the Jewish people. A Church that did not see and act upon its solidarity with the Jewish people could hardly be said to be living and walking under the guidance of the Spirit of the Holy One of Israel. It could hardly be accepting the lead of the Spirit of him who "became a servant to the circumcision" (Rom. 15:8). Because the Spirit is the Spirit of the covenantal God, it leaves room for the Church's disobedience, the Church's "freedom" to go where the Spirit does not lead. So the Church in its long history as the anti-Judaic Church may not properly be said to have been without the Spirit. What can and must be said, however, is that the anti-Judaic Church was to that extent a disobedient Church, a Church that did not let the rule of Jesus Christ and of the Father guide its course.

In that the Church today, since *Nostra Aetate,* has begun to see the error of its ways and is trying to follow the lead of the Spirit, it can begin for the first time in nineteen centuries to show that its life is lived in the history of God's covenantal involvement with his creatures. It can do so by showing that it understands its own life covenantally, taking responsibility for its own words and actions. As it moves to recognize and act out of its solidarity with the people of God's Sinai covenant, it will therefore not pray for the Spirit to tell it what to do. It will rather act in the conviction that it is commanded to decide what to do, because it walks in the light of the Spirit of the God of Sinai and of Jesus Christ in his solidarity with his own people.

iv. The Spirit in the world

The Church knows the Spirit as *Creator Spiritus:* in the words of the Nicene Creed, the Spirit is "the Lord, the giver of life." As the Spirit brooded over the waters of Creation, so all the world is hers. The Spirit of the covenantally self-determined God is out there in the world, not just in the Church, stirring things up, sharing covenantally in all created life, and so suffering with all that suffers in this world. Paul wrote that the whole creation groans with longing for its restoration (Rom. 8:22), and that the Church, which has the first fruits of the Spirit, joins in this groaning (v. 22). That could mean that the Spirit also groans with the pain of this world. Surely the Giver of life would suffer when any life is one of suffering.

The Church has not been told just how the Spirit of God is present and active in the world. The Spirit, it has been told, blows where it wills (John 3:8), so the Church can only remain open and attentive to hearing in the world sounds the tone of which it has come to learn from the Word God has spoken to it. It will listen for the echoes of the covenant of Sinai when men and women assume responsibility for ordering life according to the ways of peace and justice. It will listen for the echoes of God's covenantal act in Jesus Christ, inviting men and women to take responsibility for doing works of trust, mercy, and forgiveness, as the Church has learned these from Christ. It will look for any signs of solidarity with the Jewish people and the purposes of God in entering covenantally into human history. When it hears such sounds it will not know, but it may surely suspect, that it has come across the work of the Holy Spirit in the world.

The implications of these reflections is that it may in fact be possible to make "theological discoveries through interfaith dialogue"; so reads the subtitle of the study guide *My Neighbor's Faith—and Mine* prepared by the Dialogue Subunit of the World Council of Churches. It may happen that the Church will learn better to understand and accept the Lordship of Christ through discovering what Christ's Spirit has been accomplishing outside the Church. If such discoveries are possible, it will be because the Church is clear that the lordship is covenantal and will therefore be discoverable in the fruits of the Spirit.

3. FREEDOM IN THE SPIRIT

i. Freedom through transformation

The principal work of the Holy Spirit, thought Calvin (*Institutes*, III, I, 4), is faith. Certainly a sure trust in God's goodness is a constituent part of the freedom into which the Spirit calls the Church. In a passage touching on the freedom of the Spirit, however, Paul moves on from there to speak of what that freedom amounts to. "The Lord is the Spirit," he wrote (2 Cor. 3:17–18), "and where the Spirit of the Lord is, there is freedom. And we all . . . reflecting the glory of the Lord, are being changed into his likeness. . . ." Faith may be chronologically the first work of the Spirit, but the principal effect of the presence of the Spirit, as Paul seems to have understood the matter, is a human transformation of being conformed to Christ.

It seems at first sight that Paul saw this transformation as something that happens *to* us: "we are being changed." Yet he says this is our freedom, which sounds as if we have something to do with it. This is confirmed when Paul says later in the same letter (2 Cor. 6:1) that he, surely as one who has the freedom of the Spirit, was "working together with" God. And in another place (Gal. 6:25, emphasis added) he says, "If we live by the Spirit, let us also *walk* by the Spirit," and again (Gal. 6:16, emphasis added), emphatically, "*Walk* by the Spirit!" The transformation that Christian freedom makes possible, then, appears to be decidedly an activity in which the Christian engages. "Do not be conformed to this eon, but be transformed by the renewal of your mind" (Rom. 12:2). We are being changed, and we are to change. The freedom for transformation of which Paul speaks is through and through covenantal.

This conclusion is supported dramatically by Galatians 5:13–14: "For you were called to freedom, brothers; only do not use your freedom as an opportunity for 'the flesh,' but through love be servants of one another. For the whole Torah is fulfilled in one word, 'You shall love your neighbor as yourself.' " The freedom to which the Galatians were called by the Spirit, according to Paul, is one that they may use or misuse. The right use of the Spirit's freedom is the choice to be servants to each other, as Christ served his fellow Jews and even an occasional Gentile. Further, they are to serve as Christ served, under the guidance of Torah and so seeking to follow Torah's great and radical commandment: love your neighbor as yourself. Do this, but really *do* this, and you shall live! (Luke 10:28). Israel's freedom in God's covenant is to do the *mitzvot*, the commandments of the Sinai tradition. The Church is called into the same covenantal freedom through the Spirit of its one Lord, who interpreted the freedom, as Paul evidently understood it, as concentrated in the single commandment of love. Conformed to Christ, they would have all they needed to live the freedom of covenantal life.

Walking by the Spirit, serving one another as Christ served his people (Rom. 15:7–8), fulfilling the freedom of Torah by loving the neighbor, all this means taking up covenantal responsibility. It means doing things, things that Paul could call "the work of the Lord" (1 Cor. 15:58, 16:10), "good work(s)" or "work(s)" (Rom. 2:10, 13:3; 2 Cor. 9:8; Phil. 1:6. Cf. Eph. 2:10; Col. 1:10), and even "doing the Torah" (Rom. 2:13). Paul seems to have been deeply concerned that his Gentile converts understand that the God and Father of Jesus Christ is the God of Sinai, a covenantal God who wants his Church to be no less concerned than Israel about taking up their responsibility to live, to walk, to act according to the pattern he holds up before them in Jesus Christ as their Lord.

To object that Paul was a champion of justification by grace alone, to be received in faith, is to confuse the issue. There is no question here about justification, and certainly not about grace. The sheer grace of God lies in his making covenant with his creatures at all. Sinai is pure grace, a sheer unmerited initiative by God to call Israel to be a co-worker with him in his cause. So also is the calling to freedom by which God awakens his Church through Jesus Christ. What is in question is neither the grace of the covenantal God nor the justification or acceptance by God of his people Israel and his Church. The question is rather how one is to live by grace, how the justified person is to respond.

The answer that Paul gave was not a new one. He gave a Jewish answer, as is to be expected. You have been rescued by the Lord, he said in effect, so you belong to the Lord, as the Lord belongs to the covenantal Father. Therefore walk by the Spirit given you; enter into the service to which you have been called; exercise the freedom of the Spirit that is yours. That will show what the lordship of Jesus Christ actually looks like.

ii. Covenantal service

The items that comprise covenantal service were called by Paul (1 Cor. 12:1, 7) "spiritual gifts" and "manifestations of the Spirit." He called each of them a gift, yet what he went on to speak of were varieties of active service that he was urging the members of the Corinthian congregation to exercise toward one another for the good of the whole community (1 Cor. 12:7, 25–26).

When we compare the list of these "spiritual gifts" with what he elsewhere called "the fruits of the Spirit" (Gal. 5:22, to be considered in the following subsection), we might fairly conclude that the list before us comprised the agenda of the Corinthian community, rather than Paul's own and preferred summary of the matter. This list of the "gifts of the Spirit" may be more interesting, then, not for its content, but for what Paul did with it.

Common, not only to the introduction to this passage on these gifts of the Spirit, but also to their articulation, is the theme of unity: these "gifts" are all from the same one Spirit (1 Cor. 12:4), and they are all given "for the common good" (1 Cor. 12:7). They are all "varieties of service" to "the same Lord" (1 Cor. 12:5). If it be asked in what the lordship of Christ consists, at least within the categories familiar to the Corinthian congregation, Paul's answer was a rigorously communal interpretation of what they were in fact already doing. He asked them not to do less, but to go on doing what they were already doing, only in a way that built community. The covenantal note is clear: they were to continue exercising active responsibility, but they were to do it with a view to the One with whom they had this covenant. There are a vast variety of services, but they are to remember that there is only one Lord (1 Cor. 12:5). In Paul's view, that is, Jesus is for this community a ceaseless reminder of the One God who set Israel into its many forms of service. Remembering that it may be the agenda of the Corinthian church, not that of Paul, we review the list of "gifts of the Spirit" that Paul, as we shall see, continually reinterpreted covenantally as services.

The Corinthian community seems to have seen its members as variously gifted with wisdom, knowledge, faith, healing power, the ability to work miracles (not further specified), prophecy, "tongues" (evidently outbursts of ecstatic utterances), and perhaps also—although these could have been Paul's additions— "the ability to distinguish between spirits" and "the interpretation of tongues" (1 Cor. 12:8–10). Three times in this short passage Paul reiterated that these were gifts of "the same" or "the one" Spirit. Whatever may have been the exact nature of these gifts, they were all varieties of the way the one Spirit showed itself, and they were all given for "the common good." From what Paul emphasized, it may be surmised that the Corinthians tended to think competitively, or possibly enviously, of their various gifts, as if the one who only had faith was less "gifted" than one who spoke in "tongues," for Paul's metaphor of the community as a body repeatedly touches on each of its parts being necessary to the well-being of the whole.

Fundamental to Paul's interpretation of the gifts of the Spirit is their translation into services on behalf of the community. This shift is underscored by his turning from all of them and asking the Corinthians to consider "a more excellent way," presumably more excellent than any gift prized by the Corinthians, but especially more excellent than the competitive and envious manner in which they had been received. That more excellent way is love, a term developed in the so-called "hymn to love" of 1 Corinthians 13 so as to show what sort of service results when Christ's lordship is effective through the Spirit.

The list of features of love-in-action (the only sort of love in question) is not that of the Corinthians' catalogue of gifts. Indeed, Paul's list is not only different; he uses his to de-emphasize theirs. As a *halakhic* teacher, as an instructor for the Church in how to walk the way of the covenantal God, Paul gives here his rules for covenantal action and behavior. He does not say that the Corinthians' gifts were nothing, only that they were utterly secondary to the way of love.

This "more excellent way" was formulated by Paul in a presumably later letter to another community, under the heading "the fruit of the Spirit" (Gal. 5:22–28). We turn to this other passage to continue our reflections on a covenantal interpretation of the lordship of Christ, one that makes room for and calls forth responsible life under that lordship.

iii. *Covenantal fruit*

As God's gracious gift of his Torah to Israel is meant to produce results, so also God's gracious gift in Christ through the Spirit to the Church is designed to produce fruit. As God's dealings with Israel are covenantal, calling for and making possible a joyful and responsible people, so God's dealings with the Church are covenantal, leading to an equally joyful and responsible community. Set free from former slavery to pagan immorality, the Church is called to responsible walking. Paul called this walking "the fruit of the Spirit" (Gal. 5:22).

This fruit, this walking by the Spirit, is the visible form of the lordship of Christ, and it stands in radical opposition to what Paul called "the works of the flesh" (Gal. 5:19). "Flesh" here as elsewhere in Paul's writings means not the body or even so-called "natural" desires, but that which works contrary to the purposes of God. The conflict is between "flesh" and "sin" on the one hand, and Spirit or God on the other. The conflict is between God's good will for his creation and the terrible corruption that has crept into God's good creation and turned it into opposition to God. "Flesh" stands for that from which the Christian has been set free. Works of the flesh are what the lordship of sin looks like.

It should be noted that Paul does not set the fruit of the Spirit in opposition to the Torah. He makes it clear that the freedom the Church has is not that of Torah (Gal. 5:18), not that of Israel, but its own particular freedom with its own particular responsibilities. The "works of the flesh" that Paul enumerates are opposed to the fruit of the Spirit, but they are just as contrary to the commandments of the Torah, consisting as they do of, among other things, immorality, impurity, licentiousness, idolatry, and sorcery (Gal. 5:19–20). The gift of and responsibility under Torah for Israel and under the Spirit for the Church are certainly different, but they are in no sense opposed to each other. What they are opposed to, both of them, are the "works of the flesh."

Paul then gives us his agenda, which he takes to be the agenda of God for the Church: the fruit of the Spirit. They are just what we are led to expect from what Paul wrote in 1 Corinthians 13. At the head of the list is love, with all the following items interpreting what love is. Here, as there, love means "joy, peace, patience, kindness, goodness, faithfulness, gentleness, self-control" (Gal.

5:22–23; cf. 1 Cor. 13, especially vv. 4–7). There can be no conflict here with the Torah, Paul adds (Gal. 5:23). And indeed a more telling lack of conflict may be pointed out: Paul's list is profoundly covenantal. The terms are sweeping and require that the Church accept the responsibility to work out for itself what it means to be joyful (Paul did give a halakhic indication as to how to begin in 1 Cor. 13:6), to be peaceful, to be patient, kind, and the rest. The Church will look to its Lord, as Paul seems to have done, to take its clues, but it accepts responsibility for its covenantal response when it accepts the freedom of the Spirit.

I believe it is correct to say that we have here Paul's own agenda, because it reflects what he was so concerned to present to his churches: not just the words and teaching of Jesus (he knew a few of these, although possibly not as many as we!), but Jesus' life, his own person crucified, as the Church knew him in the apostolic witness. The fruit of the Spirit, as Paul presented it, is the very life of his "little children, with whom I am again in travail until Christ be formed in you" (Gal. 4:19). Paul's catalogue of the fruits of the Spirit depicts the life of those who are using the freedom of the Spirit to begin to conform their lives to Christ (cf. the old observation that 1 Corinthians 13 can be read as well by substituting the name of Jesus for the word "love"). The fruit of the Spirit is the result of accepting covenantal responsibility as God's gracious gift of Jesus Christ as Lord.

"No one can say 'Jesus is Lord' except by the Holy Spirit" (1 Cor. 12:3). The logic of this claim should by now be clear. To say truly—not just with the lips, that is—that Jesus is Lord is to accept his lordship, to have taken up covenantal responsibility before God to turn around and away from one's pagan past and present environment and to begin life in the freedom that is the gift of the Spirit. The Church, like Israel, is not left to wander in a wilderness of confusion about how to live and what to do. Like Israel, the Church has been shown a path to walk, "the Way," as it may have been called at first (Acts 9:2, 22:4. Cf. Mark 10:52; John 14:6; and 1 Cor. 12:31!). Like Israel, the Church is called to responsibility in taking up its yoke (that which makes work easier).

For Israel that yoke is the Torah; for the Church it is Christ, but the two are not at all opposed.

The tragedy of so much of the Church's history is that it did not, until so recently, see this complementarity, and so prevented Israel from seeing it. The cost to the Jewish people has been obvious. The cost to the Church is that it failed to do justice to the insight that the gift of the Spirit is precisely this freedom: to take up full responsibility for living by grace.

As an example of this failure a diocesan convention, recently called for the purpose of electing a new bishop, was opened with prayer for the Holy Spirit to come and, in effect, tell the members how to vote! As if the members had no direct, covenantal responsibility in the matter! Better had the prayer been for the Spirit to stir up hard thought and careful discrimination on the part of all concerned (not to speak of workable political agreements), that they take full responsibility for the decision that they, not the Spirit in their place, were called upon to make.

What has been given the Church in the lordship of Christ is the freedom to start living as servants of this Lord and so as servants of all whom he served and serves: Israel first of all, then the Church, and then all the poor and wretched of this earth.

The Church gave itself and all others a misleading image of the lordship of Christ when it began to celebrate a feast day of Christ the King. It would have done better to declare a feast of Christ the Servant, but it may have been the leading of the Spirit, responsibly followed, that has caused it to celebrate Christ's servanthood every time it celebrates the Eucharist, for when it does this, it "proclaim[s] the Lord's death until he comes" (1 Cor. 11:26).

4. UNFINISHED CONTINUITY

i. *The continuity of the covenantal story*
The Church's confession of Jesus Christ as Lord has at least two implications that merit attention here: the Church discovers itself as having been taken into Israel's covenantal story, and that story

is not over. The Church finds itself taken into Israel's story, because it confesses as Lord one who lived out of and for the sake of that story. It confesses Jesus as Lord to the glory of the Father, the covenantly self-determined God, because the apostolic witness to him, especially that of the synoptic Gospels, presents him as desiring only the success of God's cause. The confession of Christ as Lord also implies that the story is not over, because that cause of God, which Jesus made his own, has yet to be realized. Christ has not yet appeared (to use the normal apostolic term, *parousia*), or he has not yet returned (to use the usual ecclesiastical term). If we think of this in covenantal terms, we may conclude that this delay is at least in part due to the fact that Christ's Church has yet to submit sufficiently to his will that it take upon itself the responsibility of serving him by serving all he served. Both implications need elaboration, and we shall begin with the first, turning to the second in the next subsection.

The Church confesses Jesus as Lord, referring of course to the actual Jesus, Jesus in his context. Jesus apart from his past would not be the real Jesus, and his past was that of his people. Lordship is confessed of a Jew in his full Jewishness, in his presumed self-understanding as a Jew living under the conditions of the Roman occupation. As all of Jewish history before and after Jesus teaches us, his Jewishness certainly included a sense of his solidarity with all his people. Further, Jesus is confessed as Lord not apart from his present, which must still include that solidarity with all Jews— unless Jesus is no longer the real person he was. And finally, he is confessed as Lord not apart from his future—his future as Israel's future: the age to come, the Messianic age, "the Kingdom of God." If the apostolic witness to him is at all to be trusted, surely he made that hope of Israel his special concern. Whether he saw himself as the coming messianic figure, or whether that was the interpretation of his disciples, is a secondary question and probably beyond a historical answer, because we have no historical access to him except by way of their understandings of him. What is primary is the consensus of his witnesses, that he made Israel's hope his own, giving his whole life to it.

The story in which Jesus is presented as standing, and in which therefore his Church must see itself, is Israel's. It is the story the beginning of which unfolds in the Scriptures. It is, therefore, the covenantal story. In their different ways, each of the Evangelists makes this clear. The focus may at times be more on the promises of the covenant, at other times more on its commandments that God's will be done. Together, the witness is to Jesus as the embodiment of the covenanting God and covenanted Israel. This covenantal story is now proclaimed to the world in order to draw in the Gentiles. If the Church were to say that the story does not continue, it would deny the reality of its own as well as Israel's further history. It excludes such a course by confessing Jesus Christ as Lord.

ii. An unfinished story

The second implication of the Church's confession is that the story is not over. In different ways, each of the witnesses to Jesus as Lord made this clear. Mark did so with his repeated note of "Watch, for you know not when the master of the house will come" (Mark 13:35). Matthew pointed ahead by concluding his Gospel with the command that the disciples go and make more disciples "from among all Gentiles . . . teaching them to observe all that I have commanded you" (Matt. 28:19–20). Luke closed the first part of his story on a note of waiting, in Jerusalem; the second part (Acts) finishes without any marks of an ending: Paul is teaching in Rome "quite openly and unhindered" (Acts 28:31). Nor is the conclusion of the Fourth Gospel any more an end: rather, the story is told so that the reader may believe and have life. And for Paul, the end of the story was certainly still out ahead, even if it "is nearer to us than we first believed" (Rom. 13:11). In a word, the story goes on.

The Church, of course, has always known, in a sense, that the story into which it came to be and lives is unfinished. The eschatology of the apostolic authors has been reflected in the creeds, for example, with their words about Christ coming "to judge the living and the dead," and belief in "the resurrection of the dead and the life of the world to come." (Christian "other-worldliness" is not without creedal foundations!) The difficulty with the Church's vision, however, is that it is so fixed on the final end. When so much emphasis is placed on the end of the story, the intervening chapters are in danger of being taken with less than full seriousness. The story from Creation to Easter is recalled; the last end is looked forward to as God's victory. What about the intervening chapters, including especially the one being written in the present? Without questioning the need for an ultimate hope, would not Church do well to develop a more intermediate hope?

To develop an intermediate hope, a Church that believes that it lives in a story that is not over may find it profitable to reflect on the central place of the covenant in that story. That could help it to see not only the continuing role of the Jewish people in the story, but also its own role. If the covenant reveals a distinctive feature of God's purpose—namely, to include his covenantal partners in and give them responsibility for the future of God's cause—that hope will always include what I shall call "covenantal expectation." This has been developed in Judaism as an expectation that God is now, and will be in the immediate future, good to Israel, and that Israel will commit itself all the more joyously and seriously to praise God and walk in his commandments, today and tomorrow. Covenantal expectation for the Church would mean expecting not only that nothing present or future can separate it from the love of God in Christ, but also expecting that the Church and each of its members will assume responsibility to serve its Lord by serving all whom he served and serves. Covenantal expectation would be hope for a contribution from the Church, as well as from Israel, to God's cause in the present day and tomorrow.

To live in an unfinished story is to realize that one is contributing to its writing by that living. It is to realize that the story's development and its future course depend not only on God but also on God's partners. Such an awareness, as I see it, makes for excitement because risk is involved. When the Church or some of its members fail to promote God's cause, to that extent God's cause is set back. A covenantal God is not necessarily going to override the failings of his creatures. More likely, being covenantal, God will let those failings stand. He may be able to do something constructive with them, but not without creaturely cooperation. What the creaturely partners of the covenant do and fail to do thus become highly important. Therein lies risk, but with it comes the consolation of knowing that one is joining God in the risk he has already assumed in determining himself to be a covenantal God.

iii. The open future of the covenant

If the story is unfinished, the future of the covenant is open. How it will develop has not been predetermined. How it will proceed is up to the Church and to Israel, not just to God, and this by God's covenantal choice. If that is even close to the truth, it would seem wise for the Church and the Jewish people to put their collective heads together and share what they are able as they face the next steps to be taken on their respective paths. The few who have already begun to try this have clearly learned things they did not know before, or are seeing the way ahead differently from how they saw it before.

One of the principal truths that Christians have been learning from their conversations with Jews in recent years is that the Church needs practice in attending to the immediate future, rather than the distant future. It needs practice in giving only such attention to "salvation," or "redemption," or to the End, as will allow it to concentrate on the historical future and the tasks for today and tomorrow. With respect only to the Church's relationship to the Jewish people, the Church has here a rather full agenda. Without worrying about some ultimate form of that relationship, there is a staggering amount of repair work to begin at once, due to the deterioration caused by the Church's behavior over so many centuries. If the Church wants to serve a Lord of whom Paul wrote that he became a servant of the Jewish people, then it has its work cut out for it. In its liturgy, lectionary, preaching, educational work, in its budget, planning and policy making, the Church has scarcely begun to repair the damage it has done to itself, not to speak of that done to the Jewish people, by its anti-Judaic tradition. With but a few exceptions here and there, the Church has hardly begun to turn seriously to the service of those to whom Christ became a servant. That means that on the whole, the Church confesses Christ as Lord only with its lips, but it blocks that lordship with its life.

Near the end of the great apocalyptic vision of the Revelation to John (Rev. 20:4, 6), it is said that at a "first" resurrection, the martyrs will come to life and reign with Christ for a thousand years. But if Christ reigns as a servant, that must mean that they will serve with him. Or to put it the other way, Christ reigns or serves with his saints, his co-workers. The lordship of Christ is in every respect covenantal. To paraphrase a rabbinic saying about Israel and God, we might say that if the Church serves Christ by serving those whom he serves, he is Lord, and if the Church will not serve him by serving them, he is—so to speak—unable to serve and so is not Lord. Along such lines will the Church think when it learns to conceive of Christ's lordship in covenantal terms.

More important than its thinking, however, is the Church's behavior, for there is where the covenantal lordship of Christ becomes actual and therefore visible. When the Church as the body of Christ sets itself in the service of the Jewish people, then it will be the case that Christ is once more able to continue the work he began and that Pilate cut short. Once more in his body he will have become a servant of the circumcision. Then may come the time when the Church and Israel together could cooperate in his service to the whole world. For the range of Christ's serving lordship is not confined to just the Church, or just the Church and his people Israel; it has its goal in the service of all creation.

CHAPTER TWELVE

All in All

The Church has no cause of its own because its cause is Christ's. Christ has no cause of his own because his cause is God's. It may be that God has no cause of his own because his cause is that of creation. Then the realization of Christ's lordship would be his total service to the God whose lordship would be a total service of self-giving love for all creation. In which case the goal of "the things concerning Jesus of Nazareth" would appear to be the triumph of humble love, the end of all domination in all creation. Such a goal may surpass our imagination, but it can guide the Church as it walks toward it.

1. THE GOAL OF GOD'S STORY

i. A vision of the end

In the midst of his longest reflection on the end of the story (1 Cor. 15:12–58), Paul (playing on Psalm 8:6 and referring this to Christ) presented a remarkable picture of its conclusion: "When all things are subjected to him [i.e., the Son], then the Son himself will be subjected to him [i.e., the Father] who put all things under him, that God may be all in all" (1 Cor. 15:28).

Rosenzweig remarked that this was merely a theological idea that had no meaning for Christian life because it looked so far into the future as to lose all touch with the present (*Star*, 412). That may stand as a correct judgment about the anti-Judaic Church of the past. For a Church that means to come to a better relationship with the Jewish people, the picture may have much to do with the present, as we shall try to show.

What are we to make of (literally) "all in all?" The Revised Standard Version (RSV) tried "everything to everyone," but most translations have not attempted to interpret this mysterious expression. Does "all in all" mean that God will be alone, the totality of all that remains, or does it mean something like the RSV interpretation, that God, who by his Creation refused to be alone, will be the center and total concern of a creation utterly in his service? Does the expression catch something of the tone of, and is it meant to correspond to, the opening of Scriptures, "In the beginning God created the heavens and the earth . . . and behold, it was very good"? Such a correspondence seems appropriate to Christian hope, which, like Jewish hope in the context of which it arose, is always grounded in memory (see Ritschl, *Hope*). To speak of God being all in all may be a way to speak of a final realization of God's original creative purpose, in which all creation comes to find its center in God, who will indeed be everything to every creature.

We may set beside this verse from 1 Corinthians also the great doxological ending of Romans 9 to 11, 11:33–36. As Krister Stendahl pointed out some years ago, neither in that doxology, nor indeed in the whole concluding paragraph beginning with v. 25, is there a single christological reference. All Israel will be saved (v. 26) because its Deliverer, the God of Israel, will come to rescue it (vv. 26–27). The call of that God is irrevocable (v. 29) and, in the end, the mercy of that God will rule (v. 32). "From him and through him and to him are all things," and to him alone will be the glory for ever (v. 36). Paul's vision of the end is unqualifiedly theocentric in Romans 11 and in 1 Corinthians 15. In this as in so much else, "Paul's religion" was none other than "the religion of Jesus." That is hardly a surprising agreement, seeing that they were both devoted Jews. For both of them the end of God's story could only be God the Father.

ii. The end of the story?

What can it mean to speak of the end of God's story? Here the Church needs to be clear about what it knows and just as clear about the limits of its knowledge. It can know first hand, for example, from its own lived experience with God, that Jesus is the way to the Father. How could it possibly know that no one, ever, in any place, can come to the Father except by him? The lover has adequate evidence that the beloved is enchanting, but if the lover goes on to say, "No one can compare with you," those words express the strength of love, not a result that the lover would even care to test by exhaustive investigation. So, the Church has learned of the story of God and Israel because it has found itself drawn in (on new terms) into that story. Of the end, or even of *an* end, it knows only a promise.

To know the end only as a promise is not to know nothing. If it has learned to know of God through, and to rehearse what it knows as, a story, then the logic of narrative at least implies an end. The implication, however, is not ironclad. There can be stories that simply stop or trail off into silence. We may judge such stories unsatisfying, but they would still be stories—stories without an ending. Could the story of God be such?

While not logically impossible, it would seem that God's story would not just stop or trail off into silence. The first argument for such a supposition is that God is its subject, the Creator of heaven and earth. The story is of one who is purposeful, and who wrestles with his creatures to bring them to cooperate with their God. The story, further, is of a God who is reliable and may be trusted. God does not give up on what he sets out to do, no matter how many delays and frustrations may disrupt the forward movement of the tale. That is clearly an implication of the narration on which Israel and the Church rely when they seek to speak of God. The story of God moves in narrative fashion towards an end, even if that end cannot be seen with much clarity, certainly not face to face, as it were, but only dimly, as if reflected in a polished bronze, a first century "mirror" (1 Cor. 13:12).

The metaphor of reflection is a reminder that Jewish and Christian hope is grounded in memory. Hope is "remembering forward," as Ritschl put it (*Hope*). What is hoped for is shaped by what one remembers. Or, to use the terms I developed in chapter 8 above, novelty is expected within the terms of continuity. The end may be beyond anything in the past, but it will be recognized when it comes as the ending of precisely the story known. Every novelty incorporated into the story thus far has been just that: incorporated into the story, so that the novelty fits into a continuity. Thus it is with the Church's hope and its way of speaking of the end of God's story. It knows no details, but it knows of a continuity within which to speak of the end.

Since the story is God's, so the end will be seen as God's: God will be all in all, or everything to everyone. Does that spell victory? Again, the memory, the continuity must be recalled. The story is of a covenantally self-determined God. The continuity of a covenant, however, does not depend on the trustworthy God alone; it depends also on the most untrustworthy partners of that covenant. An element of suspense and uncertainty must necessarily be included in any story including such partners. Israel's story of Creation contains an element of risk, as we saw in *People Israel.* The ending of such a story cannot be imagined otherwise. We simply do not know that all will turn out for the best. It must be left open whether it may not turn out to be the best that could be done under the circumstances, circumstances yet to be determined in part not only by the trustworthy God but also by the rather untrustworthy partners to whom God has committed God's own future.

This consideration opens us again to the ambiguity of 1 Corinthians 15:28. It may be that God will be everything to everyone, which could be taken to stand for the covenant in all its fullness. It may also turn out, however, that God may have to be content to be all in all, all that there is, because his covenant partners had seen to it that they were no longer part of God's story, that the story would indeed no longer be remembered or told, because there were none left to tell or hear it. The truth is that we do not

know how the story will end. Perhaps it will not have a fitting ending, but most unfittingly taper off—or burn out—into silence; or
perhaps it will have a fitting ending.

iii. Another vision

There is another and rather different vision of the end contained in the last book of the Church's canon, The Revelation of
John. The difference lies not only in the vivid and dramatic imagery, but also in the new situation of Roman persecution of the
Church that it reflects and the note of vengeance that the author
sounds. Following preliminary letters to seven churches, that
note is heard (6:10) as the vision of plagues, pestilence, woes, and
war begins to unfold (chapters 8–16), leading to the triumph of
the wrath of God over the great harlot, clearly Rome (chapters
17–18), and the victory of one "who is called the Word of God,"
whose sword smites the nations and who rules over them "with a
rod of iron" (chapter 19). This warrior-Word then rules with the
saints for a thousand years (chapter 20) until finally at the end
there appears a new heaven and a new earth (chapter 21) when
God is with his people in a new Jerusalem, in which "the Lord
God the Almighty and the Lamb" take the place of the Temple,
the sun and the moon, and occupy together the throne.

This vision of the end differs from Paul's, perhaps largely because it is the ending of a story the principal events of which, as its
author saw it, had happened since Paul's time. Abraham, Moses,
Sinai, even the person and life of Jesus have all receded behind
Roman persecution and Christian martyrdom. The end of that
story of Roman domination is seen as the domination of the warrior-Word of God who "will tread the wine press of the fury of the
wrath of God" (19:15). Gone is one who will be Lord as one who
serves (Mark 10:45; Rom. 15:8). In his place is one who will rule
just as do "those who are supposed to rule over the Gentiles" and
"lord it over them" (Mark 10:42), in contrast to whom Jesus was
once understood to have set his own model of lordship.

There are still to be heard here faint echos of the covenantal
story, but they are overpowered by the clashing cymbals of Ro-

man power and warfare. This is a vision conjured up by and for victims of oppression, a vision that has been cherished again and again over the centuries and into our own day by Christians under oppressive conditions. Psychologically understandable as it may be, it has let Rome shape its hope, with the result that revenge and the fury of the wrath of God come to dominate the picture. Indeed, domination as the Gentile world knows it and as Israel and the Church are always tempted to practice it has taken over the vision and has, in historical fact, too often become the model for the Church's practice.

One clear note from the other vision, and from the story to which it was conceived as the end, is that the key figure is called the Lamb, indeed "the Lamb that was slain" (Rev. 5:6, 9, 12; 13:8), but this is a Lamb of wrath (6:16), in whose presence those who "worship the beast" are tormented eternally (14:9–11). And in striking contrast to Paul's vision, this is a Lamb who in the final scene shares the praise and the throne of God (22:1, 3). It follows logically enough that the last words of the vision tell us that the servants of the Lamb "shall reign for ever and ever" (22:5).

For all the power and even beauty of this somewhat grim apocalyptic vision, it has distorted seriously, in my judgment, both Israel's witness to the covenantal God of Sinai and the apostolic witness to Jesus of Nazareth and his Father. Notes of vengeance and the seduction of dominating the oppressor are certainly to be found in both those witnesses, but unlike in Revelation, they do not control the story. On the contrary, the path chosen in this apocalypse by God Almighty and the warrior-Lamb is precisely the one that appears to have been rejected by the God of Sinai and by Jesus Christ and his Father. The Church, even when it finds itself oppressed, should reflect on that.

iv. The place of the end and the role of hope
The Church has thought itself entitled and even called to hope for the ultimate victory of Christ and God. Perhaps it is, but what is victory? Does the Church draw its image of victory from Rome, or now from Washington, with bands playing and banners flying?

Or if it draws it from the cross and Easter, how are the cross and Easter to be portrayed? Western inconography has presented Easter rather triumphalistically; has it done well in doing this? Are the fear, confusion, doubt, and uncertainty of the first Easter now all behind us, because a triumphant Church has won its way in the world?

In Paul's vision of the end with which we began this chapter, he said that before the Son surrenders himself to the Father, God will see to it that "all things are subjected to" the Son. Paul was applying to the Son what the Psalmist had said of all God's sons and daughters:

"When I behold Your heavens, the work of Your fingers, . . .
what is man that You have been mindful of him, . . .
that you have made him little less than divine,
and adorned him with glory and majesty;
You have made him master over Your handiwork,
laying the world at his feet . . . .
O LORD, our Lord, how majestic is Your name throughout the earth!"
(from Ps. 8, Jewish Publication Society trans.)

Psalm 8 is built in turn on Genesis 1, and especially on verse 26: "And God said, Let us make man in our own image, after our likeness. They shall rule the fish of the sea, the birds of the sky, the cattle, the whole earth, and all the creeping things that creep on earth." Genesis 1 sees human beings as authorized by God to rule over all life, as God's agents, so to speak. Genesis 2 presents Adam as the caretaker of the earth. Psalm 8 stresses the ruling authority of human beings more than their caretaking responsibilities, but it does set this clearly within the framework of God's creative work from which all is derived.

Paul's vision of the end draws upon this language, but he has set it in the framework of a discussion of death and resurrection. Christ is going to "deliver the kingdom to God the Father" but only "after destroying every rule and every authority and power. For," Paul continued, Christ "must reign until he has put all his enemies under his feet," the last of which is death (1 Cor. 15:24–26). And this he supports, in what would become not untypical rabbinic fashion, by more or less quoting Psalm 8: "for God has put all things in subjection under his feet" (1 Cor. 15:27). The applicability of the quotation is hardly obvious.

The dominion referred to in Psalm 8 is that of humanity over other forms of life (of which death is not one), but neither they nor death are presented as enemies. "Rule," "authority," and "power" are terms used by Paul and his followers a number of times, and they appear to stand for unearthly, perhaps angelic, forces that are part of the problem, not the solution, of this corrupted world. They cannot undo God's work (Rom. 8:38), for they also are God's creatures (Rom. 13:1), but they must be contended with (Eph. 1:21, 6:12; Col. 2:15). Paul has extended the divinely appointed domination of humanity over all living creatures, established in Creation, to a future dominion of Christ yet to be established over these hostile forces, the last of which is death. Paul's free interpretation of Psalm 8 is decidedly apocalyptic.

Paul may have shared with the author of Revelation more of an apocalyptic spirit than we may wish, but at least he spared us the latter's theme of vengeance. Of equal importance is the fact that for Paul the reign in his vision of the end will be that of God alone. God may reign for the good of his creatures and in full covenantal cooperation with them. He may be everything to everyone. But his throne is his alone, however humbly he may choose to sit upon it. Neither the Church's distinctive Lord nor the Church share that throne. Paul did say, in another connection, that the saints would cooperate in God's judgment of the world and even of angelic forces (1 Cor. 6:2, 3), but in the vision of the end that we are examining, he has managed to resist the temptation of dominion that has marked and marred the witness of both Israel and the Church to the God of Sinai and to Jesus and his Father.

We are left, then, with a question about Christian hope: whether it can so be focused in Israel's witness to the God of Sinai and the apostolic witness to the Father of Jesus Christ as to rise above a vision of dominion, a vision perhaps of all-too-characteristically male dominion. It may yet be that the Church will need to see far more clearly a female vision than it has allowed thus far in order to free itself for a Christology that will let God be the humble God she (he) has shown herself (himself) to be in the covenant with Israel and in the face of Jesus Christ.

2. THE GOAL OF THE SON

i. Christ the Son

The irony of the classical christological tradition is that it made of the designation son of God—a Jewish term of service, intimacy, fidelity, and humility (which may have been Jesus' own term for his role and was certainly one used of him by his disciples)—a title of power, dominion, and assertion. It would appear to be a fixed item in the earliest tradition concerning Jesus that his designation as son was connected with his acceptance of baptism by John, surely an act of self-identification with those in need of repentance and mercy, and committed to the cause of God's renewal of Israel. If one were to boast of that, then it would be, with Paul (2 Cor. 11:30), boasting of one's weakness. The glory in such a designation could only be that of God the Father. Consistent with this is the witness to Jesus as one who had no cause of his own but lived and died entirely for the cause of God. Jesus was therefore at one with his Father (John 10:30), but this in no sense qualifies the confession that the Father is greater than the Son (John 14:28). The Son is just that; the Son is not the Father.

The misunderstanding that can arise and has often enough arisen at this point, that the Son cannot be "of God" if he is said to be inferior or subordinate to the Father, may rest upon an unconscious projection onto God of human (especially male?) conceptions and practices of power, control, and dominion. To be superior is to be on top and in physical control. To have power is to be able to bend another to your will. The superior gives orders; the inferior obeys. So if the Father is greater than the Son, the Son is inferior, weaker, only in some derived sense "of God." Due to some such presupposition, the classical tradition found itself resisting every sort of subordinationism, insisting that the Son must be considered fully God, in the sense that the Son is in all respects (other than that of having been "begotten") the equal of (i.e., as high on the power scale as) the Father.

If we could resist the pull of this idea of superiority, however, we might be free to see that the glory of the Son is that he wanted to be nothing other than one wholly in the service of God, and that this is not being inferior to God. It is being God's partner as God would have it. For the Church needs to recall ever anew that it is in seeing this lowly Jew that it sees the Father in the glory of God's own humility. God's "superiority" consists in the abandonment of superiority. God is God precisely in making Israel to be his full partner in God's cause of the well-being of all creation. God is God precisely in extending his "dominion" by drawing a Gentile Church to take up, alongside of Israel, responsibility for that cause as God let them see it in the Jew from Nazareth. But if that is the God with which the Church—and Israel—has to do, then there is every reason for the Church to let the Son be the Son, not his Father. There is every reason for the Church to rejoice in and give thanks for the "subordination" of the Son to the Father.

ii. The revelation of Sonship

At stake in the question of the subordination of Jesus Christ to the Father is the heart of what the Church discovers in and finds it must say about the things concerning Jesus of Nazareth. To call Jesus "the Son of God" is not to apply a known predication to an otherwise unknown figure. It is not as though the Church knew already what it is to be "Son of God" and then decided that Jesus measures up to that term. On the contrary, the Church in its beginnings and ever since has been confronted by the Jew Jesus, first in the flesh, then in the witness of word and sacrament, and from him learns what it is to be the Son of God. Either he is the revelation and so the full measure and definition of Sonship, or the Church has learned from some other lord how it may construe him.

If I have the logic of Christian claims concerning revelation and Christology correctly here, then it may be clear why it is so misleading to speak of "the divinity of Christ." That phrase sounds as if the Church knew something reliable about divinity and so felt it was justified in predicating this of Christ. The fact of the matter, of course, is just the opposite: the

Church has first learned whatever little it may know about divine matters from the things concerning Jesus of Nazareth. It might well speak of the Christ-likeness of divinity, or, more boldly, the Jesusness of God. On this, Donald Baillie (*God*) was sound. It has no grounds whatsoever for speaking of the divinity of Christ.

The Sonship that Jesus makes known to the Church is his own, which he has as a Jew standing with his people in their eternal covenant with God. That is why in chapter 9 we felt it necessary to reinterpret the traditional doctrine of the eternal Sonship of Christ in covenantal terms. Sonship, precisely in the Church's doctrine of the Triune God, will be grounded in and defined by God's covenantal self-determination, if the Church means to confess that in Christ it has been graciously confronted, blessed, called, and claimed by the God and Father of Jesus Christ, the God of Sinai.

iii. The meaning of Sonship

Sonship for Israel meant and means belonging to God, but belonging to God as God's beloved. Sonship, be it that of all Israel, of each Israelite, or of such representative figures as Israel's king, priest, or prophet, names the role of one bearing the joy and responsibility of having been made God's covenantal partner. This was the Sonship bodied forth for the Church in Jesus. To confess Jesus as the Son of God is to confess that he belongs to his Father as the Jew fully authorized by God to confront his Church with the gift and claim of God's gracious love. Jesus is the Son of God precisely because he leads the Gentile Church to the God of Israel. The meaning of his Sonship is that he stood and stands only for the Father. Therefore, it must be said of the goal of the Son what we have said of his cause: he had and has none of his own; his whole goal was and is the goal of the Father.

Such a conclusion is expressed well in the verse from 1 Corinthians 15 with which we began this chapter: in the end, Christ, along with all else in creation, will also be subjected to the Father, so that God may be everything to everyone. The Son will be subjected to the Father, and that will be the fulfillment of the goal of the Son. And precisely in this subjection, the Son would be the fullness of the revelation of the Father, the God who has determined to be the sort of Lord who refuses to lord it over his creation.

In the terms and conceptual framework of the classical tradition, Paul's vision of the end, in which the Son is subjected to the Father, bespeaks of a low or subordinationist Christology. That would account for the fact that so little notice has been taken of it traditionally. The question should be put to the tradition, however: is it not the highest possible Christology that sees the Son so fully reflecting the Father? The highest possible Christology will be one that sees in the lowly crucified one the very heart of God the Father. His lowliness is the image of God's humility. The lowliness of this crucified Jew is his "divinity," his Godliness, and just this is what is confessed by the Church when it says of this Jew, "God of God, Light of Light, true God of true God." The subjection of the Son to his Father is therefore fittingly presented as his goal. He could have no higher.

The consequence of the Son's goal for ecclesiology should be clear: the servants of the servant of God and of the Jewish people (Rom. 15:8) would have no other calling than to rejoice *with* the Jewish people (Rom. 15:10) and with them glorify God alone (Rom. 15:9, 11). With Israel, such a Church will "abound in hope" (Rom. 15:13) for the coming age of the Messiah. It will pray, "Thy kingdom come, Thy will be done on earth." When the Messiah comes, the Church believes it will already know his name, but in the meantime, the Church can only hope in and work for his coming, recalling that, if it turns out to be right about the Messiah's identity, his coming will be not to his own glory but to the glory of God the Father.

"He will come again in glory to judge the living and the dead, and his kingdom will have no end." So sings the Church in its doxological, confessional creed. The glory in which the Son will come would have to be that of God the Father, if it is really the same one who will "come again." And the "judgment" will be that setting-things-right that is the judging of the God of the eternal covenant. The kingdom without end, finally, would have to be the kingdom for which he lived and died, the one in which God alone is king, and a king not as among the Gentiles. Only along such lines can the Church sing its doxology of the end, if it would conform its praise to the goal of the Son.

3. THE GOAL OF THE FATHER

i. Creator of all

If the Church dares to speak of the end of the story, it will hardly do to tell it otherwise than as the end of the story that opens with those remarkable words, "In the beginning, God created the heavens and the earth." Israel and—*a fortiori*—the Church were not there to witness that beginning, and the end has not yet come. So Israel—and therefore the Church too—speaks of that beginning, not to describe how it happened, but to say that however it happened it is all of God, the God whom Israel knows basically from Sinai and the Church discovers through Jesus Christ. The beginning, therefore, is the beginning of what this God wills: partners for his covenant and a place for that covenant to be lived. The end of the story will be told so as to accord with that beginning.

The end of a story with such a beginning would therefore center appropriately in God the Creator and include the creation in full covenant with God. Paul's vision of the end and even that of the book of Revelation do this each in its own way, but their differences should remind us that in fact the end is unknown. Israel, and the Church with Israel know of God's covenantal self-determination. The Church sees the glory of that self-determination vividly presented in the face of the crucified one. How the story of God's covenantal self-determination will look in the end is something that can only be left open. There is no place for knowledge, but there is room for hope, because the end will be that of the story of the God who is Creator of all.

ii. The glory of humility

Perhaps no word occurs more often in that story as a summary term for the goal toward which God is moving than "glory." In the end, God will be glorified, for God's glory is already his and is told of by the heavens. In the end, the world shall be full of the glory of God as the waters cover the sea. The end of the story will be God in his glory. But what is glory?

In the Hebrew Scriptures, the word is widely and variously used in the sense of the awesome splendor and majesty of God. Sometimes it is compared to a cloud (Exod. 24:15, 40:34, etc.), or more dramatically to a great thunderstorm (Ps. 97:1–6). Sometimes it seems to be a great light that fills the Temple (Ezek. 43:1–5; cf. Isa. 6:3). Yet in a crucial passage, Moses on Mt. Sinai asks to see God's glory and, although he is told that he may not look on God's face, nonetheless God answers his request by saying, "I will make all my goodness to pass before you, and will proclaim before you my name, 'The LORD,' and the grace that I grant and the compassion that I show" (Exod. 33:19, Jewish Publication Society trans.). Was God's glory in that which Moses was not shown, or could it be that for all the talk of dazzling light and awesome thunderstorm, the glory of the God of Sinai consists in all his goodness, in his graciousness and compassion? The passage is ambiguous.

The same ambiguity continues in the way in which the Greek Apostolic Writings speak of glory. It can also be said to shine as a great light (Luke 2:9), and when the word is used of Jesus, it refers generally to the risen Jesus. On the other hand, the Fourth Gospel may be referring to Jesus' crucifixion as his glorification at 12:23–24 and 17:1 (cf. 21:19). Could it be that it was in the face of the crucified that Paul thought that the glory of God was to be seen (2 Cor. 4:6)?

The vast majority of references to God's glory in the whole Bible point in the direction of awesome splendor, majesty, and power. There is an undertone, however, of glory of another sort, as different from human conceptions of human or divine glory as God's thoughts and ways are said to differ from human thoughts and ways (Isa. 55:8–9). The undertone points in the direction of the glory of humility or, we could also say, a humble glory. The goal of God the Father may therefore be the free reign of all his goodness, his graciousness and mercy, his self-giving for the well-being of his whole creation. In the end, God's goal may prove to be his full sharing of all he is and has with all his creatures, thus becoming everything to everyone.

iii. The meaning of Fatherhood

It is said that Abraham called God "the judge of all the world" (Gen. 18:25). The image of the judge, whether referring to the Father or the Son, has had a long history in Christian thought and iconography, and the image of the judge and of the judgment has been less than heartwarming. The image has drawn heavily on human experiences of human judges. It has paid little heed to those whose story is told in the biblical Book of Judges. There we hear of those whom God raised up to restore Israel's fortunes, to bring order out of chaos, to protect the weak, and in general to promote righteousness. If God is the judge of all the world, that means that he is to restore justice and peace to his world. The world's Creator is also the world's Redeemer (cf. Isa. 44:24, 54:5). The goal of the Father, then, must be to be the restoration of the whole world. That is the meaning of his Fatherhood.

I concluded the first part of *A Theology of the Jewish-Christian Reality* by reviewing the place of the Church and the Jewish people before God in the light of the parable (Luke 15:11–32) of the Prodigal Son, as it is so often called. It is fitting that we return to the story near the end of this volume, for if the two sons held my attention at the end of the first volume (*Discerning*), it is well to recall here that it is the father who appears first and has the last words in the story. The story may be read as being primarily about an incredibly humble and self-sacrificing father.

This man who had two sons, one of whom asked for his share of his inheritance, proceeded to divide his estate between them. That meant that he now had nothing! He was left as a guest of his elder son in what had once been his own house. Yet when the younger son returned in rags, he rushed out to receive him and claim him as his own.

The elder brother was angry because of the feast prepared for his brother, but it should be recalled that he was paying for all of it. The fancy clothes, the gold ring, the fatted calf, all were from his share of the estate. His father had been "generous" with the elder son's inheritance. Yet the father's response makes it clear that he is well aware of this fact, that all that is his is already his son's. All he asks is that his elder son join him in the same generosity out of which he had divided all he had with his two sons. The father set before us in this story is one whose father-hood is dedicated to the good of his children. They are his whole goal. He has no other.

iv. Walking toward the end of dominion

We have hazarded the judgment that the goal of the Son in the end is to be dissolved into the goal of the Father, whose goal is totally the good of his creation. All this is speculative hope, not knowledge, but it is a hope grounded in the covenantal self-deter-mination of God that is revealed to the Church in Jesus Christ, alive as the crucified Son of his Father. Perhaps no human vision of the end of the story onto which the Church has been grafted can or need count for much. What matters far more is that the end be seen to be in the care of one whose hands are the best pos-sible ones to provide for his creatures. Trusting in him, the Church may then turn its attention to the road before it and the next steps it must take.

With these reflections on the end, I have said as much as I can—perhaps more than I should have—for and to a Church that wishes to push open wider and walk through the door that was so barely cracked open with the fourth section of the declaration *Nostra Aetate* of the Second Vatican Council. These reflections on Christology have been made with as much concern for such a Church as I can muster. I have tried to take the great tradition with utmost seriousness, and I have tried to be faithful to the Church's canon of Scripture. But I have read, interpreted, and reinterpreted both in the light of the Church's relatively recent affirmations of the eternal covenant between God and the Jewish people. It may be that I have taken these recent affirmations too seriously. Many members of the Church seem to be quite unaware that anything new has been said on the subject of the relationship between the Church and the Jewish people. Many who are aware of what has been and is being said do not seem to see that there are far-reaching implications of that affirmation, touching the heart of the Church's understanding and teaching. In this third part, I have suggested what those implications may be for the Church's Christology. I certainly do not think that any of what I have said can be anything more than an invitation to the Church to think further and better than I have been able to in this central area of the Church's faith. So I ask, if not this, then what? I do not ask that as a rhetorical question.

There is much to be done before the world will even begin to notice that the Church has altered from its old, traditional anti-Judaic course. Some Jews see that at least a beginning has been made and are thankful; other Jews see how slowly the turn is being made and remain skeptical. What is more serious is that so many of the Church have yet to join in making the turn. I have had especially these Christians in mind over the past few years of writing this book for my hope has been to show them that the novelty of God's gracious act in Jesus Christ appears even more wonderful and awesome when it is set in the context of the continuity of God's covenant with the Jewish people.

With this final chapter, I have tried to take seriously the vision of the end which Paul presented of the subjection of the Son to the Father. The consequences for Christology that I have explored seem in every respect to take us back to the humility of Christ, and thus to the humility of God. That should open for the Church the possibility of rethinking and reshaping its own life so as to make it far clearer than the Church has made it in the past that it is on the road toward the end of all dominion, not to speak of domination. A Church that would share the humility of its Lord and of his Father might then be in a mood to be of service in God's cause of mending his threatened creation. How the Church and the Jewish people together are to understand and respond to that wider world of which they are but parts will be, after further study and long reflection, the subject of the last part of *A Theology of the Jewish-Christian Reality.*

Abbreviations

Adv. Marc. Adversus Marcionem
Anti-Semitism Anti-Semitism and the Foundations of Christianity
Art The Art of Biblical Narrative
"Asterius" *"Asterius: A New Chapter in the History of Arianism?"*
BCP The Book of Common Prayer
Beginnings The Beginnings of Christology
Beloved Disciple The Community of the Beloved Disciple
Canon Canon and Community
CD Church Dogmatics
Christ Christ in the Light of Christian-Jewish Dialogue
Christology Christology in the Making
"Cloud" "Cloud of Smoke, Pillar of Fire"
Covenant A Living Covenant
Deity In Search of Deity
Dialogue Dialogue with Trypho
Dieu Dieu ou le Christ
Discerning A Theology of the Jewish-Christian Reality. Part 1, Discerning the Way
Doctrine The Nature of Doctrine
"Dying" "Dying He Lives: Biblical Narrative and the Redemptive Jesus"
"Erneuerung" "Zur Erneuerung des Verhältnisses von Christen und Jüden"
Fourth Gospel The Fourth Gospel
Gentiles Summa Contra Gentiles

God God Was in Christ
Grundzüge Grundzüge einer Theologie im christlich-jüdischen Gespräch
"Heart" "Anti-Semitism is the Heart"
Hebrew Hebrew in the Church
Hope Memory and Hope
Identity The Identity of Jesus Christ
Institutes Institutes of the Christian Religion
Investigations Philosophical Investigations
"Israel's Enemies" "Israel's Enemies in Pauline Theology"
J & C Jews and Christians
Judaism Jesus and Judaism
Lectures Lectures and Conversations on Aesthetics, Psychology, and Religious Belief
Logik Zur Logik der Theologie
Memory In Memory of Her
"Oekumene" "Oekumene nach Auschwitz"
Origins The Origins of Anti-Semitism
Outline Dogmatics in Outline
People Israel A Theology of the Jewish-Christian Reality. Part 2, A Christian Theology of the People Israel
Pharisee Jesus the Pharisee
Proclaimed Christ Proclaimed
Rabbinic A Rabbinic Anthology
Reality The Reality of God
Rechtfertigung Rechtfertigung und Recht
Rejected Has God Rejected His People?
Relations More Stepping Stones to Jewish-Christian Relations
Sabbath From Sabbath to Sunday
Schweigen Das Schweigen der Christen und die Menschlichkeit Gottes
"Scientist" "God and the Physical Scientist"
Secular The Secular Meaning of the Gospel
Sermon The Sermon on the Mount
Sinai Sinai and Zion
Spirit God as Spirit
Star The Star of Redemption

"Temple" *"Temple Cleansing and Temple Bank"*
To Mend To Mend the World
Tradition The Christian Tradition. Vol. 1, The Emergence of the Catholic Tradition 100–600
Works Works of Love

Bibliography

Alter, Robert. *The Art of Biblical Narrative*. New York: Basic Books, 1982.

Anselm of Canterbury. In *Library of Christian Classics*, vol. 10. Edited by Eugene R. Fairweather. Philadelphia: The Westminster Press, 1956.

Aquinas, Thomas. *Basic Works of Saint Thomas Aquinas*, 2 vols. Edited by Anton C. Pegis. New York: Random House, 1945.

Athanasius, "On the Incarnation of the Word," in *Library of Christian Classics*, Vol. 3. Edited by Edward R. Hardy. Philadelphia: The Westminster Press, 1954: 55–110.

Bacchiocchi, Samuele. *From Sabbath to Sunday*. Rome: Pontifical Gregorian University Press, 1977.

Baillie, Donald. *God Was in Christ*. New York: Charles Scribner's Sons, 1948.

Barth, Karl. *Church Dogmatics*. Edited by G. W. Bromiley and T. F. Torrance. 13 vols. Edinburgh: T. & T. Clark, 1936–1939.

———. *Dogmatics in Outline*, London: SCM Press, 1949.

———. *Rechtfertigung und Recht*. Zürich: EVZ Verlag, 1970.

Bethge, Eberhard. "Bibelarbeit über 2 Korinther 3, 12–18 und 4, 6." In *Zur Erneuerung des Verhältnisses von Christen und Juden. Handreichung Nr. 39*. Düsseldorf: Die Evangelische Kirche in Rheinland, 1980: 56–71.

Borowitz, Eugene. *Contemporary Christologies*. New York: Paulist Press, 1979.

Brown, Raymond. *The Community of the Beloved Disciple*. New York: Paulist Press, 1979.

Calvin, John. *Institutes of the Christian Religion*. Translated by Ford Lewis Battles. 2 vols. Philadelphia: The Westminster Press, 1960.

Church of England. *Articles of Religion*, first published 1571, adopted with modification by the Episcopal Church in 1801, and reprinted in its *The Book of Common Prayer*. New York: The Church Hymnal Corporation, 1977.

Croner, Helga, comp. *More Stepping Stones to Jewish-Christian Relations*. New York: Paulist Press, 1985.

Davies, Alan T., ed. *Anti-Semitism and the Foundations of Christianity*, New York: Paulist Press, 1979.

Dunn, James D. G. *Christology in the Making*, Philadelphia: The Westminster Press, 1980.

Eckardt, A. Roy. "Anti-Semitism is the Heart." *Theology Today* 41 (No. 3, October 1984): 301–308.

———. *Jews and Christians*. Bloomington: Indiana University Press, 1985.

Efroymson, David. "The Patristic Connection." In *Anti-Semitism and the Foundations of Christianity*, edited by Alan T. Davies. New York: Paulist Press, 1979.

Encyclopedia Judaica. Jerusalem: Keter Publishing House, 1972.

The Episcopal Church. *The Book of Common Prayer*. New York: The Church Hymnal Corp., 1977.

Evangelische Kirche in Rheinland. *Zur Erneuerung des Verhältnisses von Christen und Juden. Handreichung Nr. 39*. Düsseldorf: Die Evangelische Kirche in Rheinland, 1980.

Fackenheim, Emil. *To Mend the World*. New York: Schocken Books, 1982.

Falk, Harvey. *Jesus the Pharisee*. New York: Paulist Press, 1985.

Fiorenza, Elisabeth, Schüssler. *In Memory of Her*. New York: Crossroads, 1983.

Frei, Hans W. *The Identity of Jesus Christ*. Philadelphia: Fortress Press, 1975.

Gager, John. *Kingdom and Community: The Social World of Early Christianity*. Englewood Cliffs, N. J.: Prentice-Hall, 1975.

———. *The Origins of Anti-Semitism*. New York: Oxford University Press, 1983.

Gaston, Lloyd. "Israel's Enemies in Pauline Theology." *New Testament Studies* 28 (1982): 400–423.

Goldberg, Michael. "God, Action, and Narrative: *Which* Narrative? *Which* Action? *Which* God?" Mimeographed paper, 1986.

Greenberg, Irving. "Cloud of Smoke, Pillar of Fire." In *Auschwitz: End of an Era?*, edited by Eva Fleischner. New York: KTVA Publishing House, 1977.

Gregg, Robert C. *Arianism: Historical and Theological Reassessment.* Philadelphia: The Philadelphia Patristic Foundation, 1985.

Hall, Douglas. "Rethinking Christ." In *Anti-Semitism and the Foundations of Christianity,* edited by Alan T. Davies. New York: Paulist Press, 1979.

Hamilton, Neill Q. *Jesus for a No-God World.* Philadelphia: The Westminster Press, 1969.

————. "Temple Cleansing and Temple Bank." *Journal of Biblical Literature* 83 (No. 4, 1964): 365–372.

Hanson, R. P. C. "The Arian Doctrine of the Incarnation." In *Arianism: Historical and Theological Reassessment,* edited by Robert C. Gregg. Philadelphia: Philadelphia Patristic Foundation, 1985: 181–211.

Hartman, David. *A Living Covenant.* New York: Free Press, 1985.

Hoffmann, R. J. *Marcion: On the Restitution of Christianity.* Chico, California: Scholars Press, 1984.

Hoskyns, E. C., and F. N. Davies. *The Fourth Gospel.* London: Faber and Faber, Ltd., 1947.

Justin Martyr. "Dialogue with Trypho." In *The Ante-Nicene Fathers, vol. 1,* edited by A. Cleveland Coxe. New York: Charles Scribner's Sons, 1899.

Kee, Howard. *Community of the New Age.* Philadelphia: The Westminster Press, 1977.

Kierkegaard, Søren. *Works of Love.* Translated by David F. Swenson. Princeton: Princeton University Press, 1946.

Lampe, G. W. H. *God as Spirit.* Oxford: Clarendon Press, 1977.

Lapide, Pinchas E. *Hebrew in the Church.* Grand Rapids: Eerdmans, 1984.

————. *The Sermon on the Mount.* Maryknoll: Orbis Books, 1986.

Levenson, Jon D. *Sinai and Zion.* San Francisco: Harper & Row, 1987.

Lindbeck, George. *The Nature of Doctrine.* Philadelphia: The Westminster Press, 1984.

Macquarrie, John. *In Search of Deity.* New York: Crossroads, 1985.

Marquardt, F. W., and Friedlander, Albert. *Das Schweigen der Christen und die Menschlichkeit Gottes.* München: Chr. Kaiser Verlag, 1980.

————. *Die Gegenwart des Auferstandenen bei Seinem Volk Israel.* München: Chr. Kaiser Verlag, 1983.

————. "Was haltet ihr von Christus?—Jesus Zwischen Juden und Christen." Paper presented at the Kirchentag, Hamburg, Germany, June 19, 1981.

Marxen, Willi. *The Beginnings of Christology.* Philadelphia: Fortress Press, 1969.

Metz, Johann B. "Oekumene nach Auschwitz." In *Gott nach Auschwitz,* edited by Eugen Kogon. Freiburg/Basel/Vienna: 1979.

Miles, Maurice F., in collaboration with Robert C. Gregg, "Asterius: A New Chapter in the History of Arianism?" in *Arianism: Historical and Theological Reassesment,* edited by Robert C. Gregg. Philadelphia: Philadelphia Patristic Foundation, 1985: 111–151.

Milet, Jean. *Dieu ou le Christ?* Paris: Trévise, 1980.

———. *God or Christ?* New York: Crossroads, 1981.

Montefiore, Claude G., and Herbert Loewe, eds. *A Rabbinic Anthology.* New York: Schocken Books, 1974.

Monti, Joseph. *Who Do You Say that I Am?* New York: Paulist Press, 1984.

Neusner, Jacob. *Messiah in Context.* Philadelphia: Fortress, 1984.

Ogden, Schubert. *The Point of Christology.* San Francisco: Harper & Row, 1982.

———. *The Reality of God.* New York: Harper & Row, 1963.

Pawlikowski, John. *Christ in the Light of Christian-Jewish Dialogue.* New York: Paulist Press, 1982.

Pelikan, Jaroslav. *The Christian Tradition,* Vol. 1, *The Emergence of the Catholic Tradition (100–600).* Chicago: University of Chicago Press, 1971.

Piddard, Brian. "God and the Physical Scientist." *Times Literary Supplement.* No. 4338. (May 23, 1986): 555–56.

Pines, Shlomo. "The Jewish Christians of the Early Centuries According to a New Source." *Proceedings of the Israel Academy of Sciences and Humanities,* vol. 2. (1968): 237–310.

Ritschl, D. *Memory and Hope.* New York: Macmillan, 1967.

———. *Zur Logik der Theologie.* München: Chr. Kaiser Verlag, 1984.

Root, Michael. "Dying He Lives: Biblical Narrative, and the Redemptive Jesus." *Christology and Exegesis,* edited by Robert Jewett (155–169): *Semeia* 30. Decatur, GA: Scholars Press, 1985.

Rosenzweig, Franz. *The Star of Redemption,* trans. by William Hallo. Boston: Beacon Press, 1964.

Rubenstein, Richard. *After Auschwitz.* Indianapolis: Bobbs-Merrill, 1966.

Sanders, E. P. *Jesus and Judaism.* Philadelphia: Fortress Press, 1985.

Sanders, James A. *Canon and Community.* Philadelphia: Fortress Press, 1984.

Schillebeeckx, Edward. *Jesus*. New York: Seabury Press, 1979.

Second Vatican Council. "Nostra Aetate." In *Stepping Stones to Further Jewish-Christian Relations*, edited by Helga Croner. New York: Paulist Press, 1977.

Sloyan, G. "A Response" (to Pinchas Lapide). *Face to Face* 9, New York: Anti-Defamation League (Winter, Spring 1982): 13–16.

Tertullian. "Adversus Marcionem." In *Ante-Nicene Fathers*, vol 3, edited by A. Cleveland Coxe. New York: Charles Scribner's Sons, 1899.

Tocqueville, Alexis de. *Democracy in America*. New York: Harper & Row, 1966.

van Beeck, F. J. *Christ Proclaimed*. New York: Paulist Press, 1979.

van Buren, Paul M. *The Secular Meaning of the Gospel*. New York: Macmillan, 1963.

———. *A Theology of the Jewish-Christian Reality*, Part 1, *Discerning the Way*, San Francisco: Harper & Row, 1980.

———. *A Theology of the Jewish-Christian Reality*, Part 2, *A Christian Theology of the People Israel*, San Francisco: Harper & Row, 1983.

von der Osten-Sacken, Peter. *Grundzüge einer Theologie im christlich-jüdischen Gespräch*. München: Chr. Kaiser Verlag, 1982.

Wilkins, Robert. *The Myth of Christian Beginnings*. Notre Dame: University of Notre Dame Press, 1971.

Williamson, Clark. *Has God Rejected His People?* Nashville: Abingdon, 1982.

———. "A New Context for Christology." *Religion and Intellectual Life* (vol. 3, No. 4, Summer 1986): 72–76.

Wittgenstein, Ludwig. *Lectures and Conversations on Aesthetics, Psychology, and Religious Belief*. Edited by Cyril Barrett. Oxford: Basil Blackwell, 1966.

———. *Philosophical Investigations*. Oxford: Basil Blackwell, 1958.

World Council of Churches. *My Neighbor's Faith—and Mine: Theological Discoveries through Interfaith Dialogue*. Geneva: World Council of Churches, 1986.

Wyschogrod, Michael. *The Body of Faith*. New York: Seabury, 1983.

General Index

Name Index

Scripture Index